**Praise for *The Penguin State of the Middle East Atlas*
and Dan Smith:**

"A brilliant, accessible up-to-date resource: everything you need to know to fuel your understanding of this complex region."   – Jon Snow

"A concise, wise, and accessible guide to the region . . . Change has burst on us so rapidly and dramatically since the Arab Spring that we need all the help we can get in trying to make sense of it. This book, with its combination of good maps, clever graphics and judicious text, will aid understanding of a part of the world which is even more pivotal today than it was in the past." – Martin Woollacott

"Dan Smith has been teaching me about geography for almost as long as I can remember – there is no one I would trust more to map the Middle East."
– Danny Dorling,
Halford Mackinder Professor of Geography, University of Oxford

"I can't think of a better introduction to the complexities of the Middle East than Dan Smith's *The Penguin State of the Middle East Atlas*. It sets out the background to present-day developments clearly and concisely. The narrative is highly readable, and the beautifully presented maps and diagrams, together with the brief chronologies, provide a user-friendly complement to it. All in all, highly recommended."   – Greg Shapland,
former Head of Research Analysts, Foreign & Commonwealth Office (UK),
and visiting research fellow at the University of Sussex

Praise for previous atlases:

"*The Penguin State of the World Atlas* is something else – an occasion of wit and an act of subversion. . . . These are the bad dreams of the modern world, given color and shape and submitted to a grid that can be grasped instantaneously."
– *New York Times*

"Unique and uniquely beautiful . . . a discerning eye for data and a flair for the most sophisticated techniques of stylized graphic design; the atlas succeeds in displaying the geopolitical subtleties of global affairs in a series of dazzling color plates . . . tells us more about the world today than a dozen statistical abstracts or scholarly tomes."   – *Los Angeles Times*

"Coupled with an unusual non-distorting map projection and a series of brilliant cartographic devices, this gives a positively dazzling set of maps. It deserves to be widely used."   – *New Society*

"A super book that will not only sit on your shelf begging to be used, but will also be a good read. To call this book an atlas is like calling Calvados, applejack – it may be roughly accurate but it conveys nothing of the richness and flavour of the thing. Its inventive brilliance deserves enormous rewards."   – *New Scientist*

"A striking new approach to cartography . . . no-one wishing to keep a grip on the reality of the world should be without these books."
– *International Her...*

Also available from Penguin

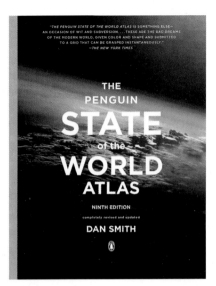

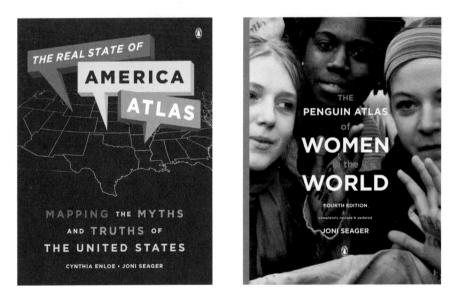

"No-one wishing to keep a grip on the reality of the world should be without these books." — *International Herald Tribune*

"Invaluable . . . I would not be without the complete set on my own shelves." — *Times Educational Supplement*

"Fascinating and invaluable." — *The Independent*

"A new kind of visual journalism." — *New Scientist*

THE PENGUIN STATE OF THE MIDDLE EAST ATLAS

Completely Revised and Updated

Third Edition

DAN SMITH

PENGUIN BOOKS

PENGUIN BOOKS

An imprint of Penguin Random House LLC
375 Hudson Street
New York, New York 10014
penguin.com

This third edition first published in Penguin Books 2016

ISBN 978-0-14-312423-8

Produced for Penguin Books by
Myriad Editions
59 Lansdowne Place
Brighton, BN3 1FL, UK
www.myriadeditions.com

Edited and coordinated by Jannet King,
Dawn Sackett and Candida Lacey
Designed by Isabelle Lewis and Corinne Pearlman
Maps and graphics by Isabelle Lewis

Printed in Hong Kong

1 3 5 7 9 10 8 6 4 2

CONTENTS

ABOUT THE AUTHOR

Dan Smith is the Director of the Stockholm International Peace Research Institute. He is also a Professor at the University of Manchester's Humanitarian and Conflict Response Institute. From 2003 to 2015 he was Secretary General of the London-based international peacebuilding organization International Alert, and before that Director of the International Peace Research Institute in Oslo. He has also held fellowships at the Norwegian Nobel Institute and Hellenic Foundation for Foreign and European Policy and was, for over a decade, the Chair of the Institute for War and Peace Reporting.

As well as *The State of the Middle East*, he is the author of successive editions of *The State of the World Atlas* and *The Atlas of War and Peace*. At International Alert he produced the path-breaking *A Climate of Conflict* (2007) report on the links between climate change, peace, and war. He was Chair of the Advisory Group for the UN Peacebuilding Fund in 2010 and 2011.

He was awarded the OBE in 2002, and blogs on international politics at www.dansmithsblog.com

INTRODUCTION

THE MIDDLE EAST AND THE WORLD

A moment of great hope and promise unfolded in the Middle East in 2011 – the Arab Spring, as it was quickly called by participants and observers alike – as millions of people took to the streets. They demanded that rulers who had no accountability and who showed little sense of responsibility should step down. Four years later, it is only in Tunisia that, despite extreme pressures, the flowers are still in bloom.

In other countries, events flow fast in a variety of directions – towards re-establishing the old order, into war, into chaos. There is a confusing array of actors with shifting loyalties and hidden agendas. They seem to act out of complex combinations of conviction and pragmatic compromise. The result has been, so far, to blight the Arab Spring in most countries.

The forces that drove change in 2011, however, have not gone away. People did not rise up against their rulers whimsically but because so many saw no option other than to take the enormous personal risks of publicly demonstrating their opposition and voicing their demands. In too many countries, chaos, war and the forces of political and religious reaction have exhausted energy for change. But that situation will not necessarily endure for long. After hope has taken a short break, those same driving forces of change will be at work. In five years, ten or twenty, nobody can know exactly when, it is highly likely that the region will see renewed popular movements and new opportunities for change, even though the same opposing forces will also persist.

The events of 2011 and thereafter gripped us. People all over the planet respond to what happens in the Middle East in a way that we don't respond to distant events in other regions. People who don't live there have opinions about the Middle East in a way that we don't about West Africa or East Asia. Sometimes, as with the beheadings on video and massacres at beaches, museums, mosques and on the battlefield, we are fascinated and revolted at once. We have feelings and emotions, we feel a stake.

The reasons for this connectedness operate at quite different levels. The most obvious is the wars – Israel against the Arab states and the Palestinian movements, the implosion of Lebanon in the 1980s, Kurdish wars of identity and recognition, Iraq and Iran, the US-led coalition against Iraq in 1991, the civil war in Algeria, the first and second *intifada* of Palestinians, a second US-led coalition against Iraq in 2003, followed by a decade of mayhem, the uprisings in Libya, Syria and Yemen. Wars, it can seem, without end.

These wars very often engage our emotions. But there are other equally violent wars that do not. Why the difference? The simplest reason is oil. Everything that runs, runs on energy, and, as well as having multiple other uses in agriculture and industry, oil has been a key source of energy for a century, replacing coal if not quite rivalling the sun. Because of oil, what transpires in the Middle East can have profound economic impact the world over. Accordingly, outside powers have interests there that often go deeper than those they have in other areas. Thus also, conflicts in the Middle East have a way of involving other parts of the world. Outsiders intervene routinely

---

Hope has taken
a short break

---

with power and influence if not always with direct force, and Middle Eastern conflicts have exported violence to other areas for almost half a century.

At a somewhat deeper level, history and strategy play a part. Simply due to location, the region was important for growing European empires in the 18th and 19th centuries. The very term, 'Middle East' reflects European imperial history – middle of what, east of where? It was initially a British term, but is now widely translated and used. The region was in the middle of a swathe of the world from Morocco to the Philippines that European powers fought to bring under their sway. When 19th-century industrial technology rose to such a level that it could dig a canal through the Sinai isthmus at the northern end of the Red Sea, the region's centrality went from being an interesting geographical fact to a prime strategic consideration. For the British empire, based on sea power, the Suez Canal was the main artery. Down at the southern end of the Red Sea, Aden was an essential coaling station and staging post. The Middle East was strategically important for foreigners long before oil came on the scene.

For the European corner of the world, the Middle East had also been important as a source of threat. It was the power base of the Ottoman Empire that, at its peak, held almost as much territory in Europe as outside it. But, of course, to reflect on that history necessarily takes us to a third, deeper level, that is more subtle, less tangible but probably fundamental.

This is the region where three world religions began. The rivalry and confrontation between the Ottomans and the European powers – from the Ottoman heyday of the 16th and 17th centuries, through the stagnation of Ottoman power in the 18th century and its erosion in the 19th – was a matter of both power and religion. The rivalry was between Islam and Christendom as much as it was between Istanbul and Vienna, Paris or London.

The religious dimension is equally unavoidable today. Various locations in the Middle East feature in what has been called the *sacred geography* of Judaism, Christianity and Islam, and Jerusalem has a special place for all three. It is a region where for many people – both those who live there and those who do not – spirituality and politics come together. And because religion has been and remains a shaping force in culture and in ethical norms that guide our ordinary behaviour, the impact of this dimension is real even in highly secular society, even for many people who are not themselves religious. Middle Eastern issues get under the skin of rational discussion in a way not many others do. They generate a quite evangelical fervour among people with no obvious stake in the region other than their emotions.

All this – oil, history, religion, war – means the region is rarely out of the international news headlines. It is the focus of numerous expert studies and official reports. And since the Middle East has a long history of civilization and has long been a region of special global significance, it is the subject of a plethora of scholarly books as well. Yet understanding the region is not easy for most people outside it and the welter of information and analysis does not actually help.

An enormous part of the daily reality of most people in the Middle East is – just the same as elsewhere – of little interest to international news managers. So what we find when we look at what is available for most people to read or watch is a very detailed but strangely two-dimensional picture – full of facts,

———
**Middle of what?
East of where?**
———

———
**Middle Eastern issues get
under the skin
of rational discussion**
———

without much context – when we actually want and need something simpler yet three-dimensional. That is what this book tries to provide. Amid the welter of changing daily facts and contending and contentious interpretations, the aim is to offer not a definitive explanation but a doorway towards understanding things a bit better.

The Middle East as it is today has been shaped by the interplay of six key historical, cultural and contemporary factors – Islam, the Ottoman Empire, European colonialism, the foundation of the state of Israel, oil and the role of the USA. The result of these factors is to tie a region together in a series of closely related economic, political, strategic and social challenges. These are the features around which this book organizes itself.

Venturing out with a broad overview and general guide that consciously omits a lot of important detail means getting into the territory of controversy. Religious difference and political conflict breed controversies, and around the Middle East they are particularly fervent. The heated disputes that result affect not only political leaders but also reporters, commentators, experts and scholars. The arguments are bitter and are often simply a contest of slogans. Instead of acknowledging that there can be genuine misunderstandings or confusion and uncertainty about facts, accusations of bad faith abound. In a part of the world where there has been so much disputation, conflict and

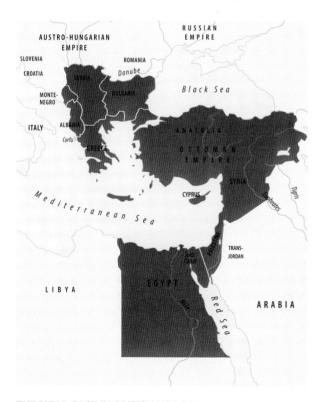

THE NEAR EAST IN BRITISH USAGE
early 20th century

misery over the past 70 years, let alone further back, partisans of different positions have plenty of facts to choose from to support their viewpoint and attack the rest. The implication often is that not already holding the right view is inexcusable. This is inescapably alienating for anybody who has doubts about what is happening, about its causes, about the balance of rights and wrongs, and about what can or should be done.

This book focuses on conflicts. It looks at where they have been, how they started, how they progressed, when, how and why they ended. Facts without context – especially today's facts without the context of history – do not really aid the process of understanding issues as complex and deep as those in this region. The atlas is about the contextual outlines within which events day to day can be more readily understood.

——

Six factors shape the modern Middle East: Islam, the Ottoman Empire, European colonialism, the foundation of Israel, oil, and the role of the USA

——

There is controversy and often confusion over just about everything to do with the Middle East. Let's start with its size and shape.

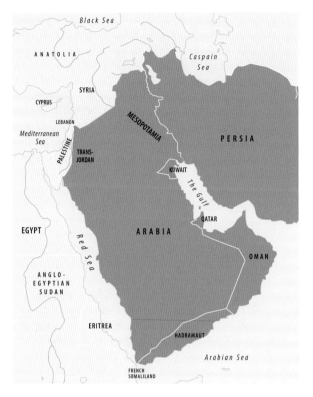

THE MIDDLE EAST IN BRITISH USAGE
early 20th century

In British usage in the early 20th century, the term 'the Middle East' referred to Arabia, Mesopotamia, the Gulf and Persia. The term 'Near East' was used to refer to the Balkans, Anatolia, the Levant and Egypt (and further away, there was the 'Far East' covering South-East Asia, China, Korea and Japan).

In some contemporary usage, the term 'Middle East' goes as far west as Morocco, takes in Cyprus and Turkey to the north and Sudan to the south, and reaches to Pakistan and Afghanistan in the east and even Tajikistan. The National Geographic *Atlas of the Middle East* reflects the uncertainty because it used to leave out Pakistan, Afghanistan and Sudan but included them in the second edition. Among other authorities, the *Encyclopaedia Britannica* includes Cyprus and Turkey while the BBC does not; Wikipedia includes nothing west of Egypt nor east of Iran; the CIA includes nothing in Africa, not even Egypt. The area covered in this book is the area the US State Department, followed by the Council on Foreign Relations, refers to as the Near East, and except for Mauritania (which is to the south of Western Sahara) it is exactly the same as the area the BBC calls the Middle East.

The reason why there is no universally agreed definition of the region is that the very concept of the Middle East is political. In defining it, judgements are made about some of the key issues that preoccupy it and the key factors that constitute it. Over time, the influences of Islam, the Ottoman Empire, European colonialism, the foundation of Israel, oil and the USA have tied a diverse area together and unified it as a region facing a series of closely related economic, political, strategic and social challenges.

**CHANGING VIEWS OF
THE MIDDLE EAST**
early 21st century

 countries included in first edition of the National Geographic *Atlas of the Middle East*

additional countries included in the second edition of the National Geographic *Atlas of the Middle East*

further countries often regarded as part of the Middle East

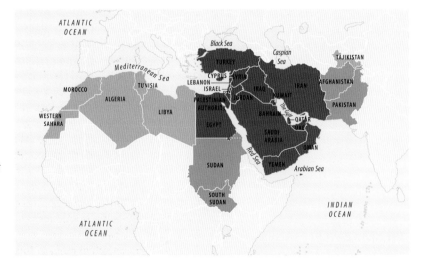

**THE MIDDLE EAST
IN THIS ATLAS**

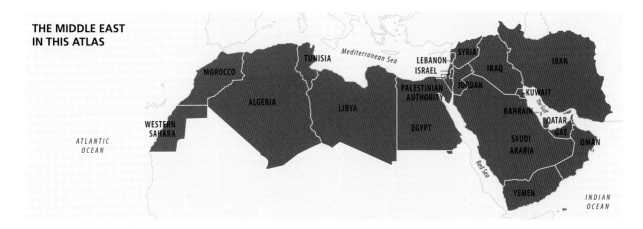

The North African states to Egypt's west share much of the same culture and politics and many of the same dilemmas. They are equally part of the Middle East. Iran is likewise intricately and inextricably part of the region's political, social and cultural development. On the other hand, it would be misleading to include Sudan, whose development dilemmas and pathway are distinctively different from those of the Middle East. Similarly, it is inappropriate to bring in Pakistan or Afghanistan. They are both Islamic countries, but their recent histories and current dilemmas are shaped by forces and problems that are in key respects distinct from those of the Middle East.

Economic, political, strategic and social challenges combine to unify the Middle East

---

This much will be generally agreed, if only because many books make the same judgements. American readers may be less used than European readers to the idea of the Maghreb being in the Middle East but have probably come across treatments of North Africa and the Middle East as a single region, so it is not a particularly unfamiliar concept.

Equally straightforward is a decision not to include Cyprus in an atlas on the Middle East. Including it could only be because of geographic proximity; the island's strong Hellenic links and the European orientation evident among Turkish Cypriots and Greek Cypriots alike make it more relevant to see it as part of Europe. More contentious, perhaps, is the decision not to include Turkey except when its present or past touches closely the affairs of the region, in much the same way as Britain, France and the USA are included.

To European and North American eyes and ears, there is much that is Middle Eastern about Turkey. However, Turkey looks at its most Middle Eastern if the comparison is made with the Western Europe of London, Paris, Berlin, Amsterdam, Rome and Madrid. To anybody who is familiar with south-eastern Europe, there is much in modern Turkey that looks, sounds and feels strikingly familiar. That is hardly surprising, since the history of the Balkans is yoked as securely to Turkey's by the Ottoman Empire as is the history of the Middle East. The result of the long period of Ottoman domination, can be tasted in the cuisine, seen in some of the architecture, heard in the music and, more subtly, experienced in many aspects of custom and attitude.

Though the Ottomans were long called Turks, Turkey was not formed until after the Ottoman Empire had perished. Mustafa Kemal Atatürk, the brilliant general and charismatic leader who led Turkey to independence and dominated its politics for a further decade and a half until his death, turned the new country towards Europe. He enforced modernity and secularism. Turkey was never colonized by Europeans, was no more affected by the foundation of Israel than its neighbour Greece, and has been a member of NATO for over 60 years. Its trajectory is not that of the Middle East.

———

This is an atlas of today that uses the past to explain and tentatively attempts to look ahead. It uses a variety of techniques for presenting information and analysis – text, maps, other graphics and chronologies – which are intended to be read alongside each other. It draws on history to explain how the region arrived at where it now stands. Part One focuses on issues of power that have created the region today, looking at each of the prime influences on the region. Part Two looks at a series of cross-cutting regional issues of identity, power, faith and war that define where the Middle East stood when the wave of change started in 2011. Part Three explores the contemporary conflicts within the region, their background, evolution and prospects, looking at successive waves of war as they have unfolded since the late 1940s. Finally, a brief conclusion scans the horizon ahead.

GLOSSARY

al-Aqsa Martyrs Brigades Palestinian militant group. An offshoot of Fatah, the largest group within the Palestine Liberation Organization.

al-Qaeda Militant Islamic organization and network responsible for the September 2001 attacks on the USA. Led till his death by Osama bin Laden and now by Ayman al-Zawahiri, it is classified by the USA, EU and UN as a terrorist group.

Alawi Secretive religious group primarily based in Syria, with pre-Islamic origins, which appears to have drawn on Islamic fundamentals.

Amal Shi'a Muslim militia formed in Lebanon in 1975. Its fight against Palestinian refugees and Hezbollah led to Syria's re-intervention in Lebanon in 1987.

Druze Islamic confessional group with origins in Shi'a Islam and its Ismaili version, but also influenced by Greek philosophy and Christianity.

Fatwa A ruling on Islamic law given by a recognized Islamic scholar.

Hamas Palestinian Islamic political organization with origins in the Muslim Brotherhood, winner of the 2006 Palestine legislative elections. Listed by the USA and EU as a terrorist organization.

Hashemites Arab dynasty, hereditary sherifs (guardians) of Mecca for a millennium until 1925; the Hashemite family is the royal family of Jordan.

Hezbollah Shi'a group formed in 1982 and based in Lebanon with both a civilian and a military branch. The USA has labelled Hezbollah a terrorist organization.

Intifada Spontaneous Palestinian uprising. First *intifada*: 1987–93; second *intifada*: 2000–05.

ISIS The Islamic State of Iraq and ash-Sham – a *jihadi* group originating in Iraq, then expanding to Syria, then developing active branches in other countries. The richest and most powerful *jihadi* group in 2014–15 (see Transliteration and usage below for comment on terminology).

Islamic Jihad Militant Islamist group, based in Syria and active in the Occupied Territories of Palestine, which rejects any accommodation with Israel. Labelled a terrorist organization by the USA and EU.

Ismaili Shi'a group that split from mainstream Shi'ism in the 8th century CE.

Jihad A contested term that at its core is the duty of all Muslims to maintain the Islamic religion, within themselves and within their communities. Generally interpreted as referring to an inner struggle but sometimes interpreted as endorsing a violent struggle against those who are seen to oppose true Islam.

Jihadi A member of a militant group of Sunni Muslims that acts on the violent interpretation of the idea of jihad.

Likud Conservative party of Israel.

Majlis Arab term for legislative assembly, also used by countries with strong Islamic ties.

Maronites Members of the Eastern Catholic Church and largest Christian group in Lebanon.

Palestinian Authority Political unit with limited authority over the administration of Gaza and parts of the West Bank. It grew out of the 1993 Oslo Accords and was established in 1994.

Popular Front for the Liberation of Palestine Nationalist organization with Marxist–Leninist ideology. One of the constituent groups forming the PLO.

Salafist A Sunni Muslim who follows an ultra-conservative doctrine taking its inspiration from the Prophet Mohammed and his earliest followers – al-salaf al-salih, the 'pious forefathers'.

Sunni Islam Largest Islamic denomination. Sunni Muslims believe the first three successors (caliphs) to Mohammed, while not directly related, were rightly chosen from the community for their leadership abilities.

Shi'ism Second largest Islamic denomination. Shi'a Muslims do not recognize the legitimacy of the initial three Sunni caliphs. They regard members of the family of the Prophet Mohammed as his natural and rightful successors.

Wahhabism Puritanical Sunni Islamic movement, dominant in Saudi Arabia and Qatar.

TRANSLITERATION AND USAGE

There are at least 12 different systems for transliterating from Arabic to Latin script. They differ in, for example, their choice of vowels or their use of 'g', 'gh', 'k', 'kh', and 'q' for the same Arabic letter and sound. Though each system has its devotees, there is ultimately no correct way to spell Arabic words in Latin script. To illustrate the result, the BBC website lists 21 different ways of spelling the second name of the late Libyan president who is referred to in this book as Qaddafi, the form of his name used by the *New York Times* and *Economist* among others (representing a change from the first and second editions of this book, which used the form Qadhafi that it seems nobody else uses). With less spectacular diversity, accepted usages include, for example, both Muslim and Moslem, both Mohammed and Muhammad, both Hizbollah and Hezbollah, both Nasser and Nasr, and so on. In general, including in this book, system is put aside when it comes to the name of a person, movement, institution or place that is particularly well known internationally and for which one form predominates in common usage.

Media outlets across the world have tended to use a variety of titles and associated acronyms for the militant group in the Middle East that has been the focus of most attention since 2013. Four terms have been commonly used: 'ISIL', standing for the Islamic State of Iraq and the Levant; 'ISIS', combining Arabic with English and standing for the Islamic State of Iraq and ash-Sham (a classical Arabic term referring to an area based on but larger than modern Syria); 'Islamic State', since ISIL/ISIS rebranded itself as such in June 2014; and 'Daesh', based on the Arabic acronym al-Dawla al-Islamiya fil Iraq wa'al Sham (which translates as the Islamic State of Iraq and ash-Sham. Because it is close to the term 'dahes' (one who sows discord), it is used to insult the group. In this book, ISIS is used as a name that feels easy to say and remember.

PART ONE

THE MAKING OF THE MIDDLE EAST

The Middle East contains some of the first places where people gathered together in towns, some four to five thousand years ago. It is the birthplace of three world religions – Judaism, Christianity and Islam. It has been both the source and the possession of great empires. In every part of it, the past is important, both in lived traditions that shape everyday life, and in the histories of power and conflict that have swept across it. The rights and wrongs of some of today's conflicts – not least between Israel and Palestine and between Sunni and Shi'a Muslims – are routinely discussed in terms that reach back more than a millennium into the past. To understand the Middle East today, it is important to understand how it was made.

In the fabric of the region's history it is possible to discern a number of patterns, factors that have shaped the region and continue to do so today. The first is Islam. Adherence to the faith broadly unites the region and distinguishes it from neighbouring regions, yet internally also marks out lines of division, not only between Muslim and Jew, for example, but between Sunni and Shi'a. Historically, the spread of Islam and the spread of Arabic from the Arabian peninsula to the borders of modern Turkey and through North Africa were a single process. Arabic, the language of the Quran, is the language of most Middle Easterners.

Two further historical moulders of the region are the great empires which have left their marks there. The ones whose legacies live on today are the Ottoman Empire from the 14th century CE until World War I, and the 19th- and 20th-century European empires of Britain and France. The political culture of the region owes much to the Ottomans while its political structure was effectively defined by the Europeans.

As decolonization unfolded in the mid-20th century, three further factors emerged. The state of Israel was founded in 1948, a fact that created a running wound for the Arab world. In the 1950s, the exploitation of oil gathered pace and started to generate enormous wealth. And in the same decade, the USA began to move in to replace the fading French and British powers, doing much to set the terms of how the new wealth would be used, with Western-orientated economic development and *status quo* politics. No attempt to understand conflict and the prospects for peace or disaster in the Middle East can be complete without understanding the impact of Israel, the USA and oil.

THE OTTOMAN EMPIRE

Osman, the founder of the Ottoman Dynasty and Empire in the early 1300s, was the ruler of a principality in western Anatolia on the borders of the fading Byzantine Empire. He was leader of one of the groups of *Ghazis* – holy warriors for Islam – whose ethnic origins lay in central Asia. The early mission of the Ottomans was to extend the Abode of Islam.

Compared to European armies of the time, Ottoman forces were professional and efficient. There was consistent expansion in the Balkans and Anatolia throughout the 14th century, until the Ottoman Sultan unwisely challenged the invincible central Asian armies of Timur the Lame (Tamerlane) in 1402 and was crushingly defeated. The Ottoman state tottered and there was a decade of internal warfare.

Ottoman leadership, however, showed resilience as well as efficiency; central authority was steadily reasserted and expansion renewed. After a further 40 years, the Ottomans took Constantinople, completing the destruction of Byzantium. The city, renamed Istanbul, became the new Ottoman capital.

In its prime, the Ottoman Empire controlled almost as much territory in Europe as in Anatolia and the Arab lands

---

The Empire's golden age was the reign from 1520 to 1566 of the 10th Sultan, Suleiman – known in the Empire as 'the Lawgiver' and in Europe as 'the Magnificent'. His 46 years of rule involved constant military campaigning, and though his ambitions were ultimately baulked in Europe, his forces were never defeated in open battle. He extended Ottoman territories as far north as Budapest, and expanded the Empire in the Middle East.

In its prime, the Ottoman Empire controlled almost as much territory in Europe as in Anatolia and the Arab lands. Both its armed forces and the quality of its administration began to deteriorate soon after Suleiman's death, but the Empire remained formidable.

In terms of territory, the Empire was at its peak when it suffered its first important defeat since Timur. Ottoman forces were repelled by a better-trained and more motivated Habsburg army in 1683 outside Vienna, followed by a further defeat in 1687 at the battle of Mohács, which freed Hungary from Ottoman control.

The next 230 years of its history told a tale of decline, but the Empire was a major factor in European and Mediterranean politics throughout the 18th century. From the early 19th century, in both North Africa and the Balkans, the Ottomans lost further territory. They lost out to European nationalists in Greece, Serbia, Croatia and ultimately Bulgaria, and to breakaway rulers in North Africa, who were themselves displaced, bullied or corrupted by European power as the 19th century wore on. Where the Ottoman Empire in its glory had threatened Europe with conquest, now the European powers risked war in picking over its pieces.

The Sultan was in principle the absolute ruler, but the reality depended on his capacities and his will. Increasingly, the Sultan merely reigned rather than actually ruling, and the centre of Ottoman power was weakened by competing factions. Attempts at reform in the 19th century failed repeatedly, because to be successful, reform had to overturn the existing order. The reformers themselves were members of the Ottoman elite and not fully committed to that upheaval. By the time of the Empire's final demise – its fate sealed first by the Balkan War in 1912 and then by World War I – the Sultan had no executive power. The Sultanate was finally abolished in 1922 as modern Turkey was formed under the leadership of Mustafa Kemal Atatürk.

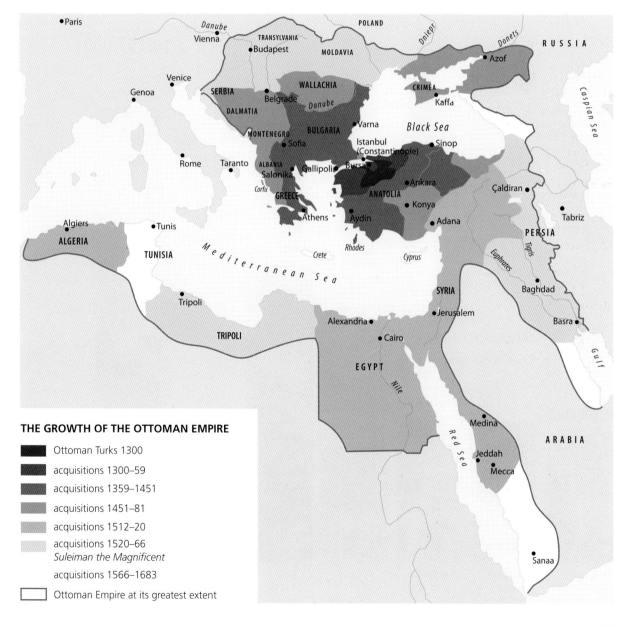

THE GROWTH OF THE OTTOMAN EMPIRE

- Ottoman Turks 1300
- acquisitions 1300–59
- acquisitions 1359–1451
- acquisitions 1451–81
- acquisitions 1512–20
- acquisitions 1520–66 *Suleiman the Magnificent*
- acquisitions 1566–1683
- Ottoman Empire at its greatest extent

Decline and legacy

The decline of the Ottoman Empire was marked by moments of extraordinary cruelty and brutality – the massacre and depopulation of the Aegean island of Chios in 1822, massacres by Turkish irregulars in the Bulgarian uprising of 1876, massacres of Armenians in Istanbul and other cities in 1895 and 1896, and of 600,000 to 1 million Armenians in 1915.

One reason for this cruelty was that Ottoman power was arbitrary. Even when the absolute power of the Sultan was more rhetoric than reality, the power of his representatives and army commanders was complete and they brooked no opposition. As opposition to Ottoman power grew, the reaction was sometimes extreme.

THE STRENGTH OF EMPIRES

Comparative extent of major empires in square miles and duration in years

There is no neat statistical way of comparing the power of the great empires. In general, empires are regarded as mighty because of both their expanse and their longevity. One non-scientific way of comparing them is by combining each one's duration and its size at its greatest extent into a single perspective.

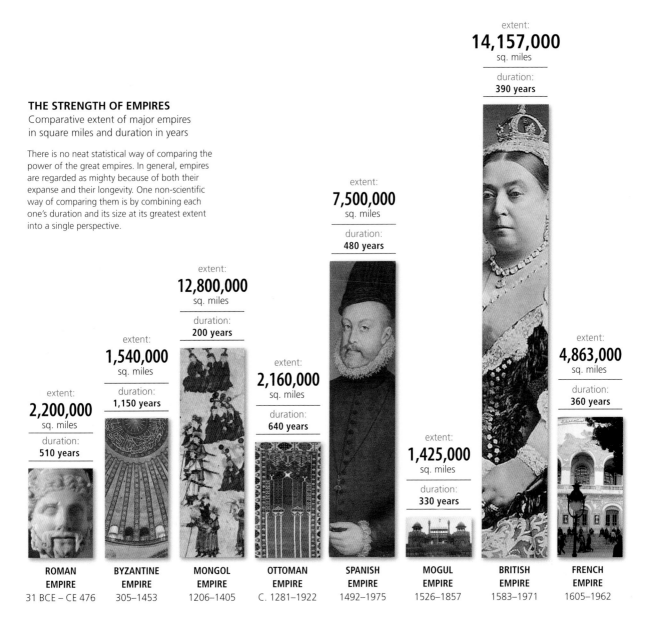

	extent:					extent:	
						14,157,000 sq. miles	
						duration: **390 years**	

extent:
7,500,000
sq. miles

duration:
480 years

extent:
12,800,000
sq. miles

duration:
200 years

extent:
1,540,000
sq. miles

duration:
1,150 years

extent:
2,160,000
sq. miles

duration:
640 years

extent:
4,863,000
sq. miles

duration:
360 years

extent:
2,200,000
sq. miles

duration:
510 years

extent:
1,425,000
sq. miles

duration:
330 years

ROMAN EMPIRE	BYZANTINE EMPIRE	MONGOL EMPIRE	OTTOMAN EMPIRE	SPANISH EMPIRE	MOGUL EMPIRE	BRITISH EMPIRE	FRENCH EMPIRE
31 BCE – CE 476	305–1453	1206–1405	C. 1281–1922	1492–1975	1526–1857	1583–1971	1605–1962

Yet the Empire was also characterized by an extraordinary degree of cosmopolitanism and showed relative tolerance to its diverse population. Compared to the religious wars and pogroms of Europe, tax discrimination against Jews and Christians in the Ottoman Empire was a modest and tolerable form of second-class citizenship. Though they often faced discrimination, they rarely suffered outright persecution and in the age of the Ottomans, the Jews faced nothing to match the Nazi Holocaust. The right existed for people to have a different religion from that of the ruler, a principle that was inconsistently applied but was centuries ahead of the European standard of the day.

Cruelty and cosmopolitanism are important features of the Empire's lasting impact on the Middle East. Its existence helped maintain the Middle East as a single region, united along overlapping axes of language, religion, government, education and cultural assumptions. Within this unity, the Empire also fostered the region's diversity and complexity. Minority groups, including religious minorities, could find a reasonably comfortable place within it. Unlike Europe, which went through a century of warfare and barbarism in the struggle between the Catholic and Protestant versions of Christianity, the Ottoman Empire allowed different forms of Islam to coexist relatively peaceably. In many ways, the Greek Orthodox Church received more prestige and authority under the Muslim Ottoman Empire in its prime than ever under the Christian Byzantine Empire.

In the 18th and 19th centuries, the Empire faced the challenge of Wahhabism in the Arabian Peninsula – a movement based on the demand for a return to early Islamic values and principles. In response it put increased emphasis on the religious role of the Sultan as Caliph. Even then, the Empire remained tolerant of religious difference.

At the same time, the form of government and the culture of power that were bequeathed to the region were arbitrary, aloof and capable of despotic repression of dissent. Despite the widespread appeal of democratic principles since the late 19th century, the archetypal and most common form of power in the Middle East remains arbitrary. That is a large part of what the wave of change in the region since late 2010 has been about – a demand for accountable rather than arbitrary authority.

But the arbitrary nature of their authority leaves Middle Eastern states ill-suited to adapting to new challenges through steady reform. This leads to frustration of popular demands and radicalization of popular movements, against which the elites resort to their old ways.

The dilemmas that the Middle East has faced and been unable to resolve – the high degree of illiteracy, the inability or unwillingness in most cases to use oil wealth for the general wellbeing, the uncertainty about how to face the modern world, and challenges such as the empowerment of women – in part, these can be traced back to the lasting influence of one of world history's greatest Empires.

REMAINS OF THE OTTOMAN EMPIRE
Country names and borders 2015

territory remaining in 1915

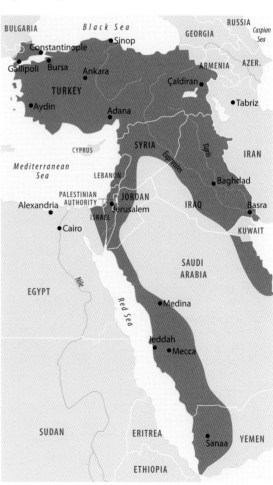

EUROPEAN COLONIALISM

The long decline of the Ottoman Empire opened the door for the rising force of Europe to push its way into the Middle East. To begin with, the pressure was almost surreptitious; it was hard to recognize and it was not part of a strategy for weakening the Empire but for gaining a tiny share of its fabulous wealth.

In the 16th century, special trading rights and tariff concessions granted to foreign governments – known as 'capitulations' – were initially an indication of Ottoman power. The poorer West came to the Sultan to seek special permission to trade. But the system meant that profitable trade increasingly fell into Western hands and by the 19th century, the capitulations were both a cause and a symptom of the Empire's economic weakness and its inability to modernize in the face of the European challenge. Increasingly during the 19th century, European trading and financial strength was not simply overwhelming the Ottoman grip on its peripheral regions, but weakening its economic core.

After trade came raw power. Suleiman the Magnificent had been baulked outside Vienna in the 1530s. A later Caliph was defeated 150 years later in the same place and the Empire's European dominions began to contract. A further century later, a French force landed in Egypt as an outgrowth of a Western European war and batted aside a much larger Egyptian force, bringing to an end six centuries of power held by the Mamluks, who controlled Egypt but were subject to the Ottomans. Napoleon Bonaparte's Egyptian victory was tarnished by the arrival of a British fleet that destroyed his supply system and cut short his Middle East venture. Were it not for that, the consequences of Bonaparte's victory might have been more lasting.

As it was, Bonaparte not only brushed aside the Mamluks but smashed the image of Ottoman superiority. This was a decisive blow to Ottoman self-confidence and capacity to exercise far-flung power – and by the same token, a fillip to Western European self-confidence and ability to win local allies.

―――

Bonaparte smashed the image of Ottoman superiority and boosted Western European self-confidence

―――

On the back of trade and military superiority came – selectively at first, more or less comprehensively in the end – the urge to influence, control and rule. Through a combination of treaty agreements with local elites and military presence, the web of European influence and control spread. Algeria was the first major territory to come under direct European occupation, but further to the east the British were already nibbling at the fringes of Ottoman territory in the Arabian Peninsula.

That reflected a basic geostrategic pattern of European colonial expansion. The British focus was on the eastern half of the region, the French on the west. Not until after World War I – when France's rights as an ally were hard even for the British government to deny – was France able to gain direct control of formerly Ottoman territories outside North Africa, though it had pressed for influence in modern-day Lebanon and Syria for much of the 19th century.

Britain's economic and strategic interests in the region were intensified by the opening of the Suez Canal – designed by a French engineer – which allowed the world's largest empire to achieve a quicker trade link with India and the rest of its Asian possessions. Following World War I, with its gains from the collapsed Ottoman Empire (as well as gains in Africa and Asia at the expense of defeated Germany), the British Empire reached its greatest extent, just as it entered a war-weary, economically broken period of unprecedented weakness.

COLONIAL POWER AND THE OTTOMAN EMPIRE ON THE EVE OF WORLD WAR I
Country names and borders 1914

- British
- French
- Italian
- German
- Spanish
- Ottoman Empire
- independent state

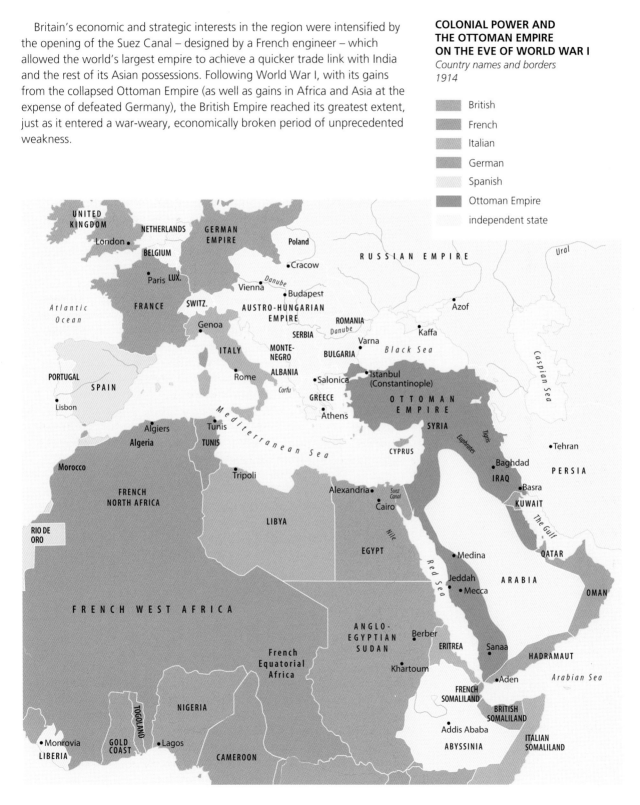

Colonial impact

The British and French authorities did not always describe their colonial possessions in straightforward language. They called them protectorates (Tunisia and later Morocco 'protected' by the French, Kuwait and later Egypt by the British) and after World War I their power in former Ottoman territories was endorsed by mandates from the League of Nations.

Whatever the name, the reality was colonial – and it became a very supple reality. In Egypt, nominal independence in 1922 was completely consistent with continuing British control of everything it most valued. When World War II came, British control expanded to encompass the whole of Egypt, in case Egyptians might not automatically take the British side.

In general, the British sought to protect their strategic interests with as little intrusion as possible into the societies whose acquiescence they demanded. French colonial authorities attempted to reach deeper into the fabric of the society and culture of the people they aimed to dominate. They both encouraged more French settlers and did more to attempt to reconstruct parts of Arab society according to the French model. In Algeria, this included insistence on French schooling and compulsory military service.

Opposition was ruthlessly suppressed. The 1871–72 Kabyle rebellion against French rule in Algeria was a major uprising involving over 100,000 insurgent fighters, after which land seizure and denial of legal rights were used to punish and control the Algerian population. Despite their different approach, the British authorities in Egypt also had no compunction in asserting their will. Notoriously, in 1906, a fight involving five British army officers who were out hunting led to 32 Egyptians being convicted of premeditated murder: four were hanged and the rest were flogged.

Throughout the 19th century and even after they were allies from the beginning of the 20th century, Britain and France were imperial rivals in Africa and the Middle East. Each sought to gain territory before the other could, risking an armed clash as late as 1898 in southern Sudan, for example. As the Ottoman Empire weakened, they manoeuvred against each other, mutually determined to keep other powers (especially Russia) out, each trying to concede to the other as little as possible. As they picked over the pieces of the Ottoman Empire, Germany took a position of advantage in Istanbul, provided copious military assistance and gained an ally for World War I.

**The power of the new colonial masters
was every bit as arbitrary as
that of the Ottoman Empire**

The deepest similarity between British and French colonialism in their respective Middle Eastern territories was the contradictory content and impact of what they brought with them from their Western European homelands. The power of the new colonial masters was every bit as arbitrary as that of the Ottoman Empire. It was in no whit based on popular consent, though in both the British and French colonial elites there were those who prided themselves on knowing Arab society, knowing what Arabs wanted and needed, and knowing individual Arabs who would agree with the colonial diagnosis and treatment. As the years of colonial dominion wore on, the threadbare nature of those pretensions was ever more sharply exposed as colonial power met increasingly fierce resistance.

But arbitrary power was not the full story of the colonial impact. Britain and France both brought modernity into the Middle East, which came in the form of the products of the industrial age – not least, to begin with, greater wealth and superior military technology. It also came in the form of a modern way of thinking that emphasized organization, efficiency, discipline and the importance of achieving concrete results in every endeavour.

Even while modernity continued to upturn old ways of life in Europe, it was being exported with profoundly destabilizing effects. Among Arab thinkers it initiated a long, and in many ways still unresolved, debate about how the Arab ways of life, the Arab identity and Islam could survive against modernity: was the best strategy to accept modernity, to confront it head on and reject it, or to attempt to co-opt and use those components of modern thinking that were not incompatible with Arab culture and religion?

———

Britain and France both brought modernity into the Middle East

———

Modernity, in short, was simultaneously troubling and tempting, made even more so by the third aspect of the West's contradictory impact – liberal and progressive political philosophy that stressed liberty, individual human rights and, by widely accepted extension, independence from colonial rule. These were not necessarily the views of even a small fraction of those Europeans who came to the Middle East in service of colonial government or for trade. And even those Europeans, whether living and working in the Middle East or back home, who did hold progressive political views in domestic matters – such as the extension of voting rights to all adults – did not necessarily believe such views applied to Arabs as well as Westerners.

But selectiveness and inconsistency could not mask the fact that the authority exerted by the colonial powers abroad was of a type that was, as time passed, increasingly unacceptable at home. In the period between World War I and World War II the right to hold colonies became a matter of political controversy in Europe in a way that had been unknown in the early days of their empires. And this philosophical uncertainty became increasingly visible in the Middle East and increasingly encouraging to those who sought independence, and who challenged the Western powers on the basis, in part, of Western ideas of freedom.

THE NEW MIDDLE EAST AFTER WORLD WAR I

World War I was not only a war of unprecedented devastation and global reach, it also re-shaped world politics. Its impact on the Middle East was profound, with effects still felt a century later.

The war was born out of rivalry between the great European empires, and detonated by the particular rivalries in the Balkans – as great and medium powers fought to capitalize on the opportunities created by the culmination of the long Ottoman decline. War shattered three empires (Germany, Austria-Hungary and the Ottoman Empire itself), reshaped one through revolution, civil war and terror as a new form of dictatorship (Russia), and exhausted two – Britain and France, who were the victors along with the USA and other allies, including Italy.

The peace settlement divided up the defeated powers' territories both in their homelands and their empires. Some of this re-alignment process created new states, some allotted control of extra territory to neighbouring states or to greater powers. This diplomacy continued for four years, from 1919 to 1923.

Faced with the slow weakening of the Ottoman Empire during the 19th century, it had been British policy to ensure that no other power gained a

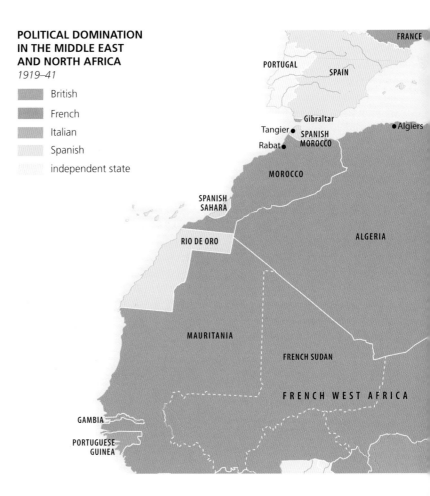

POLITICAL DOMINATION IN THE MIDDLE EAST AND NORTH AFRICA
1919–41

- British
- French
- Italian
- Spanish
- independent state

decisive advantage. Early in World War I, British policy swung from stopping others gaining an advantage and set out to gain regional advantage for itself.

———

War shattered three empires, reshaped one and exhausted two

———

In the course of this, the British government started to make promises, beginning in 1915, when it agreed to a special French role in the area of modern-day Lebanon and Syria. Between 1915 and 1916 it promised Hussein, the Sharif of Mecca, support for the establishment of an Arab kingdom in exchange for a revolt against the Ottomans. The kingdom was to stretch from the Indian Ocean in the south-east to what is today the northern border of Iraq, with the exception of the Syrian / Lebanese coast, the Holy Places in Palestine, and with special access for Britain to key points such as Baghdad and Basra (see map p 32). Finally, in 1917, the British government promised to the British Zionist movement, and through it to the world movement, support for establishing a national Jewish home in Palestine.

(see map p 32)

CHRONOLOGY continued

1923 Treaty of Lausanne sets boundaries of modern Turkey and supersedes the Treaty of Sèvres. No provision made for independent Kurdistan. Proclamation of the Republic of Turkey with Mustafa Kemal named president.

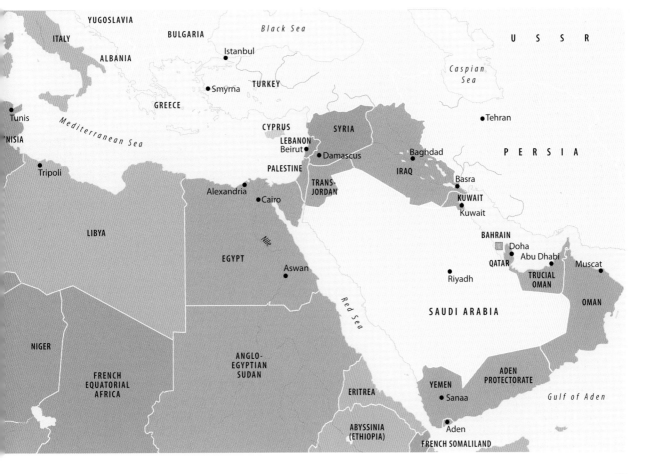

A new regional order

Britain's promises to Arab and Zionist leaders were made amid the exigencies of a war from which it was far from certain that Britain would emerge victorious. Not surprisingly, they contradicted each other and could not all be fulfilled.

The historical record appears to indicate that the promise to the Arab leaders was the shallowest. In a six-week period at the end of 1915 and the start of 1916, Britain and France negotiated an outline agreement – the Sykes–Picot agreement – on their shares of the spoils to come. France was 'given' control of a significant area of Anatolia and the eastern Mediterranean coastline, and influence in the northern and north-western parts. This included areas already promised to Hussein, Sharif of Mecca, by the British. Meanwhile, Britain 'received' most of the rest of the promised Arab kingdom, including the Gulf coast, leaving the rest of the Arabian Peninsula, except Aden, for the Arabs.

The assumption behind these agreements was that, once the war was won, the victors could divide up Ottoman territory as they wished but the diplomatic process turned out to be more complex than that. As well as the rising power of the USA, there were the interests of Italy, who joined the Allies in 1915, and Greece to consider. Italy received some of the Dodecanese Islands in the Aegean, and Greece gained control of what territory it could in the traditional Hellenic areas of south-western Anatolia.

The British and French governments appear to have genuinely believed that their rule would not only be good for Arabs but also popular. While British officials were rightly scathing about French expectations of a unanimous welcome from Arabs who would come under the latter's dominion, they retained parallel delusions about their own popularity. Whenever and wherever it was possible to gauge Arab opinion, the preferred option was Arab rule.

The most important constraint upon British and French plans after the war was fatigue. They took on new imperial roles they no longer had the capacity to fulfil. Britain could not run both Egypt and Iraq and control the rest of its empire. By 1922 Britain opted instead to allow internal autonomy for Egypt under a friendly king, and the same in Iraq ten years later. The carve-up of Anatolia foreseen in the Sykes–Picot agreement never happened and, with British forces in the Middle East region rapidly shrinking after the end of the war, the decisive leadership of Mustafa Kemal drove out the Greek forces and constructed a new republic. Nor was it possible for Britain and France to maintain the commitment of the 1920 Treaty of Sèvres to give part of Anatolia to the proposed new state of Kurdistan; again, Mustafa Kemal's forces prevailed.

**Whenever and wherever it was possible
to gauge Arab opinion,
the preferred option was Arab rule**

With grand plans, inadequate forces, and a lofty disdain for the people's will, Britain and France set out to impose a new regional order. The post-war settlement after World War I – while it actually left almost nothing settled – created the basic system of states and state borders that continues to shape the region's political geography today.

THE SYKES-PICOT AGREEMENT OF 1916 FOR THE PARTITION OF THE MIDDLE EAST

Negotiations between Britain and France over the partition of the Ottoman Empire took six weeks, starting in late November 1915.

British negotiations were led by Sir Mark Sykes. Widely travelled in the Middle East, especially Turkey, he gained the confidence of the British War Minister, Lord Kitchener, and dominated the government committee that in 1915 worked out British policy.

The French negotiations leader was François Georges Picot, an official in the foreign service. His father and brother were influential figures in French policy in Africa and Asia respectively and he spoke for a combination of commercial, political and religious interests seeking a leading role in Lebanon and Syria.

The agreement was approved in early February 1916. It referred to the possibility of an independent Confederation of Arab states, but contradicted earlier promises made by Britain to the Sharif of Mecca.

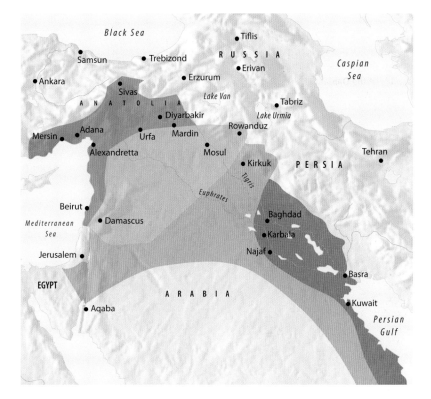

- Blue zone direct French control
- A zone under French influence
- Red zone direct British control
- B zone under British influence

THE STATE OF KURDISTAN

Proposed by Treaty of Sèvres *1920*

- proposed state
- to be given choice of joining after 1922

In parcelling out the Ottoman Empire, Britain and France, the victorious powers, intended to create a Kurdish state. The Treaty of Sèvres fixed a two-stage process, with the Anatolian part given independence immediately and Iraqi Kurds being given the choice whether to join after 1922. For the new Turkey, Mustafa Kemal refused to cede any land and Britain and France backed down. In 1925, 25,000 died in a failed Kurdish uprising in Turkey.

29

DECOLONIZATION AND ARAB NATIONALISM

European colonialism reached its zenith and began to decline at approximately the same time. Britain and France emerged from World War I with more territory and less capacity for wielding power than ever. The colonial grip was starting to slacken.

Developments in the Middle East unfolded within a larger context. Before World War I, Britain had already fought a bitter war to retain control in South Africa, and had then granted considerable autonomy to the white colonial class there and the other settler colonies of Australia, Canada and New Zealand. In Ireland it had faced the prospect of mutiny in the army before the war over plans for partial independence, and the 1916 uprising was followed by the war of independence between 1919 and 1922. In the Indian sub-continent – Britain's largest and most important imperial possession – the struggle for independence was intense throughout the inter-war period, culminating after World War II. Similar, though less critical, pressure was also felt throughout most of the French empire.

Britain and France were victors in World War I but were badly weakened by both the unprecedented human toll of the war and its economic costs. And

INDEPENDENCE IN THE MIDDLE EAST AND NORTH AFRICA
1945–75

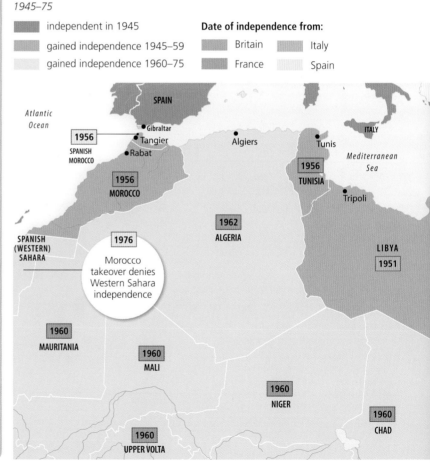

- independent in 1945
- gained independence 1945–59
- gained independence 1960–75

Date of independence from:
- Britain
- France
- Italy
- Spain

the political climate in Europe was changing, weakening the self-confidence and firmness of purpose necessary for the imperial enterprise. All this meant the victors did not directly take over formerly subject nations in Europe after World War I, agreeing instead to self-determination in the Balkans and in Central and Eastern Europe. The inter-war years therefore provided considerable impetus for Arab nationalist sentiment and movements for independence.

World War II was another blow to the already weakening colonial system; if the human costs of war for Britain and France were not as great as in World War I, the economic and strategic costs were much greater. The two decades after 1945 were the great era of decolonization – in the Middle East as everywhere. Under pressure throughout their empires, Britain and France quickly ceded power in the Levant – in France's case to Lebanon and Syria, and in Britain's case to Israel and Jordan. The colonial powers were also faced in the Middle East, more than in any other world region, by the rising power of the USA and the USSR. The region's traditional strategic importance, its contiguity with the southern borders of the USSR, and above all its oil, attracted the new global superpowers to seek to expand their influence in the Middle East. With all these factors in play, the end of the European colonial era was inevitable.

____

The two decades after 1945 were the great era of decolonization

____

ANTI-COLONIAL FORCES

Egyptian nationalism after World War I was led by al-Wafd al-Misrî, meaning 'The Egyptian Delegation'. It was formed in November 1918 to send a delegation to London to discuss Egypt's post-war status. The British authorities responded by arresting and exiling the leaders, leading to a revolt in March 1919 in which 800 Egyptians were killed.

The Wafd maintained the pressure and won formal independence though the British kept control of key ministries and the Suez Canal. In World War II, the Wafd supported the Allies on the understanding that full independence would come after the war. But British forces stayed on, Egypt was not fully independent and the Wafd was discredited. In 1952 an army coup won Egypt's full independence; among the new government's earliest actions was the dissolution of the Wafd.

In Algeria, the National Liberation Front (FLN) was set up in 1954. It carried out its first attacks in November 1954. By the end of 1955, France had committed more than 400,000 troops to Algeria. Estimates of war deaths go as high as 1.5 million. The FLN survived and opposition to the war grew in France in the late 1950s. Talks were opened in May 1961. The war ended in 1962 with a ceasefire agreement and an Algerian referendum approving independence.

French settlers had made up about one-sixth of the population. Many were bitter at this turn of events as were many in the army. As France withdrew from Algeria it faced an army mutiny and violent acts of sabotage.

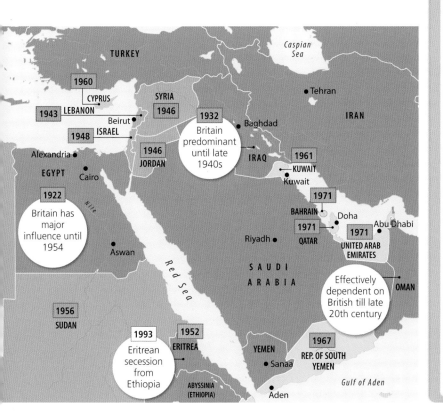

TURKEY

Caspian Sea

1960
CYPRUS
1943 LEBANON
Beirut
SYRIA
1946
1932
Britain predominant until late 1940s
Baghdad
Tehran
IRAN

1948 ISRAEL

Alexandria
1946 JORDAN
IRAQ
1961
KUWAIT
Kuwait

EGYPT Cairo

1922
Britain has major influence until 1954

Nile

Aswan

Red Sea

1971
BAHRAIN Doha
1971
QATAR
1971 Abu Dhabi
UNITED ARAB EMIRATES

Riyadh

SAUDI ARABIA

Effectively dependent on British till late 20th century
OMAN

1956
SUDAN

1993
Eritrean secession from Ethiopia

1952
ERITREA

YEMEN
Sanaa

1967
REP. OF SOUTH YEMEN

Gulf of Aden

ABYSSINIA (ETHIOPIA)
Aden

Independence and unity

For the first three decades after the break-up of the Ottoman Empire and end of World War I, the only genuinely independent Arab states were Saudi Arabia and Yemen. Some others had formal independence but were effectively dependent on the colonial power. But behind the apparently firm European grip on the region the reality was different. Following the cataclysm of World War I, the Arab world's movement towards independent statehood was inevitable.

As the pressure began to build towards independence, some Arab thinkers and politicians envisaged a larger goal than that – a vision of pan-Arab unity. For a century and a half after Napoleon's Egyptian adventure, the Middle East was confronted, challenged and, by many measures, bested by Europe. How could the Arab world respond to the challenge of European power? This became the key intellectual and political question and a central part of the argument about what kind of independence Arabs should aim for.

The pre-existing unity of the region began to influence this discussion. Though there are many differences between Arabs in the various parts of the region, there is also much that is shared in terms of language and culture, not least religion, history and experience. It is easy to exaggerate how much is shared; not all Arabs are Muslims, for example, and there are several different forms of Arabic, some of which are barely mutually comprehensible. These differences run so deep that when the idea of Arab unity began to take hold, there were many both inside and outside the country who questioned whether Egypt, let alone any area to its west, counted as Arab.

On top of these cultural differences, there were also (and still are) sharp rivalries and different interests among the Arab elites and, as everywhere, deep cleavages of class and distinctions between urban and rural dwellers.

ARAB KINGDOM PROMISED TO SHARIF HUSSEIN OF MECCA BY THE BRITISH
1915–16

territory of the promised kingdom

areas that were explicitly or implicitly not part of the promise

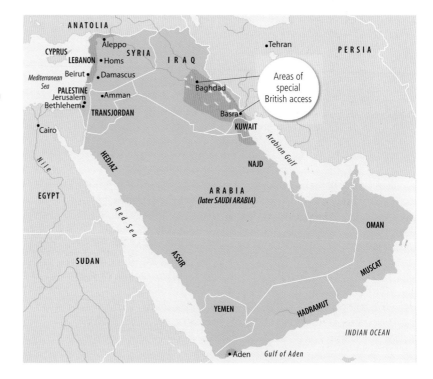

Nonetheless, Arabs in different parts of the Middle East have mutual connections that are much stronger and more real than those to be found among, for example, Europeans in different parts of Europe. Moreover, advocates of Arab unity argued that, on top of everything else they shared, the Arab world also had a common enemy – the West.

Ideas of Arab unity spread during and immediately after World War I. One of their most famous proponents, though his ideas were not especially influential at the time, was the British army intelligence officer, TE Lawrence – Lawrence of Arabia. The Arab revolt against the Ottomans, beginning in 1916, in which he played his role as a liaison officer and strategic adviser to the uprising, was a key moment in the evolution of the idea of unity. The leaders of the revolt were the Hashemite family, led by Hussein ibn Ali, the Sharif (religious leader) of Mecca; his sons, Faisal and Abdullah, led the Arab forces in the field. To win the alliance, the British promised Hussein he would have a new kingdom embracing most of the Arab world east of Egypt. This was a dynastic ambition Hussein could not have fulfilled by allying with Istanbul. It made much more sense to go with the British offer and oppose the Ottomans, even if it meant fighting with a Christian power against a Muslim one.

As it turned out, the British broke their promises straight after the war, and instead of a large single state created a patchwork of smaller ones, though Hashemite leaders took power in Transjordan, Iraq and in the Arabian Peninsula (where their grip on power was broken in 1925 by Ibn Saud, the founder of Saudi Arabia).

After the war, the unity of the Arab revolt frayed quickly under the twin pressures of internal differences among Arab leaders as they pursued their political opportunities and ambitions, and the continuing imperial presence of the British and French. But ideas of Arab unity became increasingly attractive. The reality for Arab leaders was that, even if they were leading a nominally independent government, when they had to deal with one of the two big European powers one on one, they were inevitably at a disadvantage. They could make some gains if Britain or France were distracted by events and pressures elsewhere, but as soon as London or Paris could concentrate once more, what had been gained could as easily be lost. The incapacity of each working alone led inevitably – and almost too easily – to the conclusion that it would be better for all to work together.

_____

On top of everything else they shared, the Arab world had a common enemy – the West

_____

This lesson was driven home by what happened in Palestine. In the 1930s, pressure from growing Jewish immigration led to the Arab revolt (see pp 36–41). Yet after World War II – the second European paroxysm of violence and destruction in a quarter of a century – was over in 1945, while the Europeans were weaker, the Arabs were no stronger. By the end of the 1940s, the Arab states' complete inability to prevent the foundation of the state of Israel seemed finally to underline the need for practical Arab unity.

MOROCCO AND WESTERN SAHARA

In the first two decades of the 21st century, two issues of national independence remain unresolved in the Middle East. One is Palestine. The other is Western Sahara. Spain was the old colonial power. As it abandoned Western Sahara in 1976, Morocco and Mauritania disputed possession. Both faced opposition from the Polisario Front, founded in 1973 to fight for national independence. The right of the Sahrawis to self-determination was acknowledged by the International Court of Justice in 1975. The Sahrawis are a diverse group with both Berber and Arab roots. Different sub-groups speak an Arabic dialect or the Berber language, Tamazight. Morocco did not accept the ICJ judgement and asserted its claim the same year with the 1975 'Green March' – over 300,000 people rallying at the border. Expulsions of Sahrawis began and war ensued, costing several thousand lives. By 1979 when Mauritania withdrew its claims, tens of thousands of Sahrawis had fled to Algeria. Morocco stayed, deploying an army that by the mid-1980s was about the same size as the Sahrawi population. By the end of the 1980s there was stalemate. Morocco held most of the territory but could not defeat Polisario who had safe bases in Algeria but could not prevail against a much more powerful opponent. In 1991 the UN brokered a ceasefire with a promise of a referendum so the Sahrawis so could decide their future. It was supposed to happen four months after the ceasefire. But Morocco wanted its settlers to vote. When Polisario conceded that, new obstacles were brought up. In 1996, the UN suspended the process. There followed successive rounds of talks, with international mediators producing compromises that one side or the other would turn down. In 2005 and again in 2011 popular protests against the failure to agree on a plan turned violent. By 2015, the issues had not been resolved and the referendum had not been held.

The pan-Arab dream

The high tide of pan-Arab nationalism came in the 1950s. Its advocates argued that denying Arab unity led persistently to defeat, so Arab states were unable to prevent the establishment of Israel in 1948. Responding to cultural unity with political unity was the pan-Arab solution.

Onto this platform of hope and defeat came a charismatic leader – Gamal Abdel Nasser, leader of the Free Officers' coup in Egypt in 1952, prime minister from 1954 and president from 1956. His decisive moves to force the British out of Egypt, take the Suez Canal into Egyptian ownership, and face down the combined strength of Britain, France and Israel in 1956, made him the voice of pan-Arab unity. In reality, the outcome of the Suez crisis in 1956 owed at least as much to US opposition to Britain's and France's adventurism as it did to Egyptian obduracy; even so, here at last was a victory against the European colonial powers and against Israel.

Two years after Suez, Arab unity was put into practice with the establishment of the United Arab Republic (UAR) in 1958 by Syria and Egypt. This was the pinnacle of pan-Arab nationalism – and the beginning of its end.

The union lasted only three years, partly because Syrian politicians objected to what they experienced as Egyptian dominance. Two years later Ba'athist coups in Syria and Iraq presaged another attempt – this time a federation of three states. It never got beyond a plan. Rivalry between Syria and Iraq, regardless of the regimes' shared political roots, meant that by the time a third effort was made in 1971, Iraq had dropped out and was replaced by Libya. This third effort was little more than rhetorical.

_____

The 1958 United Arab Republic was the pinnacle of pan-Arabism and the beginning of its end

_____

By then, as a practical political programme, pan-Arab nationalism was a thing of the past. In 1967, Israel once again defeated a coalition of Arab states, and did so with devastating swiftness in only six days of war. The new Arab world, it seemed, for all its talk of unity, was in reality as weak as the old. Three years later, Nasser died and pan-Arab nationalism could be pronounced dead at the same time.

Deeply appealing though the idea was to large numbers of Arabs, the practice did not match up. Many Arab leaders saw the pan-nationalists as a revolutionary threat. There was war among Arabs when Egypt went to war in Yemen from 1962 to 1967, and again in 1990 when Iraq invaded Kuwait and most Arab states joined the US-led coalition for war against Iraq in 1991.

The failure of Arab unity in practice has been profound – unity was achieved only for short periods, and even then it was never very effective (Suez, after all, was Egypt's achievement, not a general Arab success, widely though it was celebrated). Nonetheless, much of the sentiment behind pan-Arab nationalism remains important. It continues to have an important institutional vehicle in the Arab League, founded in 1945, even if the League's declarations do little more than remind Arabs of the long-term ineffectiveness of the project of unity.

Other ideologies were soon to fill the vacuum left by the demise of pan-Arabism.

The Suez crisis

CHRONOLOGY

1952 Free Officers' coup in Egypt, led by Colonel Gamal Abdel Nasser

1954 *Apr* Nasser becomes prime minister.

Oct Britain and Egypt agree timetable to evacuate the British Suez base.

1955 Escalation of Egypt–Israel conflict – Egypt blockades Straits of Tiran making Israel's port at Eilat unusable – Israeli military raids into Gaza.

East–West Cold War escalates in the Middle East. Iraq, Turkey, Britain, Pakistan and Iran form the Baghdad Pact for military strength against the USSR: Egypt begins to receive Soviet weapons via an arms deal with Czechoslovakia.

1956 *Mar* France calls on Egypt to end support for the Algerian FLN – Nasser refuses.

Apr UN Secretary-General starts process seeking to re-establish Israeli–Egyptian armistice.

June Nasser becomes president of Egypt after unopposed election. British withdrawal from the Suez Canal zone complete.

July Nasser nationalizes the Suez Canal Company. Britain and USA retaliate by withdrawing funding for Aswan Dam development project.

Oct Egypt, Syria and Jordan sign defence pact.

Britain, France and Israel finalize plan to act against Egypt.

29 Oct Israel attacks Egypt.

30 Oct Britain and France deliver ultimatum calling on parties to end fighting – as planned, Israel agrees – as expected, Egypt refuses. UN calls for ceasefire and withdrawal of Israeli forces.

31 Oct British and French forces bomb the Suez Canal zone. US President Eisenhower publicly condemns the use of force in the Middle East and threatens to use economic strength against Britain and France.

5 Nov USSR threatens to intervene with force if attacks on Egypt continue.

6 Nov British and French forces take control of Suez but the British Cabinet is informed that the value of the British currency is threatened and gold reserves have fallen by one-eighth in the attempt to protect the pound sterling against US pressure.

7 Nov End of the Suez War.

12 Nov Egypt agrees to deployment of a UN force in the Canal zone.

22 Nov Last British troops leave the Canal zone.

1957 *Apr* Suez Canal re-opens for international commerce.

THE SINAI CAMPAIGN
October–November 1956

Israel 1948 to 1967

Israeli parachute landing troops

principal Israeli advances 29 October to 5 November 1956

British and French landings in Port Said

Mediterranean Sea

Jerusalem
Dead Sea
Gaza
Rafah
Beersheba
Port Said • Port Fuad
El Arish
Suez Canal
Kantara
Abu Aweigila
ISRAEL
Negev
E G Y P T
Ismailia
Bir Gafgafa
Kusselma
Bir Hasana
JORDAN
Suez
Mitla Pass
Kalat en-Nakhel
Ras Sudr
El Tamad
Eilat
• Aqaba
S i n a i
• Humaydah
Gulf of Suez
Gulf of Aqaba
SAUDI ARABIA
Abu Zeneima
Dahab • Makna
• Tor
Sharmah
Nabek •
Tiran
Sharm el-Sheikh

Israel sea trade disrupted by Egyptian blockade in 1955

THE FORMATION OF THE STATE OF ISRAEL

CHRONOLOGY

1882 Start of politically motivated Jewish immigration to Palestine.

1885 Term 'Zionism' coined by Nathan Birnbaum, a Jewish writer.

1896 Publication of *Der Judenstaat* (The Jewish State) by Theodor Herzl.

1897 First Zionist Congress.

1909 Tel Aviv established as a twin city to Jaffa.

1914–18 World War I.

1917 Balfour Declaration promises Jews a national home in Palestine.

1918–20 British forces occupy Palestine.

1920 British Mandate to govern in Palestine approved by League of Nations.
Jewish Agency founded.

1922–23 Transjordan recognized by Britain and League of Nations as an independent entity. Borders of Palestine Mandate finalized at the Lausanne Conference.

1936–39 Arab revolt against British rule and Zionist immigration to Palestine.

1937–38 Two successive British Royal Commissions recommend partition of Palestine into two states.

1939–45 World War II. Mass murder of Jews in Europe.

1946 Jewish militants blow up the King David Hotel, Jerusalem, killing 91.

1947 *Feb* Britain refers Palestine issue to the United Nations.

Nov UN votes for partition of Palestine into separate Jewish and Palestinian states with special international status for Jerusalem. Internal violence starts.

1948 *14 May* State of Israel proclaimed.

15 May Arab–Israeli War.

1949 War ends – Israel becomes member of the UN: Knesset and the Israeli government move to Jerusalem.

1950 West Bank officially annexed by Jordan.

1964 Palestine Liberation Organization (PLO) established.

To the citizens of the new state, the declaration of Israel's independence on 14 May 1948 marked the realization of a dream and the creation of a place of survival and belonging after genocide. To Palestinians, the event is simply known as al-nakba – the catastrophe.

The term Zionism was coined by a Jewish writer a few years after the beginning, in 1882, of migration to historic Palestine by Jews with the goal not only of escaping anti-Jewish prejudice, discrimination and, at worst, pogroms, but also of ultimately establishing a homeland. Despite the political intention, the early migrations seemed innocuous and the numbers insignificant. Different population estimates show between 10,000 and 24,000 Jews living in the area later called Palestine in about 1880. Over the next three decades, perhaps as many as 1,000 Jews arrived each year. By the end of World War I, some estimates put the Jewish population as numbering about 56,000.

The meaning of this migration and its possible consequences only started to become clear during World War I as the Ottoman Empire went from decline to break-up. As plans were formulated to re-make the Middle East, and with the declaration in 1917 by British Foreign Secretary Arthur Balfour supporting 'the establishment in Palestine of a national home for the Jewish people,' Zionism became both more significant and realistic. Though the Zionist Organization's 1919 proposal for a Jewish homeland stretching well to the east of the Jordan river was flatly rejected by the great powers, the British government permitted continuing Jewish immigration into Palestine throughout the inter-war years. The British authorities did, however, make a sharp division between the areas to the west and to the east of the river, and in 1922 established Transjordan as a separate entity into which they refused to permit further Jewish immigration.

There were from time to time – both from British politicians and from Jewish leaders – statements that Jews and Arabs could and would live peacefully alongside each other. The 1917 Balfour Declaration included the 'understanding' that 'nothing shall be done which may prejudice the civil and religious rights of existing non-Jewish communities in Palestine'. But Zionists

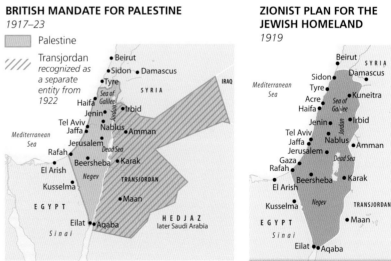

BRITISH MANDATE FOR PALESTINE
1917–23

Palestine

Transjordan recognized as a separate entity from 1922

ZIONIST PLAN FOR THE JEWISH HOMELAND
1919

did not simply want a place for Jews to live; they wanted a Jewish state, and that made hopes of easy peaceful cooperation unrealistic. 1920 saw the first Arab violence against Jewish immigrants and the first organized Jewish response. In 1929 came anti-Jewish riots. In 1936, as Jewish immigration increased after Hitler's 1933 assumption of power in Germany and the antisemitic policies of the Nazis, a major Arab uprising began, lasting until 1939. It was aimed equally against British rule and growing Zionist encroachment; particular causes of resentment were the willingness of the immigrants to pay any price for land – well above reasonable market values – and the willingness of some Arab landowners to sell, enriching themselves while weakening the position of the Palestinian community.

The British authorities suppressed the uprising and attempted to forestall a violent Jewish response and the spiral of escalation that would ensue. They also responded by studying – some 20 years after the initial commitment – how a Jewish homeland could be created. Successive Royal Commissions in 1937 and 1938 examined the question and produced proposals for partition – a two-state solution, one for the Arabs and one for the Jews.

By the late 1930s there were about 400,000 Jews in Palestine, in a population of about 1.3 million. It was no longer possible to dismiss the inflow as insignificant. It was also well understood, at least by the British authorities, that the arrival of Jews and the possible establishment of a new state was opposed by most Palestinians, and that Palestinians had no reason to think they could thrive or even co-exist in a Jewish state.

As a result, the Zionists' outline of a homeland in 1919 became less attractive to the British and partition of the area came onto the agenda with, to begin with, a quite modest area for the Jewish state and a continuing role for Britain. By 1947 much had changed and the UN partition plan provided more for Israel, less for the Palestinians and nothing for the fading empire. And within a year of Israel's formation, war had allowed it to increase its share of the area again.

COUNTRIES THAT FOUGHT AGAINST ISRAEL IN 1948

ISRAEL'S BORDERS – PLANS AND RESULT

- proposed Jewish State
- proposed Arab State
- to remain under British Mandate

BRITISH ROYAL COMMISSION PARTITION PLAN
1938

UN PARTITION PLAN
1947

RESULT
1949

Zionism and antisemitism

Over the years Zionism has displayed some striking dualities – a secular ideology that came to be buttressed in deeply religious fashion, an ideology that is as liberating for some as it is profoundly threatening for others. Only by pretending that Jews did not experience brutal persecution is it possible to deny Zionism's liberatory aspect; only by denying that Palestinians have human rights is it possible to ignore the threatening aspect of the same ideology.

THE HOLOCAUST
1941–45

countries from which Jews were sent to concentration camps

Jewish population in 1940–41 *where known*

estimated number of Jews killed between 1941 and 1945 *where known*

From 1948 until 1973, the Jewish population of Israel increased from about 657,000 to over 3 million. More than half of the population increase (over 1.3 million out of 2.4 million) was directly accounted for by immigration from at least 30 countries. In all of these countries, Jews had been minority communities, and how they lived – not least the degree of prejudice and discrimination they faced, but also many other facets of their daily lives – was shaped in part by their interactions with the majority. Though united by being Jewish and in many cases by having experienced persecution, they were also a highly diverse population, from different cultural backgrounds, speaking different languages, and brought up in different education systems. Out of this diversity, in a hostile environment, the new state of Israel set about building an Israeli nation.

Education, the projection of national symbols, the development of a historical narrative culminating in the establishment of the new state, the teaching of a new national language – all these standard tools of modern nation-building have been deployed by Israel. The identification of the establishment of Israel with the fulfilment of a religious mission adds a further dimension and greater depth to nation-building than has been available to most new states of the post-1945 era. That both the original dream of a homeland and the eventual establishment of the new state grew from persecution, and that the persecution of Jews in 20th-century Europe reached

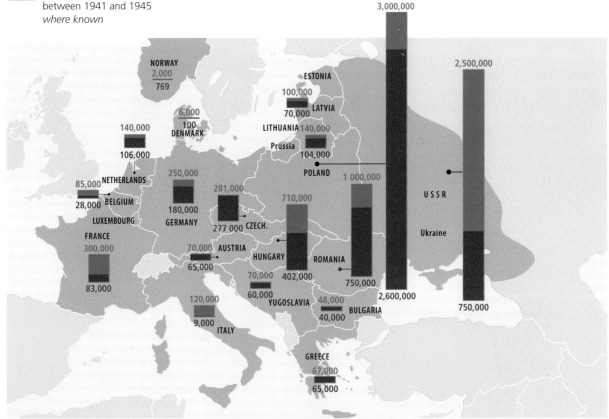

unprecedented depths of violence, together with the violence and hostility amid which Israel was established, have all contributed to the insistence within Israel that nationality is of paramount importance. And the continuing experience of hostility from the Arab world after 1948 – though not uniform – makes the maintenance of national security a definitive part of national identity.

Considerably before Israel's foundation, the ideas of Ze'ev Jabotinsky became influential. In 1923, he dismissed the optimistic thought that the Arabs would accept and even support the establishment of a Jewish homeland. He argued that an 'Iron Wall' had to be built, based on military strength, to enforce and defend statehood until Palestinians accepted the reality of Israel's existence. Then negotiations could begin and a pragmatic compromise could be worked out. Until that point, in Jabotinsky's view, Israel should be uncompromisingly reliant on its own strength.

The Palestine Liberation Organization, internationally accepted as speaking for the Palestinian people, recognized Israel's sovereignty over 78 per cent of historical Palestine in 1988. To most observers, that seemed to mean that the goal of the Iron Wall strategy had been achieved. The history of Israeli–Palestinian conflicts and negotiations since then suggests that the Iron Wall has become permanent, not a transitional strategy as Jabotinsky assumed.

In 1923 Jabotinsky argued that an Iron Wall had to be built

JEWISH MIGRATION TO THE NEW ISRAEL
1948–early 1970s

country of origin and number of Jewish migrants
rounded to 500

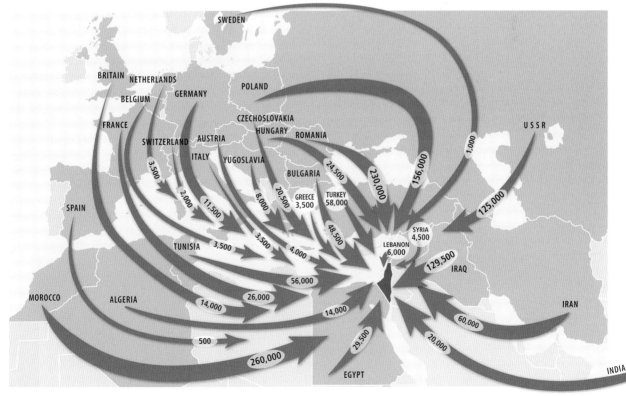

Flight and exile

Palestinians are the second largest group of refugees in the world today. A total of about 5 million are officially registered with the UN Relief and Works Agency (UNRWA) as refugees and the number grows at a rate of about 3 per cent each year, approximately an additional 150,000 people. Of the total, almost a third, about 1.6 million, live in 61 refugee camps in Jordan, Lebanon, Syria, Gaza and the West Bank. The vast majority were born refugees and have never had the chance to live in Palestine.

The first wave of flight came with the foundation of Israel in 1948. It began with the fighting that started as soon as the UN voted for partition in November 1947. During the war in 1948, over 400 Palestinian villages were cleared and destroyed – nearly half of all Palestinian villages in Mandatory Palestine at the time. In all, over 80 per cent of Palestinians living within the borders of Israel left. The second major outflow of refugees came in 1967 when Israel took control of the West Bank.

Over the years there have been fierce controversies about why the Palestinians left between 1947 and 1949. Some writers and politicians have claimed Palestinians mostly left because their leaders told them to, more to make a political point than in fear for their lives.

Detailed studies have been done based on official archives. These show very few cases in which specific orders by Arab leaders to abandon villages can be traced. Cases in which instructions were given, even when combined with those where the motive for flight is uncertain, account for less than 20 per cent of all villages abandoned. In 80 per cent or more of cases, the motives were that Israeli forces cleared the villagers out, or the village came under attack, or that the villagers were influenced by what happened down the road in another village, or that they were afraid of being caught up in the fighting, or that they were influenced by a whispering campaign, mounted by the Israel Defence Force and the Haganah group, aimed at stoking Palestinian fears.

The vast majority of Palestinian refugees have never had the chance to live in Palestine

----

Israel rejects the right of 'return' for the refugees and displaced persons. Israel wants to solve the problem with a mixture of resettlement in Arab countries, international efforts to improve the refugees' living conditions, and restricted re-admission. The Palestine Liberation Organization insists on the absolute right of return for all Palestinian refugees of 1948. Many neutral observers have agreed over the years that the best short-to-medium-term interests of Palestinian refugees themselves sometimes take second place to the political manoeuvring for this longer-term goal.

FLIGHT

1948

Detailed research reveals different numbers for how many villages were destroyed, partly depending on definitions, partly on the period of time covered. During the war in 1948, over 400 villages in the new Israel were cleared and destroyed; 418 are shown on this map.

- Palestinian village destroyed

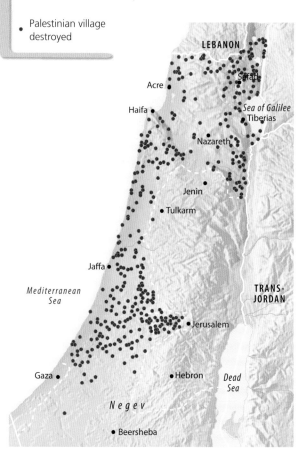

LEBANON

Acre

Haifa

Safad

Sea of Galilee
Tiberias

Nazareth

Jenin

Tulkarm

Jaffa

Mediterranean
Sea

TRANS-
JORDAN

Jerusalem

Gaza

Hebron

Dead
Sea

Negev

Beersheba

From the beginning of the 20th century to its end, the situation of the Palestinian people underwent a shattering transformation, as they went from being the well-established inhabitants of a region with family ties going back generations, to dispersal into a diaspora. This transformation unfolded because of, and at the same time as, the relocation of large numbers of Jews in their diaspora to Palestine, which was itself the result of what had been suffered by Jewish communities over centuries, culminating in an unparalleled holocaust. The response to these historical traumas has been to set group against group, placing an iron divide between them, thus germinating new agonies in the region.

EXILE

1951

When the UN Relief and Works Agency for Palestine Refugees (UNRWA) started work in May 1951, it cared for approximately 860,000 Palestinian refugees out of over 950,000 Palestinians seeking its help. There were others – numbering as many as 300,000 by some estimates – who were unable to register as refugees for one reason or another but were living in refugee-like circumstances.

flight of Palestinian refugees *officially registered refugees only*

REGISTERED PALESTINIAN REFUGEES
2013

=10,000 living in camps   =10,000 living elsewhere

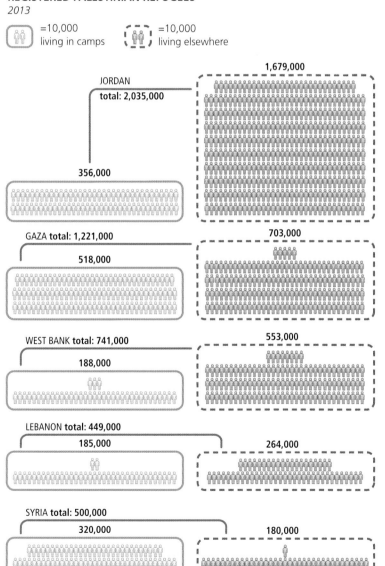

JORDAN total: 2,035,000
1,679,000
356,000

GAZA total: 1,221,000
518,000
703,000

WEST BANK total: 741,000
188,000
553,000

LEBANON total: 449,000
185,000
264,000

SYRIA total: 500,000
320,000
180,000

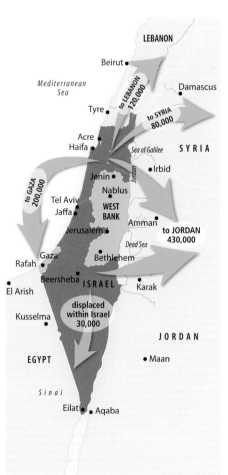

41

OIL

We depend on oil so we depend on the Middle East. That has seemed to be the simple reality behind the outside world's relationship with the region. It is subtly changing.

Crude oil is the world's most actively traded commodity. It lies at the heart of transport and is important in other ways as a source of energy and a key element of various chemicals. It is therefore at the heart of world manufacturing and the production and distribution of food.

At the start of the 21st century the Middle East's share of proved oil reserves worldwide was about 60 per cent. But new oil discoveries are always being made and by 2012 just over 50 per cent of proved reserves lay in the Middle East, almost all in the Gulf. Shifts in the pattern of consumption are also occurring as Europe and the USA reduce their reliance on Middle Eastern oil while Asian powers' consumption grows.

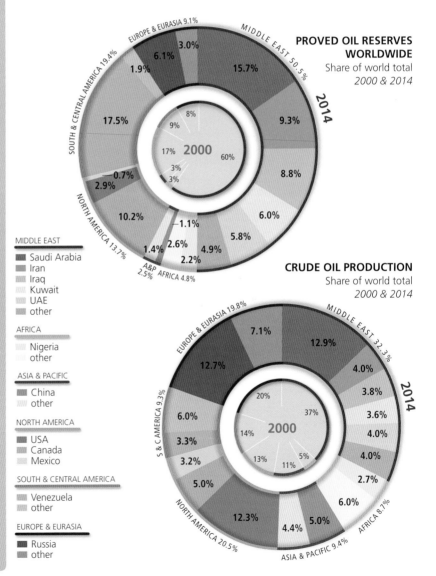

PROVED OIL RESERVES WORLDWIDE
Share of world total
2000 & 2014

CRUDE OIL PRODUCTION
Share of world total
2000 & 2014

MIDDLE EAST
- Saudi Arabia
- Iran
- Iraq
- Kuwait
- UAE
- other

AFRICA
- Nigeria
- other

ASIA & PACIFIC
- China
- other

NORTH AMERICA
- USA
- Canada
- Mexico

SOUTH & CENTRAL AMERICA
- Venezuela
- other

EUROPE & EURASIA
- Russia
- other

The first discovery of commercially exploitable oil in the Gulf region was in Iran before World War I. British interests found the oil and quickly set themselves up to profit from it. There was a surge of oil discovery in the 1930s, and the pace of commercial exploitation accelerated in the decade after World War II. Saudi Arabia's pre-war annual income from oil production was about half a million dollars; by 1950 it was over $50 million and five years later was rising above $200 million.

Control was a sensitive issue from the outset. In Iran, Mohammad Mossadeq became prime minister in 1951 with a programme of taking Iranian oil exploitation into Iranian ownership. Two years later, after considerable instability and a British boycott, Mossadeq was ousted in a coup set up by the CIA with British intelligence assistance.

The Middle East's major oil-producing states and Venezuela formed the Organization of the Petroleum Exporting Countries (OPEC) in 1960 in response to Western oil companies lowering prices the previous year. For its first decade, the new cartel could not affect prices but things began to change when the Suez Canal was closed as a result of the Six Day War in 1967. It stayed closed for six years. It was still possible for Europe and the USA to get oil from Libya because it lies west of the Canal. Libya could therefore negotiate higher oil prices with a group of US oil companies that were smaller than, and independent of, the giant transnational corporations that dominated world trade. That broke the majors' grip on world prices. Iran, Iraq and Saudi Arabia all followed suit and in 1971 a general deal was made – the Tehran agreement – setting prices for the next five years.

Then came the October 1973 Arab–Israeli War. Now accustomed to working closely together, Middle Eastern oil states agreed to reduce supplies, cutting them altogether to countries whose governments supported Israel, and also to raise prices. When the war was over and sanctions lifted, prices increased nonetheless, quadrupling in a single year. Oil income rose dramatically – from $500 million to $7 billion in two years for Iraq, and from $2.7 billion to $25 billion for Saudi Arabia.

Control and influence over oil and access to it thus became a fundamental feature of world politics. This placed the Middle East at the centre of attention and ensured outside powers would want to intervene and interfere. As long as Middle East oil is important in advanced economies, this will not change.

The USA, however, has successfully covered itself against a repeat use of the oil weapon. In the early 1970s, US reliance on oil from the Middle East was increasing as its reliance on oil from the Americas fell. Events forced a re-think and determined action soon reversed the trends. Among the richest countries, it is Japan that relies most on Middle East oil and is accordingly the most vulnerable to the oil weapon. India and China's consumption, dependence and vulnerability are also growing.

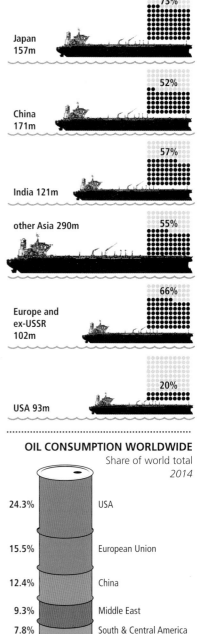

IMPORTS FROM MIDDLE EAST
Volume of oil imported from Middle East (tonnes) and as percentage of total oil imports
2014
selected major importers

Japan 157m — 73%

China 171m — 52%

India 121m — 57%

other Asia 290m — 55%

Europe and ex-USSR 102m — 66%

USA 93m — 20%

OIL CONSUMPTION WORLDWIDE
Share of world total
2014

24.3% USA
15.5% European Union
12.4% China
9.3% Middle East
7.8% South & Central America
4.7% Japan
4.3% Africa
4.3% India
3.5% Russia

The oil market

2000 Oil prices rise following attack on the *USS Cole* in Aden harbour.

2002 US Congress authorizes President Bush to use force if necessary against Iraq on grounds of its alleged weapons of mass destruction programme.

2003 US war on Iraq with UK, Australia and some other states participating – Saddam Hussein overthrown, occupation begins, resistance starts. UN ends economic sanctions against Iraq. UN sanctions against Libya lifted.

2004 Insurgents in Iraq attack the country's oil infrastructure.

2005 Oil prices at an all-time high due to war in Iraq and Hurricane Katrina in the USA. Saboteurs begin attacks on Yemen pipeline.

2011 Popular mobilization and political change in several Arab countries push oil prices to new record levels.

2012 UAE inaugurates new pipeline to by-pass Straits of Hormuz. Shamoon computer virus attacks Saudi-owned Aramco, the world's largest oil producer, erasing data on three-quarters of its computers. Documents, spreadsheets, emails and files are replaced by image of burning US flag.

2014 Iraq's oil exports reach highest volume for 35 years.

As with other commodities, the world oil market never stands still. Proved reserves worldwide have risen by well over 60 per cent since the early 1980s and more than a quarter since 2000. Most of these discoveries have been outside the Middle East so its global share has fallen. But its share of reserves is far greater than its share of current production: in other words, taken as a whole, the region is pumping its oil at a more conservative rate than the global average. So its oil will last for longer.

Oil prices have been volatile for over four decades. After the peaks of the 1970s, they remained lower for most of the 1980s and 1990s, rising from 2000 in response to the Palestinian uprising against Israeli occupation in September 2000, the increased focus on terrorist groups with roots in the Middle East after September 2001, and the US invasion of Iraq in 2003. When the situation in Iraq began to stabilize around 2009, prices fell. And when the wave of political change in the region started in 2010 to 2011, up went prices to new record levels.

In normal times, oil-producing states do not want exorbitant prices. It is in their interests that the world economy grows. Nor do they want economic incentives for rich countries to develop alternative forms of energy. They want high revenues, and although their position was hurt by declining prices in the 1980s it would suffer more if they raised long-term prices too much.

Similarly, the long-term interest of the USA, China and the other high-consuming states is in a smoothly functioning world economy. In 1990 when Saddam Hussein's Iraq occupied Kuwait, the fear was that the Iraqi dictator would then control 20 per cent of the world's proved reserves. But the spectre behind this was not that he would stop American cars running. Rather, it was that he would have too much bargaining power in world politics, which he could leverage for regional advantage.

WORLD OIL PRICE FLUCTUATIONS
1900–2014
Price per barrel of crude oil in US dollars at constant value (2014)

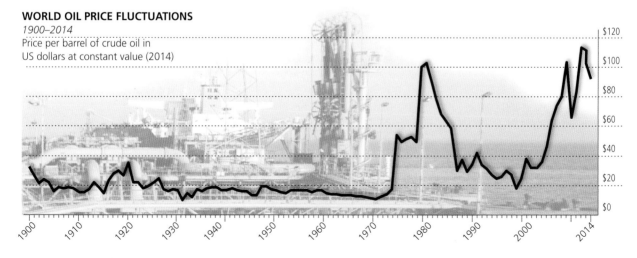

Oil is such a central commodity for the modern world that it must always be a political issue. The brutal Iran–Iraq War in the 1980s threatened to become a global conflict issue when Iran and Iraq each tried to disrupt the other's oil exports in the 'tanker war'. Oil infrastructure is also a natural target for attack, as Iraq showed as it withdrew from Kuwait in 1991, and as insurgents have shown in occupied Iraq since 2003 and in Yemen. And political instability and violent conflict in the world's major oil-producing region makes markets nervy and pushes up prices. But whereas these risks were once routinely depicted as posing a direct threat to the USA and European countries and their citizens' well-being, the real risk now is a broader, more diffuse and systemic one.

For the people who live where oil was discovered and tapped, the success of the oil-producing states in taking control of their own oil resources has had important but mixed consequences. Oil income has given the state a preponderant role in the economy of its country; this has held back the non-oil sectors of the economy. There has been relatively little diversification and nothing that is at the cutting edge of modern industry, technology or services. In the Gulf States, oil income has gone into the hands of the ruling families who controlled the state at the point when income surged. Even where some of the new wealth has been used for the general good, it has also helped to ensure the longevity of undemocratic systems of government by allowing ruling elites to defer problems and buy off potential opponents. The quietly changing global geopolitics of oil are part of the backdrop as forces for social and political change continue to be active throughout the region.

TRANSPORT AND CHOKE POINTS

Each day about 60 million barrels (over 8 million metric tonnes) of crude oil are transported by sea. About 45 million barrels per day are taken through relatively narrow shipping lanes. Strategic concerns about the vulnerability of these choke points and also oil pipelines are a constant background theme in the tangled international political positioning and manoeuvring on Middle Eastern issues.

The concerns once focused on the potential for action by governments – whether of the region or further afield – that might want to strangle oil supplies to, for example, Western Europe or Japan in time of crisis. Today a greater focus of concern is the non-state groups that have demonstrated the capacity to make spectacularly destructive attacks on very high-profile targets. Were such attacks to occur, the jittery nature of world oil markets means prices would undoubtedly rise, for a period of time at least. And the importance of oil means that this could lead to serious economic and political consequences.

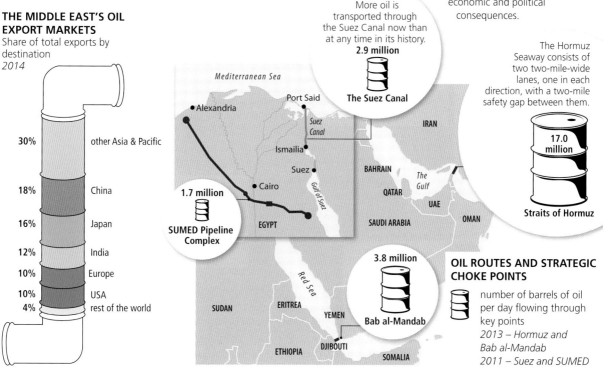

THE MIDDLE EAST'S OIL EXPORT MARKETS
Share of total exports by destination
2014

- 30% other Asia & Pacific
- 18% China
- 16% Japan
- 12% India
- 10% Europe
- 10% USA
- 4% rest of the world

More oil is transported through the Suez Canal now than at any time in its history.
2.9 million
The Suez Canal

Mediterranean Sea
Port Said
Alexandria
Suez Canal
Ismailia
Suez
Cairo
Gulf of Suez
1.7 million
SUMED Pipeline Complex
EGYPT

IRAN
BAHRAIN
QATAR
The Gulf
UAE
SAUDI ARABIA
OMAN

The Hormuz Seaway consists of two two-mile-wide lanes, one in each direction, with a two-mile safety gap between them.
17.0 million
Straits of Hormuz

Red Sea
SUDAN
ERITREA
YEMEN
3.8 million
Bab al-Mandab
ETHIOPIA
DJIBOUTI
SOMALIA

OIL ROUTES AND STRATEGIC CHOKE POINTS
number of barrels of oil per day flowing through key points
2013 – Hormuz and Bab al-Mandab
2011 – Suez and SUMED

THE US PRESENCE

The US presence has been a crucial and often defining influence on events in the Middle East for 60 years since the mid-1950s, but its role goes back much further, starting with its first foreign-policy actions and first war when it was newly independent.

The main issues at the end of the eighteenth century were trade and piracy. The British navy no longer protected American trade from pirates off the north-west coast of Africa. Trying to buy off the Barbary corsairs did not stop their raids so the new state built its own navy and went to war.

Quickly after trade came religion. The idea of spreading Christianity in the region from which it sprang gained many adherents, and the first American missionaries started work in 1819. As the century progressed, the understandable wariness of the region's rulers when confronted by Christian evangelists encouraged the latter to focus more on good works than sermons, aiming to win converts by running hospitals and schools.

_____

The USA set out to block rising Soviet influence

_____

For the USA, North Africa was an important staging post for the onslaught on Italy and Germany in World War II. But intensive US interest began later, as an off-shoot of the Cold War. The 1956 Suez crisis formed the first watershed in US policy (see p 35). The USA was, in general, warmly disposed towards Israel. It had funded Jewish migration from Europe to Palestine and was the first government to recognize the newly formed state in 1948. Nonetheless, it strongly opposed the actions of Israel, as well as those of its wartime and Cold War allies Britain and France in using military force to wrest control of the Suez Canal back from Egypt.

Different people read the decline of European colonial power differently. If Arab nationalists saw Suez as the beginning of the end of an era of humiliation, US strategic analysts saw it as opening the door to Soviet influence. The USSR was comfortable with, and supportive of, the anti-imperialism of the region, and was ready to back independence movements and fighters as part of the global struggle against the USA and its allies. To balance the effects of its rebuff to Britain, France and Israel, the USA set out to block rising Soviet influence. This political and strategic agenda was at the time more important than access to the region's oil. The USA was a major oil producer itself at the time and the sense of depending on Gulf oil only grew some 15 to 20 years later. Even so, for its allies, oil was a significant secondary motive, part of the Cold War's geopolitics.

The policy that US President Eisenhower set out a few months after the end of the Suez Crisis highlighted a willingness to use armed force to assist any state that asked for help 'against armed aggression from any country controlled by international communism'. This was an oft-repeated theme in US policy of the time. Governments that could show they were resisting international communism were treated as friends of the USA and of freedom, however little freedom they allowed at home.

The first action under the Eisenhower Doctrine was a military show of support for King Hussein of Jordan when there were anti-government riots in

1957. The following year, the Doctrine underpinned the deployment of US Marines to Lebanon.

Events in Lebanon in 1958 were the first stage in the unravelling of the constitutional compromise by which the country had gained independence, consisting of a balance of power between the political representatives of the main religious groups in the country (see p 55). This fragile arrangement fell apart in the 1960s and 1970s and the country descended into a nightmarish civil war from 1975 to 1990. The events of 1958 were a foretaste. But Lebanese President Chamoun managed to present the internal political turmoil as a matter of Soviet-backed Syrian aggression. The US administration ignored Lebanese realities, took Chamoun at face value and sent in the marines for three months.

They did little, however, as a vicious civil war was fought, killing some 2,000 to 4,000 people. In the mid-1980s in Lebanon, the USA again overlooked the complexities of Lebanese and regional politics as it again deployed marines, this time losing well over 200 American lives. And something similar happened 20 years later as US forces went into Iraq, overlooking complex local realities in favour of a global big picture.

CHRONOLOGY continued

1973–74 Arab Oil Embargo – Gulf States restrict oil exports to countries viewed as pro-Israel.

1978 Camp David Egypt–Israel Summit – Egypt completes move into US camp.

1979 *Apr* Iranian Revolution – Ayatollah Khomeini, leader of the Islamic Republic of Iran, denounces USA as the Great Satan.

Nov Iranian militants occupy US Embassy in Tehran and hold its staff hostage for 444 days.

Dec Soviet invasion of Afghanistan raises US fears of threat to regional stability.

1980 *Jan* USA announces Carter Doctrine: readiness to use force if interests in the region face direct Soviet threat.

Sept Iraq invades Iran.

1981 US strategic cooperation agreement with Tunisia.

1982 US strategic cooperation agreement with Morocco.

Israel invades Lebanon. USA leads multinational peacekeeping force in Beirut.

1983 *Oct* Suicide bomb kills 241 US marines and civilians in Beirut.

1984 US forces leave Beirut.

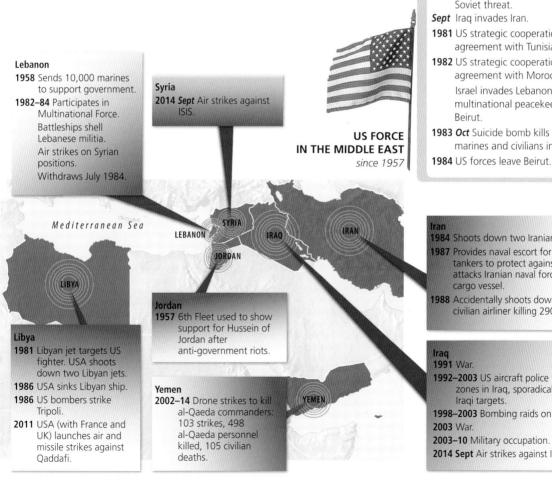

Lebanon
1958 Sends 10,000 marines to support government.
1982–84 Participates in Multinational Force. Battleships shell Lebanese militia. Air strikes on Syrian positions. Withdraws July 1984.

Syria
2014 *Sept* Air strikes against ISIS.

US FORCE IN THE MIDDLE EAST
since 1957

Mediterranean Sea

Libya
1981 Libyan jet targets US fighter. USA shoots down two Libyan jets.
1986 USA sinks Libyan ship.
1986 US bombers strike Tripoli.
2011 USA (with France and UK) launches air and missile strikes against Qaddafi.

Jordan
1957 6th Fleet used to show support for Hussein of Jordan after anti-government riots.

Yemen
2002–14 Drone strikes to kill al-Qaeda commanders: 103 strikes, 498 al-Qaeda personnel killed, 105 civilian deaths.

Iran
1984 Shoots down two Iranian fighters.
1987 Provides naval escort for Kuwaiti oil tankers to protect against Iran. US attacks Iranian naval forces, sinking cargo vessel.
1988 Accidentally shoots down Iranian civilian airliner killing 290 passengers.

Iraq
1991 War.
1992–2003 US aircraft police 'no fly' zones in Iraq, sporadically striking Iraqi targets.
1998–2003 Bombing raids on Iraq.
2003 War.
2003–10 Military occupation.
2014 *Sept* Air strikes against ISIS.

Angles of influence

The US presence in the Middle East is multi-faceted – economic, political, military and cultural. For successive US governments, politics and strategy have been key. It is the Middle East's location that does much to make it strategically vital.

It was a US strategist who popularized the term, 'the Middle East', before World War I. The region is next door to Europe, a major economic partner and strategic ally for decades, and lies conveniently south of what was the USA's greatest adversary – the former Soviet Union – much of which is now Russia, sometimes a partner, but always a tricky one, and increasingly an adversary. The Middle East has long been a good place from which to watch and – as technology advanced – listen in on the power to the north.

Israel is well established as the major US ally in the region. The relationship is not always easy. Following initial warmth, the 1956 Suez crisis introduced a note of distance. But US aid and cheap loans were major components of Israel's economic viability, and by the 1970s the USA had become Israel's biggest arms supplier.

Dependence has not made Israel visibly compliant with US preferences, however. Successive Israeli governments have shown little compunction about working against US policies they find uncongenial. Indeed, with the strength of the Israel lobby in US politics, many observers conclude Israel has more influence on US policy than vice versa.

The USA has always been careful not to let Israel be its only regional ally. The Nixon Doctrine in 1969 moved the USA away from the commitment to act with armed force, and stressed the role of local powers as enforcers of regional order. This led to US closeness with Iran under the Shah, with the Gulf kingdoms and above all with Saudi Arabia. The latter is important not only because of oil – and the importance of Saudi oil to the USA in the 21st century is considerably less than in the 1970s, when American fears arose that Arab oil producers could use oil to blackmail the USA out of its support for Israel. Rather, Saudi Arabia is an important part of ensuring a regional balance that

CHRONOLOGY

1986 USA bombs Libya following bomb in a Berlin disco used by US personnel.

The Iran–Contra scandal breaks, exposing arms-for-hostages deals between the White House and Iran's revolutionary government.

1987 The US Navy provides escorts for Kuwaiti oil tankers through the Persian Gulf in order to deter attacks from Iran during the Iran–Iraq War.

1990 Iraqi invasion of Kuwait. USA deploys major forces to Gulf for the first time, including half a million service personnel in Saudi Arabia.

1991 *Jan–Mar* US-led forces drive Iraq out of Kuwait. US and UK (and until 1998, France) maintain 'no-fly zones' in northern and southern Iraq until invasion of Iraq, 2003.

1993 US forces launch a cruise-missile attack on Iraqi intelligence headquarters in Baghdad in retaliation for the attempted assassination of former US President George Bush in Kuwait in April.

1995 USA imposes oil and trade sanctions on Iran for alleged sponsorship of 'terrorism', seeking to acquire nuclear arms, and hostility to the Middle East process.

1996 Osama bin Laden, leader of the al-Qaeda network, declares that expelling the USA from Arabia is the most important Islamic duty after faith itself.

19 American troops are killed in a terror attack on the Khobar Towers housing complex in Saudi Arabia.

2000 Al-Qaeda attack on US ship in Aden Harbour kills 17 US soldiers.

2001 US and UK disable Iraq's air-defence network

Sept Al-Qaeda attacks on New York and the Pentagon.

2002 US President Bush names Iran and Iraq as part of 'axis of evil' and mobilizes for war against Iraq.

USA commences drone strikes on al-Qaeda commanders in Yemen.

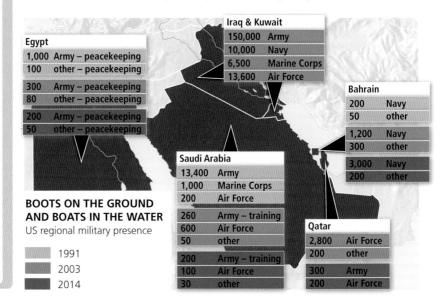

Egypt		
1,000	Army – peacekeeping	
100	other – peacekeeping	
300	Army – peacekeeping	
80	other – peacekeeping	
200	Army – peacekeeping	
50	other – peacekeeping	

Iraq & Kuwait		
150,000	Army	
10,000	Navy	
6,500	Marine Corps	
13,600	Air Force	

Bahrain	
200	Navy
50	other
1,200	Navy
300	other
3,000	Navy
200	other

Saudi Arabia		
13,400	Army	
1,000	Marine Corps	
200	Air Force	
260	Army – training	
600	Air Force	
50	other	
200	Army – training	
100	Air Force	
30	other	

Qatar	
2,800	Air Force
200	other
300	Army
200	Air Force

BOOTS ON THE GROUND AND BOATS IN THE WATER
US regional military presence

- 1991
- 2003
- 2014

meets broader US geostrategic interests. When the Shah of Iran was overthrown in 1979, the USA found Saudi Arabia was all the more important.

The USA thus has close alliances both with Israel and with Arab states in principle hostile to it, revealing the pragmatism of its policy. In the late 1970s, for example, the Carter administration responded flexibly to the decision by President Sadat of Egypt to ease Egypt out of the Soviet sphere of influence, despite the fact that Egypt had only a few years previously started a war against Israel. At the time that the first diplomatic overtures were made, Sadat's Egypt maintained a high level of anti-Israel rhetoric. As the diplomacy continued, the tune changed. US political assistance and economic support were crucial in achieving the 1979 peace agreement between Israel and Egypt.

Since then, the military aspect has again become a more important part of the US regional role. The USA supplied arms to Saddam Hussein's Iraq to support it in the war it started against Iran in 1980. Even Iraqi use of chemical weapons against both Iranian forces and Kurdish civilians did not diminish American backing. And as well as lavishly supplying arms to many states, the USA has been in almost permanent military action in the region since the early 1980s – first in Lebanon, then the waters of the Gulf, then Iraq, Libya and Syria, as well as in neighbouring Afghanistan.

There is another angle to US influence, visible at a more general, popular-cultural level, in Hollywood movies, international electronic news media and the internet. Many of the styles of consumerism – including, not least, women's dress – and ways of thinking that are projected as an integral part of cultural production worldwide offer direct challenges to Muslim traditions, as they do to all sorts of tradition everywhere.

The homogenizing force of modernity is a challenge and affront in a multitude of places, and it is widely discussed as such and directly resisted. Modernity is often perceived as essentially American. And many opponents of US policy and influence in the Middle East see the political and cultural dimensions as inextricably linked.

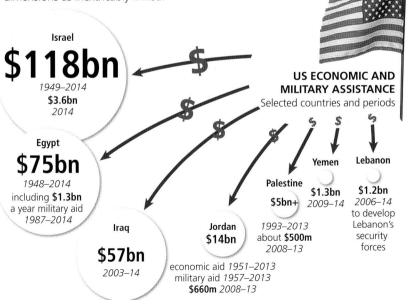

Israel
$118bn
1949–2014
$3.6bn
2014

Egypt
$75bn
1948–2014
including **$1.3bn**
a year military aid
1987–2014

Iraq
$57bn
2003–14

Jordan
$14bn
economic aid *1951–2013*
military aid *1957–2013*
$660m *2008–13*

Palestine
$5bn+
1993–2013
about **$500m**
2008–13

Yemen
$1.3bn
2009–14

Lebanon
$1.2bn
2006–14
to develop
Lebanon's
security
forces

US ECONOMIC AND MILITARY ASSISTANCE
Selected countries and periods

CHRONOLOGY *continued*

2003 USA, with support from the UK and Australia, invades and occupies Iraq.

Sept US military withdrawal from Saudi Arabia is complete.

2004 USA imposes unilateral sanctions against Syria and ends sanctions against Libya.
Two US Army sieges of Fallujah leave over 1,700 Iraqis dead.

2004–05 Insurgency against USA and allied occupation of Iraq gathers force.

2006–07 USA debates use of force to stop Iran's nuclear programme, until intelligence estimate concludes that weapons programme ended in 2003.

2007 US 'surge' strategy initiated against insurgency in Iraq.

2009 US President Obama makes a major speech in Cairo calling for a new relationship between the USA and Islam. US forces begin withdrawing from Iraq.

2010 The computer worm 'Stuxnet' – widely reported to be of US–Israeli origins – crashes Iranian government computers and nuclear enrichment apparatus.
Last US combat brigade leaves Iraq.
USA announces arms sales to Saudi Arabia worth $60 billion.

2011 *Mar* USA, UK and France launch air strikes on Libya to support rebels and oust Qaddafi.

Aug President Obama calls on Bashir al-Assad to step down as president of Syria.

2012 *Aug* Obama declares use of chemical weapons in Syria would cross a 'red line', leading to US military action.

2013 *Sept* Obama states Assad regime did use chemical weapons in Damascus suburb the previous month. Joins with Russia to support UN action to remove Syrian chemical weapons.

2014 USA launches air strikes on the ISIS group in Iraq and Syria.

PART TWO

THE REGION ON THE CUSP OF CHANGE

Anyone trying to understand the Middle East is struck by two seemingly contradictory realities: the region is both unified in many ways and highly diverse at the same time. The Middle East is bound together through the various historical, religious, cultural, economic and political influences that have shaped it. Within that unity its diversity has been shaped by the self-same influences.

The viewer from outside can all too easily lose sight of one of the two halves of that combination. What is seen from a distance is often somewhat indistinct and visible only in broad outline. Too often this can feed an essentially racist assumption that the differences between, for example, the region's ethnic groups do not matter. Yet as soon as those differences come sharply into view, in the atrocities that groups inflict on ordinary people on the other side of the region's many religious dividing lines, for example, the shared ways of living and of seeing the world that generate strong feelings of solidarity within the region can fade into the background.

One way to view the world – or any region within it – is through statistics. These permit comparisons both within a region and with the rest of the world, and they are often a fruitful way of gaining insight into broad social, political and economic trends. Statistics, however, are notoriously capable of leading the observer astray precisely by over-emphasizing some differences and under-stating others.

Statistics are not facts but a way of representing facts. The very process of gathering the data can smooth out differences and mask diversity or, by contrast, pluck out a single strand and give it too much attention. Statistical comparison involves a large amount of estimation and therefore choice about what is important. Data about the same issue from different sources are often quite incompatible with each other – sometimes for technical reasons and sometimes because of the political agendas or blinkers of the organizations presenting the data. To make matters worse, some important phenomena simply fall out of the statistics: when Iraq was internationally isolated after 1991, for example, it disappeared from some international data collection. Palestinians are also statistically invisible in some data collection as are other groups in the Middle East such as the Sahrawi of Western Sahara. Statistics have historically tended to ignore gender difference, though this is a problem that has been recognized and is steadily being resolved.

So while statistics can be useful, they should be treated with care by statisticians, researchers and readers alike.

POLITICS AND RIGHTS

CAPITAL PUNISHMENT

Number of known executions in countries with most executions *2013*

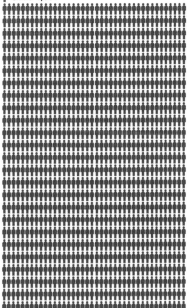

China 1,001

Iran 369+

Iraq 169+

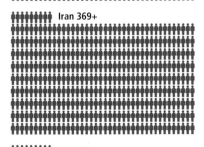

Saudi Arabia 79+

USA 39

Somalia 34+

Sudan 21+   Yemen 13+

Japan 8   Vietnam 7+

Full democracy is a rare flower in the Middle East. The acid test of democracy comes when those with power have to give it up because the majority of the people say they must; few Middle Eastern states have taken that test and fewer have passed it.

An established democracy is a state in which executive government power changes hands as the result of free and fair elections. Elections that produce a consultative assembly but not a government do not meet the criterion, so the Gulf Kingdoms (pp 134–139 and 142–143) are not regarded as established democracies. Nor does a state meet the criterion if a body that is not elected can decide who it is who gets to run for office, as in Iran (pp 94–97).

There are states where there has been revolutionary change and the new government is elected but different parties have not yet come to power: these do not qualify either. They can be regarded optimistically as transitional democracies. Algeria (pp 86–87) and Iraq (pp 100–103) have had elections that were largely free and fair but the democratic process of turn-and-turn about has not unfolded yet. In Egypt (pp 116–121) in 2013, an election confirmed in power the group that had previously ousted the elected government. In Libya, (pp 122–125) it needed great optimism to see any political system amid the country's chaos in 2014 and 2015 even though elections had happened. In Lebanon (pp 82–85) there is a strong democratic tradition but in 2013 and 2014 the parliament voted to extend its own life, finding elections too great a risk at a tumultuous time.

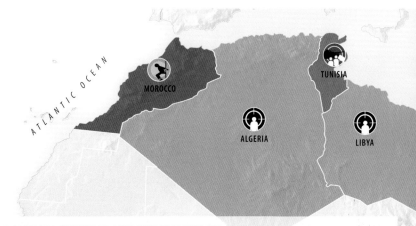

POLITICAL SYSTEMS AND HUMAN RIGHTS
2014

Political system

- established democracy
- transitional democracy
- one-party rule
- monarchy
- theocracy
- dependent territory

Reported extreme abuses of human rights
Showing only the worst abuses by each country
2011–13

 extra-judicial executions and disappearances

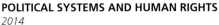 killing of protestors

 torture

In the entire region of the Middle East and North Africa, only Tunisia (pp 114–115) and Israel (pp 72–81) count as consolidated democracies and only Israel is experienced at it. In Israel, Palestinian citizens (as distinct from Palestinians living in the Occupied Territories of the West Bank and Gaza) form 20 per cent of the population. Although they face a variety of forms of discrimination and disadvantage, many of them embedded in law and others simply in the actions of both the national government and local authorities, and though they often describe themselves as second-class citizens, they are able to vote in elections on the same terms as Jewish citizens. There have been Palestinian Members of the Knesset (the Israeli parliament) ever since the first election in independent Israel in 1949. There were 16 Palestinian Knesset Members following the March 2015 elections, 13 of them representing the main Arab coalition party list.

Beyond acts of discrimination, other abuses of human rights are rife in Israel, as they are throughout the region, a product of wars and a long history of arbitrary authority, producing rage against the authorities. The formal accession by most states to international treaties forbidding extreme human rights abuse has turned out not to mean very much in all too many of them.

KEY HUMAN RIGHTS TREATIES

Almost the whole of the Middle East has acceded to them all

Convention on the Rights of the Child, 1989 ☑

International Convention on the Prevention of the Crime of Genocide, 1948 **not Oman and Qatar** ☒

Convention on the Elimination of All Forms of Discrimination Against Women, 1979 **not Iran** ☒

Convention against Torture and Other Cruel, Inhuman or Degrading Treatment or Punishment, 1984 **not Iran and Oman** ☒

The Minimum Age Convention, 1973, against child labour **not Iran or Saudi Arabia** ☒

The Convention on the Right to Organize and Collective Bargaining, 1949, providing basic trade union rights **not Iran, Saudi Arabia, Oman or Qatar** ☒

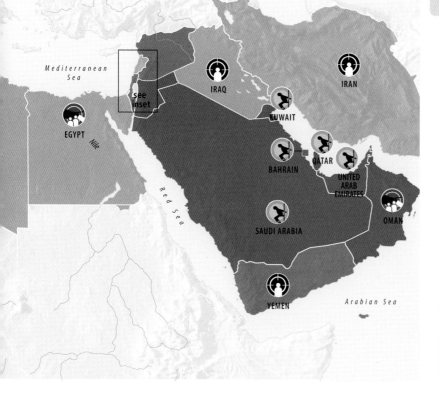

FAITH

WORLD FAITHS

Estimated number of followers
latest available data

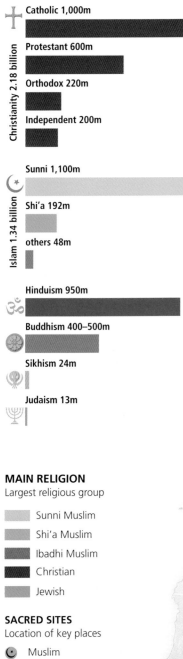

Christianity 2.18 billion

- Catholic 1,000m
- Protestant 600m
- Orthodox 220m
- Independent 200m

Islam 1.34 billion

- Sunni 1,100m
- Shi'a 192m
- others 48m

- Hinduism 950m
- Buddhism 400–500m
- Sikhism 24m
- Judaism 13m

MAIN RELIGION

Largest religious group

- Sunni Muslim
- Shi'a Muslim
- Ibadhi Muslim
- Christian
- Jewish

SACRED SITES

Location of key places

- ☉ Muslim
- ☉ Shi'a Muslim
- ✠ Christian
- ✡ Jewish

About 90 per cent of people in the Middle East are Muslims, of whom about 65 per cent are Sunni and 30 per cent Shi'a.

The division of the Islamic community into Sunni and Shi'a started with disputes and eventually war in the 7th century CE about who should succeed the Prophet Mohammed. Until the end of the 20th century, despite that violent history, the schism had generated considerably less violence than the century of bloodshed and mayhem that accompanied the Reformation and Counter-Reformation in 16th- and 17th-century Europe. The surge of violence between Sunni and Shi'a is a result in part of the tensions between the Wahhabi kingdom of Saudi Arabia (pp 134–139) and the Shi'a theocracy of Iran (pp 94–97). This upsurge in violence has expanded to bring tragedy to other religious groups such as the Coptic Christians of Egypt (p 121) and the Yazidis of Iraq.

Shi'ism is rather more structured in organization than Sunni Islam though it is not as structured as most forms of Christianity. There are different festivals and differences of theology, legal theory and culture. The theological differences are less numerous and significant than is the case in the cleavages in Christianity. Both Shi'a and Sunnis adhere to the five pillars of the faith (belief in God and acceptance of Mohammed as Prophet; daily prayer; charitable giving; an annual fast; and going at least once on a pilgrimage to

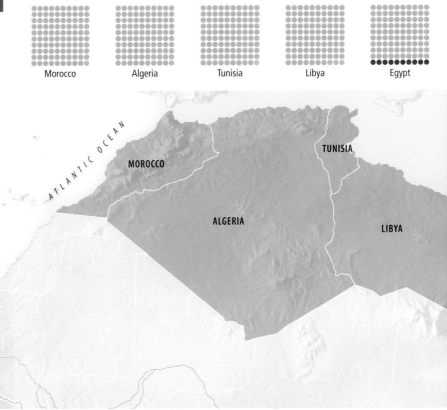

Morocco Algeria Tunisia Libya Egypt

Mecca). There are also divergences among the Shi'a and there are other Muslim groups that distinguish themselves from both the two main forms.

The Middle East is the birthplace of three world religions. The grip that Middle Eastern conflicts have on the attention of the rest of the world probably derives from religion as much as oil.

Lebanon

The unwritten pact on which Lebanon's constitutional and political practice has been based since independence allots top state positions – president, prime minister, speaker of parliament, head of the armed forces – on a confessional basis, on a formula based on the 1932 population census. While everybody acknowledges that the proportion of adherents to each faith has changed since then, it is widely acknowledged that it would risk Lebanon's fragile stability to take a new census and attempt to adjust the allocation of senior positions accordingly. At the same time, it has been politically impossible to abandon the system. The result is a tactful silence and a politically necessary uncertainty.

FAITH POPULATIONS
As percentage of total
2012 or latest available

- Sunni Muslim
- Shi'a Muslim
- Ibadhi Muslim
- Christian
- Jewish
- other

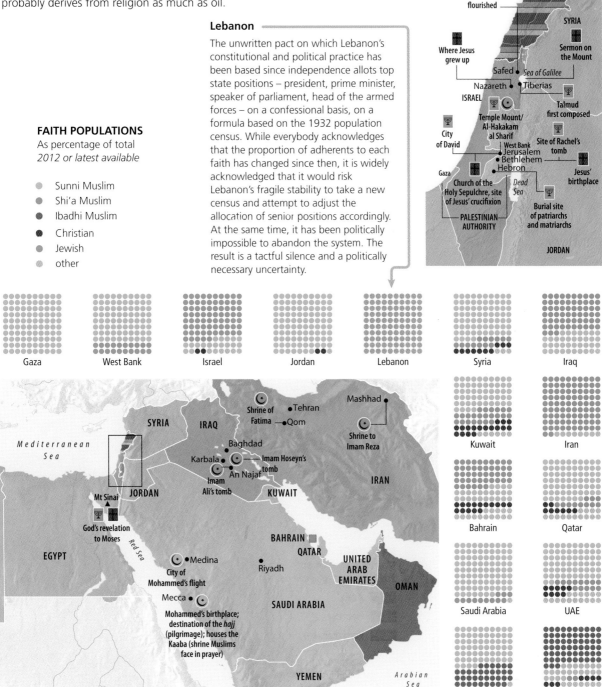

ETHNICITY

The population of the region is just over 410 million people, of whom just over two-thirds are Arabs.

The largest other population groups are Persian, Berber (speaking Tamazight), Kurdish and Azeri. Persians form over half of the population of Iran, and Jews are the majority in Israel, while there are large Berber populations in Algeria and Morocco, and significant numbers of Kurds in Iran, Iraq and Syria.

The most straightforward distinguishing feature of Arabs is the language. Arabic has been a written language since at least the 5th century CE, two centuries before the time of the Prophet. It is the language of the Quran and its dissemination throughout the region is a direct consequence of the spread of Islam. Today, standard Arabic as written, used in formal situations, and taught in schools has the same basic vocabulary and grammar as the Arabic of the Quran. For daily speech, Arabs use numerous local, colloquial forms. These vary widely enough to be mutually incomprehensible in some cases. Educated Arabs tend to be conversant in both standard Arabic and their own colloquial form.

Arabic did not become the everyday language everywhere Islam spread. In Iran, Farsi (Persian) remained the major language group and smaller populations also held onto their own languages. Iranian mullahs have traditionally learned Arabic to high levels of fluency, especially those who teach in the major religious centres.

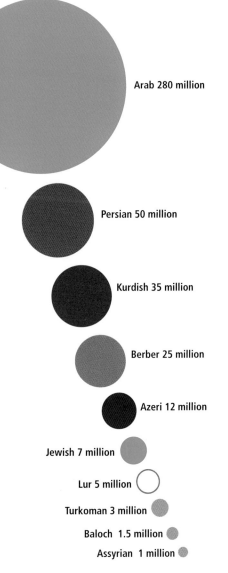

Arab 280 million

Persian 50 million

Kurdish 35 million

Berber 25 million

Azeri 12 million

Jewish 7 million

Lur 5 million

Turkoman 3 million

Baloch 1.5 million

Assyrian 1 million

POPULATIONS
Size of ten main ethnic groups
2014 or latest available data

There are considerable discrepancies between different reports on the size of population groups, a problem that dogs all studies of ethnicity, because definitions and the handling of statistics are not consistent and are often influenced by politics and prejudice. These broad estimates are based on a number of compromises between competing estimates.

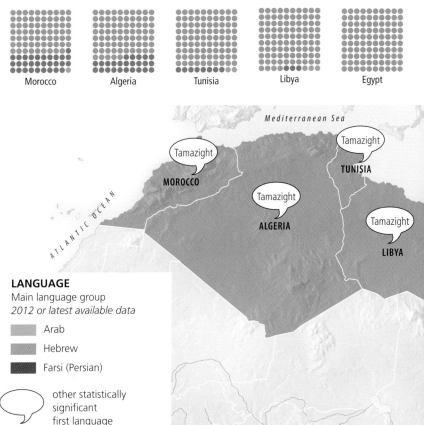

Morocco   Algeria   Tunisia   Libya   Egypt

LANGUAGE
Main language group
2012 or latest available data

- Arab
- Hebrew
- Farsi (Persian)

other statistically significant first language

A common language – even if it is the formal language rather than the everyday that is shared – has a significant unifying effect. Especially because it is linked to similarities in religious practice and because history has also generated other cultural similarities, there is a lot of fellow feeling among ordinary Arabs. The plight of one Arab group is often felt particularly intensely by others. This is part of what creates political linkages within the region so that, for example, the feelings behind the Arab Spring could spread and be shared.

Having a common formal language also provides the foundation for regional cooperation, politics and economics but the diffuse cultural fellow-feeling does not always translate into political and economic specifics. The Arab League remains a mechanism for political cooperation but Arab leaders tend to weigh many other factors before exerting themselves in partnership with each other. Thus, the unity that the Arab language and much Arabic culture might seem to offer does not by any means over-rule the division between Shi'a and Sunni or the self-interest of each country's power elite. Nor does it outweigh other political differences. Similarly, familiarity with Arabic among the political and religious leadership of Iran does not have any effect in diminishing the intensity of the Saudi–Iranian regional rivalry.

ETHNICITY

Percentage of main ethnic groups within a country
2014 or latest available data

- Arab
- Berber
- Jewish
- Azeri
- Armenian
- Kurdish
- Persian
- Lur
- Turkoman
- African
- Asian
- other

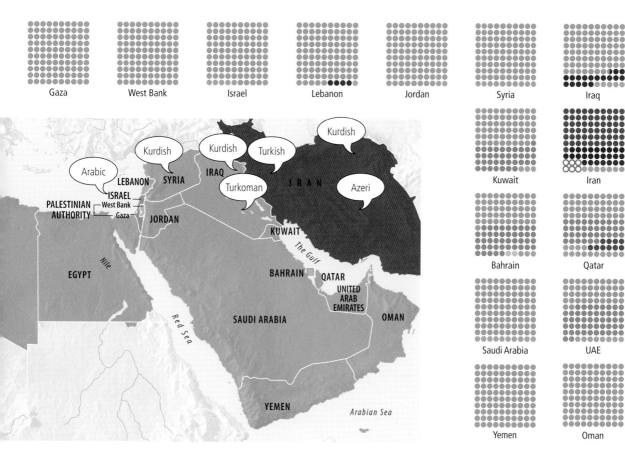

POPULATION AND URBANIZATION

Taken as a whole, the Middle East has followed the global demographic pattern of the past half century, with a fast growing population and an even faster growing urban population. Both phenomena reflect development and progress.

The growing population is the effect of, among other things, improvements in maternal health, decreased perinatal mortality and improved care for young children as well as the improved general health of the population and consequently increased longevity.

Urbanization is classically the result of growing economic wealth and industrialization, which produces a push from the land due to increased agricultural efficiency and a pull from the cities where industry provides more jobs. But other pressures, including climate variability, drive people off the land and the cities may not have enough jobs to offer. Then urbanization happens without commensurate increases in national wealth and urban centres become places where the flaws of development are felt most sharply. In the difficult transition to the city, what were hopes of betterment end in the bitterest disappointment.

It is in the contrast between hope and reality, the relationship between implied opportunity and being denied opportunity, that urban unrest grows. At the same time, a return to agricultural life is unlikely to hold many attractions. Despite urbanization, some 40–50 per cent of the Arab population remains rural, while agriculture – their primary economic activity – accounts for less than 15 per cent of Arab economic output.

The urban/rural divide is something that people have to cross in their own lives as they make the transition to the city and go through their own personal process of urbanization – of becoming part of the city. As big as it can be in the lives of ordinary people, that divide sometimes seems to get remarkably

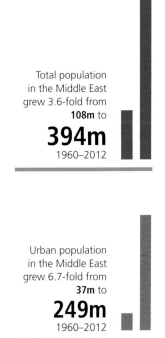

Total population in the Middle East grew 3.6-fold from **108m** to

394m
1960–2012

Urban population in the Middle East grew 6.7-fold from **37m** to

249m
1960–2012

RATE OF URBANIZATION
1960–2012
selected countries

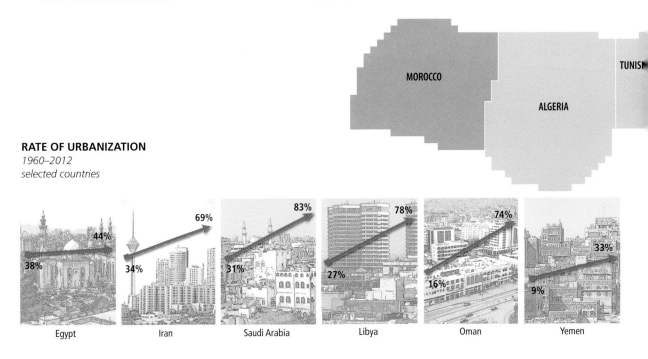

MOROCCO

ALGERIA

TUNISI▶

44%	69%	83%	78%	74%	33%
38%	34%	31%	27%	16%	9%
Egypt	Iran	Saudi Arabia	Libya	Oman	Yemen

little attention from those who would understand conflict in societies. Even where populations are homogeneous in terms of religion and ethnicity, they may be radically different in their ways of life, depending on whether they live in the cities or outside them, and even defined by whether they are recent arrivals in the city or part of a community that has been there for a couple of decades. As in Syria in the drought that was part of the build-up to civil war before 2011 (pp 128–129), a sudden influx of people into the cities can generate pressures that swell the tide of conflict.

The response to these pressures can take many different forms and be expressed in different ways. One form is that young men migrate to better labour markets in richer countries, there to experience even greater cultural upheaval and to encounter prejudice, discrimination and other new kinds of disadvantage. The region is extremely diverse in this respect, with some countries attracting very few migrants and others becoming wholly dependent on them.

A different kind of response is to join a political cause at home. Few commentators on the pressure for change in Egypt in 2011 and the course it took over the next two years (pp 118–119) would deny that one of the determining elements was the way that the pressures of life in Cairo's intense and crowded urban reality were relieved by social services provided by the Muslim Brotherhood rather than the government.

THE HUMAN SHAPE OF THE MIDDLE EAST
Size of total population *2012*

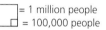
= 1 million people
= 100,000 people

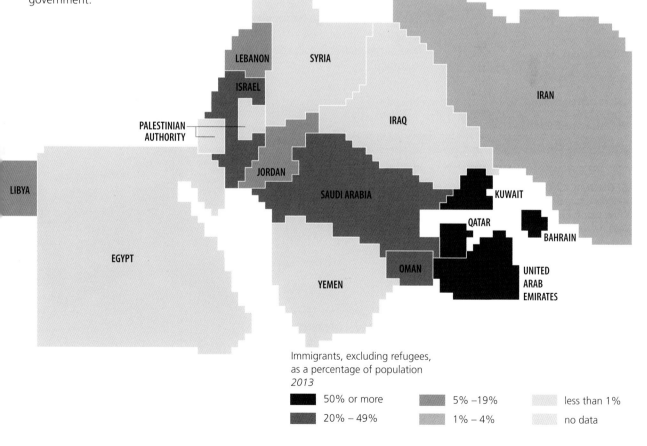

Immigrants, excluding refugees, as a percentage of population *2013*

50% or more	5% –19%	less than 1%
20% – 49%	1% – 4%	no data

59

WEALTH AND INEQUALITY

WEALTH PER PERSON

GDP per capita, PPP
2013 or most recent data
No data for Syria

Palestinian Authority	$2,810
Yemen	$3,959
Morocco	$7,198
Egypt	$11,089
Tunisia	$11,125
Jordan	$11,783
Algeria	$13,320
Iraq	$14,951
Iran	$15,590
Lebanon	$17,174
Libya	$21,046
Israel	$32,491
Bahrain	$43,851
Oman	$45,334
Saudi Arabia	$53,644
United Arab Emirates	$59,845
Kuwait	$83,839
Qatar	$136,727

For much of the Middle East the dominant economic fact is oil, and large oil reserves have generated enormous wealth. Part of the problem that the region faces is that countries with less oil have generally not found an alternative and equally effective way of generating wealth.

With small populations and massive oil reserves (pp 42–45), the six Gulf kingdoms (pp142–143) are among the 20 richest countries in the world, measured by average wealth per head of population. Yemen and Palestinian Authority, on the other hand, are among the 50 or 60 poorest, with per capita wealth of approximately the levels of Zambia and Cameroon respectively. Overall, economic fortunes in the Middle East rise and fall in line with the world average. In the oil-rich countries, economic performance fluctuates according to variations in world prices and, from one year to the next, prosperity for many ordinary people comes and goes. These peaks and troughs tend to come much closer together than the highs and lows of economic cycles in industrialized countries so there is a permanent instability built into the system.

Inevitably, it is the poor and the migrant labourers – both those from other Arab countries and those from outside the region – who feel the brunt of any downturn. Migrant labourers often face appalling living and working conditions with neither rights at work nor comfort in their lodgings. But they are paid more than they can earn at home and by living frugally can send much of their earnings home. In good times, oil-rich countries are effectively exporting a part of their prosperity in these cash remittances. In bad times, the flow of remittances slows down and many labourers go back to their home countries.

ECONOMIC GROWTH

GNI per capita 2000–10
latest year for which full regional data available

$PPP

- $17,500
- $15,000
- $12,500
- $10,000
- $7,500

Middle East & North Africa

World

2000   2005   2010

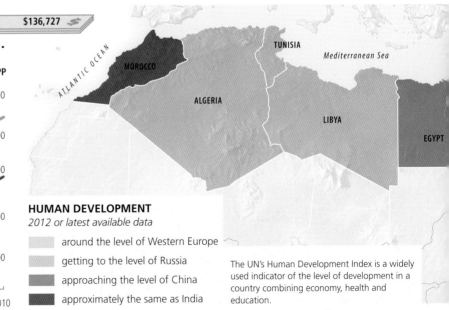

HUMAN DEVELOPMENT
2012 or latest available data

- around the level of Western Europe
- getting to the level of Russia
- approaching the level of China
- approximately the same as India

The UN's Human Development Index is a widely used indicator of the level of development in a country combining economy, health and education.

The stunning figures for wealth per head in the richest countries mask not only the dire conditions faced by migrant workers but other aspects of inequality. The standard indicators provided by the World Bank and the UN Development Programme on economic and social inequality seem to have a lot of data gaps for the Middle East.

In general terms, it appears that overall income inequality in the Middle East is greater than in Europe and North America, about the same as in East Asia and the Pacific, and less than in Africa and Latin America. Reportedly, Arab countries in general showed increasing social and economic equality from the 1950s until about 1990 and then a slow downturn. However, the relatively high rates of unemployment in some parts of the region and, less tangibly, the widespread perception of extremes of inequality in the region suggest something else is going on.

In the absence of better data, this issue can be looked at by comparing where countries stand in the league table of wealthiest countries with where they are ranked in the Human Development Index (HDI). The simple figures for wealth per head of population show how much wealth is available in a country; the Human Development Index offers a view about people's well-being. Obviously, the richer the country, the more effectively the general well-being can be looked after. And if all countries performed equally well (or equally badly), that would mean they all looked after well-being to the same degree. If some countries' HDI position is higher than their wealth per head position, they are looking after well-being with more than average effectiveness. Correspondingly, if the HDI position is lower, they care less than the global average for the ordinary citizen's well-being.

WHERE THE WEALTH GOES

Wealth per person and Human Development *2013 or most recent data*
No data for Syria

Wealth per person	World ranking	HDI
1	Qatar	31
3	Kuwait	46
7	United Arab Emirates	40
9	Saudi Arabia	34
14	Oman	56
17	Bahrain	44
36	Israel	19
58	Libya	55
68	Lebanon	65
74	Iran	75
77	Iraq	120
82	Algeria	93
88	Jordan	77
93	Tunisia	90
94	Egypt	110
116	Morocco	129
130	Palestinian Authority	107
136	Yemen	154

When a country's rank on the UN Human Development Index (HDI) is lower than its wealth rank, the country experiences more than average inequality compared to other countries.

REMITTANCES

Flows of money from the top two employers of foreign labour
2012
US dollars

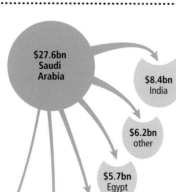

$27.6bn Saudi Arabia

$8.4bn India

$6.2bn other

$5.7bn Egypt

$3.0bn Pakistan

$2.8bn Philippines

$1.5bn Bangladesh

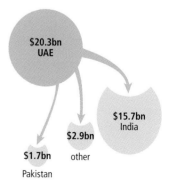

$20.3bn UAE

$15.7bn India

$2.9bn other

$1.7bn Pakistan

GENDER RELATIONS

WOMEN GAINED RIGHT TO VOTE

1948 Israel
1949 Syria

1952 Lebanon
1956 Egypt
1959 Tunisia

1962 Algeria
1963 Iran, Morocco
1964 Libya
1967 Yemen

1973 Bahrain
1974 Jordan

1980 Iraq

1994 Oman

2002 Palestinian Authority
2003 Qatar
2005 Kuwait
2006 United Arab Emirates

Inequality between the genders is rife in the Middle East as it is everywhere. Of the main indices of development, life expectancy is the only one on which women in the Middle East do better than men, which is also true almost everywhere.

Otherwise, only the United Arab Emirates offer a small bright spot for women, outperforming men on literacy by just two per cent. In earning power and in political participation and representation, the picture is characteristically one of marked inequality in favour of men.

Mostly, the countries that stand among the top 50 countries on the Human Development Index (HDI) are also least unequal in terms of gender. The standout exception is Qatar, richest country in the world per head but in the bottom half of the table for gender equality. The reverse is also true: those that are lower on the HDI tend to be most unequal in terms of gender and some stand significantly lower on the UN Gender Inequality Index than on the HDI.

Two other countries stand out. One is Israel. Generally more egalitarian than the rest of the region, it likewise comes closer than the rest to equality between men and women. The other is Tunisia. Its wealth per head is approximately at the global median (about half the world's countries are richer than Tunisia, half poorer) and so is its standing on the HDI. But its performance on gender equality is considerably better.

INDICATORS OF INEQUALITY

number of literate women for every 100 literate men *2012*	female earnings as a percentage of male *2012*
percentage of seats held by women in national representative consulting body *2012–13 or most recent data*	additional years of female life expectancy over male *2011*

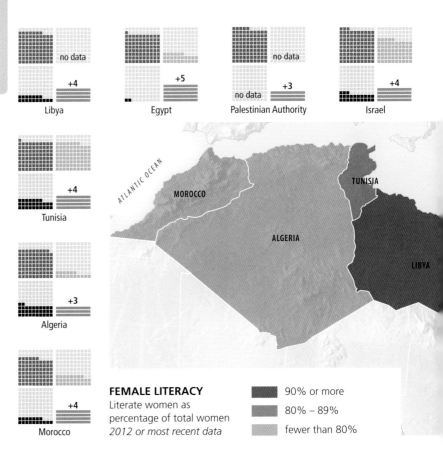

Libya — no data, +4

Egypt — +5

Palestinian Authority — no data, +3, no data

Israel — +4

Tunisia — +4

Algeria — +3

Morocco — +4

FEMALE LITERACY
Literate women as percentage of total women *2012 or most recent data*

- 90% or more
- 80% – 89%
- fewer than 80%

In the Middle East, as in many other countries, gaps between men and women in terms of earning possibilities and political participation are reducing. It is a slow, slow process that battles against entrenched social views about gender roles. Today, all countries have universal suffrage, and the literacy rates for men and women have steadily both increased and become closer in most countries, Yemen being the big exception.

The unfair conditions faced by women are defined not only by law and state policy, but also by social norms and customs. In many countries women who have been raped face the risk of murder by their own relatives to expunge the 'shame' caused by a male act of aggression. Both the local community and the authorities often turn a blind eye to these merciless killings.

In several Arab countries and also in Iran, the participation of women in public life is constrained by systems of governance that tightly control who may lead. Only Israel has so far produced a female political leader – Golda Meir from 1969 to 1974.

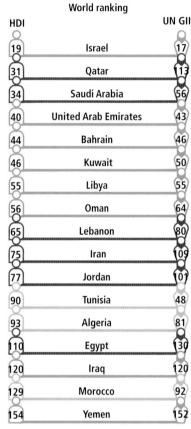

GENDER INEQUALITY

2013 or most recent data
No data for Palestinian Authority and Syria

Countries with a higher GII value have greater disparities between females and males. A higher value for GII compared to HDI indicates particular gender related disadvantage.

World ranking

HDI		UN GII
19	Israel	17
31	Qatar	113
34	Saudi Arabia	56
40	United Arab Emirates	43
44	Bahrain	46
46	Kuwait	50
55	Libya	55
56	Oman	64
65	Lebanon	80
75	Iran	109
77	Jordan	101
90	Tunisia	48
93	Algeria	81
110	Egypt	130
120	Iraq	120
129	Morocco	92
154	Yemen	152

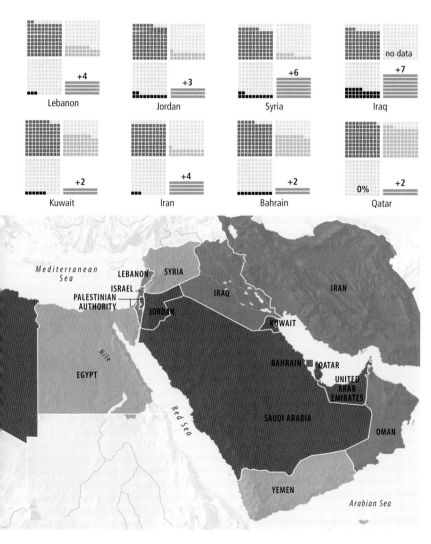

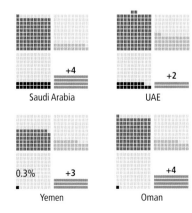

63

WATER

DRINKING WATER AND SANITATION

Access to improved water sources
and improved sanitation
2012 or latest available

100%

90% – 99%

50% – 89%

Lebanon sanitation data from 2005
Libya water access data from 2001

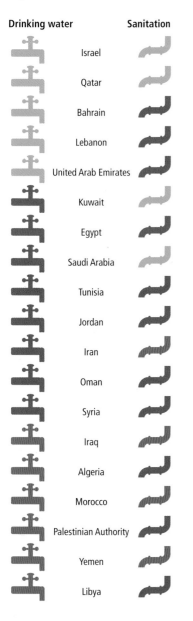

Drinking water		Sanitation
	Israel	
	Qatar	
	Bahrain	
	Lebanon	
	United Arab Emirates	
	Kuwait	
	Egypt	
	Saudi Arabia	
	Tunisia	
	Jordan	
	Iran	
	Oman	
	Syria	
	Iraq	
	Algeria	
	Morocco	
	Palestinian Authority	
	Yemen	
	Libya	

Water is essential for human life and clean water and efficient sanitation are among the basic requirements for healthy living. The Middle East is an arid region and most countries face severe water issues in the relatively near future.

Worldwide, the supply of water for human consumption has reached a critical point. Many countries withdraw more water for use than is naturally replenished by rainfall. And many also have inadequate infrastructure for delivering clean water to everybody. Unless both sets of issues are addressed, estimates suggest that by 2025 two-thirds of the world's population will experience shortages in clean water supply. Most Middle Eastern countries are at or past the critical point, while all the others except Lebanon are approaching it – and even Lebanon experiences increasing shortages of potable water with each hot summer.

The basic supply of water by nature is not expected to increase in the region in the coming decades; as a solution, desalination is still expensive and energy intensive and is not available to all. Whether governments can make the technical, economic and managerial investment required to run efficient and clean public water supply systems will do much to define their economic and social prospects in the second half of the 21st century.

WATER USE

As percentage of total withdrawals
2011

● domestic consumption
◐ industry
○ agriculture

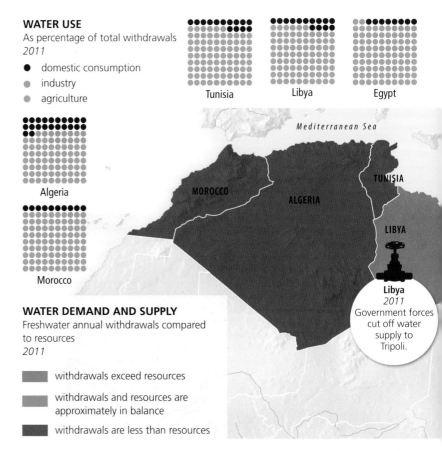

Tunisia

Libya

Egypt

Algeria

Morocco

WATER DEMAND AND SUPPLY

Freshwater annual withdrawals compared to resources
2011

withdrawals exceed resources

withdrawals and resources are approximately in balance

withdrawals are less than resources

Mediterranean Sea

MOROCCO

ALGERIA

TUNISIA

LIBYA

Libya
2011
Government forces cut off water supply to Tripoli.

Water's importance makes it critical in conflict, sometimes as a cause, sometimes as a weapon. In Israel's Occupied Territories, the imbalance in the use of water (see pp 74–75) is a constant source of resentment for Palestinians. Yet before the 1967 war when Israel occupied the West Bank, one issue in the background was the Israeli government's concern about a Jordanian proposal to divert the flow of the Jordan River. By taking control of the West Bank, Israel gained access to the river and to the area's underground water sources.

During the 1980–88 war against Iraq (see pp 98–99), Iran diverted rivers to flood Iraqi positions and bombed dams in Kurdistan. Iraq itself destroyed Kuwait's desalination plants in 1991 after its invasion and Saddam Hussein first poisoned the water source for the Marsh Arabs in southern Iraq during the 1990s, and then systematically drained the areas where they lived (see pp 104–105). The tactical use by ISIS in Iraq and Syria of its control of water supplies to put pressure on villages and opposing forces is but the latest in a long line of uses of the water weapon.

Yet worldwide and viewed in historical comparison, water is much more often a source of peace and cooperation. Though risks of conflict continue, there is a growing network of international agreements around use of the water of the Nile, and no reason in principle why the same could not happen around the Tigris and the Euphrates.

West Bank
2011
Israeli army destroyed pumps, wells and water tanks in Palestinian villages.

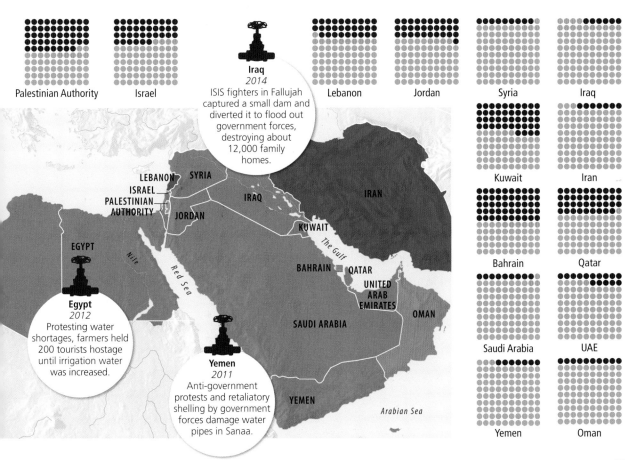

Palestinian Authority

Israel

Iraq
2014
ISIS fighters in Fallujah captured a small dam and diverted it to flood out government forces, destroying about 12,000 family homes.

Lebanon

Jordan

Syria

Iraq

Kuwait

Iran

Bahrain

Qatar

Saudi Arabia

UAE

Yemen

Oman

Egypt
2012
Protesting water shortages, farmers held 200 tourists hostage until irrigation water was increased.

Yemen
2011
Anti-government protests and retaliatory shelling by government forces damage water pipes in Sanaa.

REFUGEES

2014

2013

2012

2011
9.2 million

2010
8.9 million

REFUGEES
Total number of refugees,
IDPs and asylum seekers in
Middle East and North Africa
2010–14

OUT OF ALL PROPORTION

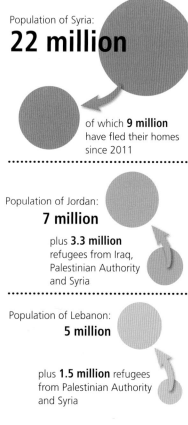

Population of Syria:
22 million

of which **9 million**
have fled their homes
since 2011

Population of Jordan:
7 million

plus **3.3 million**
refugees from Iraq,
Palestinian Authority
and Syria

Population of Lebanon:
5 million

plus **1.5 million** refugees
from Palestinian Authority
and Syria

Until the Syrian civil war started in 2011, Palestinians formed the largest single group of refugees in the world. In a world 'population' of some 51 million refugees, Palestinians are 10 per cent of the total and Syrians not much short of 20 per cent.

There were two great waves of refugee flight by Palestinians. The first came with the foundation of Israel in 1948, when 80 per cent of Palestinians within the new borders left (see pp 36–37). The second came with Israel's occupation of the West Bank in 1967 (see pp 40–41). Living outside their homeland as refugees has become a semi-permanent condition for millions of Palestinians and has lasted for two generations since the original flight in 1948. Most Palestinians living as refugees today were born refugees and what the media refer to as refugee camps are in some cases large towns.

The wars in the Gulf in 1990–1991 and the aftermath (see pp 104–105) and in 2003 and thereafter (pp 106–111) caused a comparably sized wave of refugees from Iraq. Opportunities for return have appeared and then vanished with the fluctuations of politics and conflict.

All previous experience of the movement of refugees has been dwarfed by the number of Syrians who have fled their homes, either to leave Syria or to seek some sort of sanctuary in a different part of the country.

It is a standard part of peace agreements that refugees return home. It is a fundamental human right and making it safe for those who fled in fear to return in safety is an equally fundamental part of an equitable agreement and a stable peace. But while the issue of return is paramount for Palestinians, many Israelis see it as a source of danger. And in the cases of both Iraq and Syria, whether refugees may eventually find a place back home will depend on currently unpredictable political and strategic developments. There is, unfortunately, no reason to think the scale of the refugee issue in the Middle East will soon diminish.

4,168
MOROCCO

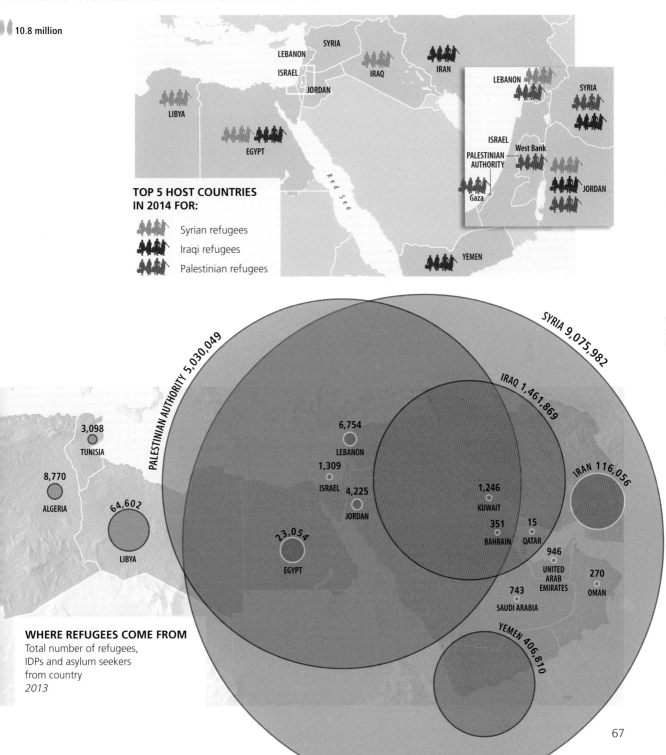

20.9 million

15.9 million

10.8 million

TOP 5 HOST COUNTRIES IN 2014 FOR:

Syrian refugees

Iraqi refugees

Palestinian refugees

SYRIA
LEBANON
ISRAEL
JORDAN
IRAQ
IRAN
LIBYA
EGYPT
Red Sea
YEMEN

LEBANON
SYRIA
ISRAEL
PALESTINIAN AUTHORITY
West Bank
Gaza
JORDAN

PALESTINIAN AUTHORITY 5,030,049

SYRIA 9,075,982

IRAQ 1,461,869

IRAN 116,056

3,098
TUNISIA

8,770
ALGERIA

64,602
LIBYA

6,754
LEBANON

1,309
ISRAEL

4,225
JORDAN

23,054
EGYPT

1,246
KUWAIT

351
BAHRAIN

15
QATAR

946
UNITED ARAB EMIRATES

270
OMAN

743
SAUDI ARABIA

YEMEN 406,810

WHERE REFUGEES COME FROM
Total number of refugees, IDPs and asylum seekers from country
2013

67

WARS

War has been a constant theme in the Middle East since the end of colonialism. Wars have come in four overlapping waves.

In the first wave from the 1940s into the 1960s, wars were part of the emergence of the new order in the Middle East. In Algeria, there was the anti-colonial struggle, and in a different way the same struggle was fought out in Egypt's 1956 Suez War to end the efforts of the old powers, the British and French, to keep running things. In both parts of Yemen there were wars to gain, retain and shape the terms of independence. But above all, the wars of the era were defined by the failed attempts by Arab states to prevent the foundation of Israel.

In the second wave from the 1960s into the 1990s, a series of wars arose out of the failure of the new order, no sooner established than fraying. The Arab states' failure to destroy the new state of Israel opened the way to half a century of Palestinian guerrilla warfare, popular uprising, mutual attack and retaliation. Lebanon collapsed into civil war in 1975 under the burden of an unsustainable political arrangement. An enormously destructive war between

Tunisia
2013 Clashes mainly in north-west border areas with Al-Qaeda in the Islamic Maghreb.

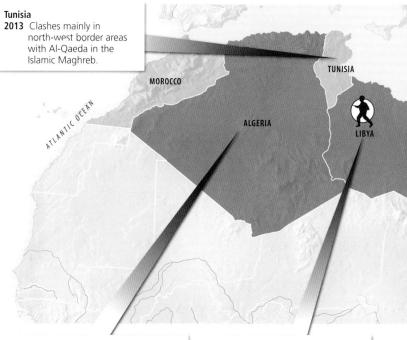

WARFARE
At any point since 1 January 2000

war in national territory

no war in national territory

 engagement in war outside national territory

 2015 Part of the Saudi-led coalition against Houthis in Yemen

Algeria
1992–Worst violence in Civil War was 1997–98. War wound down at turn of the century but has not ended. Al-Qaeda in the Islamic Maghreb (AQIM) continues attacks on police and army, economic targets, civilians and tourists. AQIM broke away from the main fighting groups when they disbanded in the early 2000s and later linked itself to al-Qaeda.

Libya
2001 Qaddafi's forces engaged in Central African Republic.

Iraq and Iran was triggered in 1980 by the ambitions of an oil-enriched dictatorship. Algeria's model of economic development proved unsustainable and the country's political set-up fell apart, triggering civil war in 1992.

In the third wave from the 1990s into the 2000s, the West, which seemed 30 years before to have dropped pretensions to a major military role in the region, preferring to act via proxies, returned in force. It aimed directly at Iraq but established a wider presence in the Gulf sub-region.

Yet this overlapped with and exacerbated the fourth wave – the uprisings, the sabotage, the global guerrilla warfare and the civil wars in which the non-state forces in the region are increasingly identified by their religious affiliation. The fourth-wave wars had two distinct yet related starting points: a widespread rejection of the right of the USA, the strongest world power, to have a major role in the region; and an equally widespread rejection of the rights of tyrants. But the forces that attached themselves to the democratic urge to overthrow tyranny have strangled what looked like an Arab spring and turned it into the start of an era of deep insecurity and instability.

Israel
2000– The violence that started in Israel and the Palestinian Authority with the second *intifada* in September 2000 has never ended though the *intifada* itself petered out in 2005. A major offensive against Hamas in Gaza because of its mostly ineffective rocket attacks on Israel led to large-scale civilian casualties in 2008–2009 but did not end the rockets, leading to a further offensive in 2014.
2006 Israel re-invaded Lebanon six years after withdrawing because Hezbollah kidnapped two Israeli soldiers. The offensive failed and Israel's forces were beaten back.

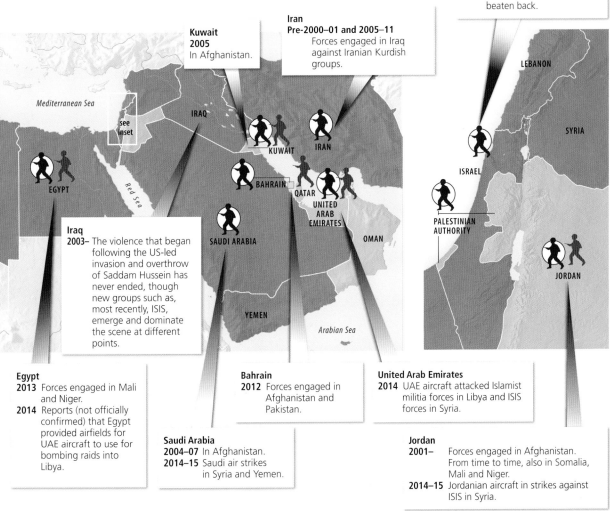

Kuwait 2005 In Afghanistan.

Iran Pre-2000–01 and 2005–11 Forces engaged in Iraq against Iranian Kurdish groups.

Iraq 2003– The violence that began following the US-led invasion and overthrow of Saddam Hussein has never ended, though new groups such as, most recently, ISIS, emerge and dominate the scene at different points.

Egypt 2013 Forces engaged in Mali and Niger.
2014 Reports (not officially confirmed) that Egypt provided airfields for UAE aircraft to use for bombing raids into Libya.

Bahrain 2012 Forces engaged in Afghanistan and Pakistan.

United Arab Emirates 2014 UAE aircraft attacked Islamist militia forces in Libya and ISIS forces in Syria.

Saudi Arabia 2004–07 In Afghanistan.
2014–15 Saudi air strikes in Syria and Yemen.

Jordan 2001– Forces engaged in Afghanistan. From time to time, also in Somalia, Mali and Niger.
2014–15 Jordanian aircraft in strikes against ISIS in Syria.

PART THREE

ARENAS OF CONFLICT

Since World War II ended in 1945, the Middle East has experienced only one year in which there was no armed conflict going on – 1947. With that exception, there has always been warfare somewhere in the region, though not everywhere. In the experience of war, as in many other ways, the region shows considerable internal diversity. Compared to elsewhere in the world, however, the Middle East does not stand out as unique in the frequency and pervasiveness of war. Nor are its wars outstandingly lethal compared to other regions. The wars with the highest death tolls in the region so far have been the Algerian war of independence of 1956 to 1962 and the Iran–Iraq war of 1980 to 1988; in sub-Saharan Africa and several regions of Asia, there have been several wars with equal or greater death tolls. The horrors that have been perpetrated during the Syrian civil war since 2011 are, indeed, horrible, but have not reached the scale of genocide in Rwanda in 1994 or Cambodia in 1975–76.

Where the Middle East does stand out is in the global significance of its wars. They brought the superpowers to the brink of nuclear confrontation during the Cold War. Some of them directly affect the economic well-being of rich and poor countries alike because of oil – sometimes because oil is used as a diplomatic weapon, and sometimes because war drives its price up. They contain an inbuilt risk of escalation and spillover, not only because the conflict issues go so deep but also because of the involvement of outside powers. Parties to some of the wars have not hesitated to export the violence to different parts of Europe, and al-Qaeda and other groups have brought large-scale terrorism to the USA and Europe in the 21st century.

In modern armed conflict, the frontline of suffering always involves civilians – killed or wounded by bombs dropped from the sky or detonated in cars and buses, by rockets and artillery, by snipers; driven forcibly from their homes or running for their lives; grieving for family members killed in action; caring for those disabled and traumatized by violence. It is questionable whether this moral concern features at all prominently in the strategic thinking of more than a handful of those who give the orders in more than a handful of conflicts. The suffering of ordinary people is itself a weapon with which political leaders attempt to impose their will.

ISRAEL AND PALESTINE

Since Israel fought its way into existence against a divided Arab enemy, warfare of various forms – open war, clandestine attacks, missile strikes, targeted assassinations, riots, snipers, bombs – has been its fundamental fact of life. There is no sign it will end soon.

Despite the outcome of the Suez War in 1956 (see p 35), Israel survived and flourished. Arab frustration grew and in 1966, with a new and more militant regime in Syria, border attacks on Israel intensified. As always, Israel retaliated and President Nasser of Egypt acceded to a Syrian request for a comprehensive defence agreement. For Nasser, the trouble was that Egypt's policy was then hitched to Syria's. He was the acknowledged leader of the Arab republics, but the Syrians were ensuring he led from behind.

To take back the initiative, Nasser escalated the conflict. He blockaded Israel's access to the Red Sea through the Straits of Tiran, asked UN forces to leave Gaza, where they had been stationed since 1956, and moved Egyptian forces across the Canal into Sinai. Other Arab states likewise moved forces close to Israel's borders.

With war clearly imminent, Israel struck. In a single day in June 1967, it destroyed most of Egypt's air force, and took control of Sinai in just four days. The Arab war effort was fragmented and uncoordinated and the result was an unmitigated Arab disaster. Egypt lost Sinai; Jordan lost the West Bank including East Jerusalem; Syria lost the Golan Heights. 200,000 Palestinians who fled across the Jordan River lost their homes, and 600,000 more who stayed in the West Bank came under Israeli military control.

Some Arab writers argued that Israel's superiority was based on religious unity and concluded the Arab world should follow suit and restore its own basis in faith. Over the next half century, the impact of these ideas was profound.

The violence did not abate after 1967. The familiar pattern of strike and counter-strike continued in the West Bank and across the Suez Canal. Leadership of the PLO, founded in 1964, changed as the dynamic Yasser Arafat became chairman. Based in Jordan, its prestige grew and it mounted joint operations with the Jordanian army against Israeli forces. But factions in the Jordanian army saw the PLO's growth and the size of the Palestinian refugee population as threats to Jordan's stability. In September 1970, mounting tensions boiled over into a one-week war that ended with the expulsion of the PLO from Jordan.

In the wake of these debacles, some Palestinian groups turned to terrorism; the most spectacular attack was when the Black September group seized and murdered 11 Israeli athletes and team officials at the Munich Olympics in 1972.

Against this backdrop, Anwar Sadat, Egypt's president from 1970, wanted to free Egypt from the burden of confrontation with Israel. But his first major move was for war, believing that would give him political room for manoeuvre. Attacking on Yom Kippur, the Day of Atonement in the Jewish religious calendar, Egyptian and Syrian forces gained the advantage of surprise and for once cooperated closely. Egyptian forces struck deep into Sinai. The political unity of other Arab states was also striking; they used their control of oil to gain concessions from Western Europe and Japan.

After early setbacks, Israel regained the military initiative. Its forces entered both Egypt and Syria. The superpowers sent arms to their respective allies. When a US-brokered and UN-approved ceasefire was not fully implemented on time, the USSR announced it was considering unilaterally deploying forces to the region. The USA responded with a nuclear alert.

The overall outcome was indeterminate. Israel prevailed but no longer looked invulnerable. Its death toll of 2,500 was over three times as high as in 1967. And despite all the USA's help, the war cost Israel the equivalent of one full year's economic output.

Sadat finally achieved the diplomatic renewal he sought by flying dramatically to Israel in 1977 to address the Knesset (parliament), paving the way for the Washington Treaty of 1979 under which Israel withdrew from the Sinai. Sadat was abused and isolated by the other Arab states, and his initiative brought to a close the first era of Israeli–Arab relations. Thenceforth, the major sources of insecurity for Israel were not to come from Arab states but from Palestinian guerrillas.

CHRONOLOGY *continued*

1978 Israel–Egypt Camp David Accord restores Sinai to Egypt.

1979 *Mar* Egypt and Israel sign treaty for Israeli withdrawal from Sinai.

July Israel declares all of Jerusalem to be its eternal capital.

1981 President Sadat of Egypt assassinated by Islamists.

1982 Israel intervenes in Lebanese civil war. PLO forced out of Lebanon, moves HQ to Tunisia.

1983 Menachem Begin resigns as PM, succeeded by Yitzhak Shamir.

1985 In Lebanon, Israel withdraws to narrow southern 'Security Zone'.

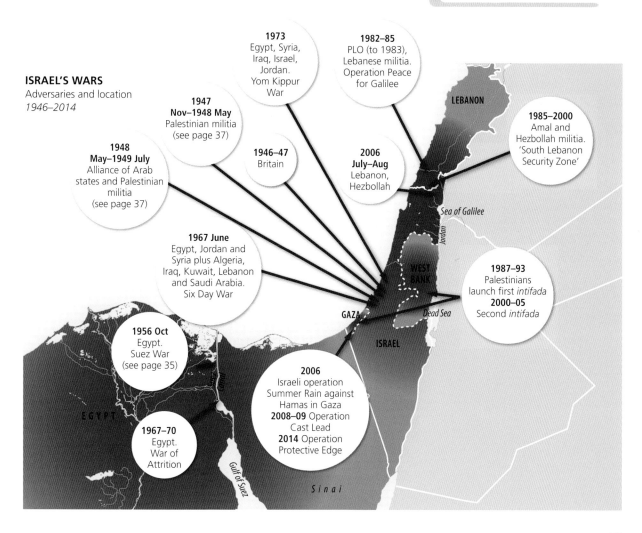

ISRAEL'S WARS
Adversaries and location
1946–2014

1973 Egypt, Syria, Iraq, Israel, Jordan. Yom Kippur War

1982–85 PLO (to 1983), Lebanese militia. Operation Peace for Galilee

1947 Nov–1948 May Palestinian militia (see page 37)

1985–2000 Amal and Hezbollah militia. 'South Lebanon Security Zone'

1948 May–1949 July Alliance of Arab states and Palestinian militia (see page 37)

1946–47 Britain

2006 July–Aug Lebanon, Hezbollah

1967 June Egypt, Jordan and Syria plus Algeria, Iraq, Kuwait, Lebanon and Saudi Arabia. Six Day War

1987–93 Palestinians launch first *intifada* **2000–05** Second *intifada*

1956 Oct Egypt. Suez War (see page 35)

2006 Israeli operation Summer Rain against Hamas in Gaza **2008–09** Operation Cast Lead **2014** Operation Protective Edge

1967–70 Egypt. War of Attrition

LEBANON

Sea of Galilee

WEST BANK

GAZA

Dead Sea

ISRAEL

EGYPT

Gulf of Suez

Sinai

Land *vs* Peace

The fundamental problem is land – who can live there and who controls its use. Israel has spread when it has been able to and after the 1967 war it was as determined to hold onto its newly occupied territory as it had been in 1948 to assert control over its territorial core.

The basic incompatibility of each group wanting to control the same area of land has by now been overlaid by decades of contention. Every fact and every statistic, every legal interpretation of every resolution, judgement and document – everything is contested. What is incontestable is that both sides have used frightening violence against the other, and that ordinary citizens as well as fighters have suffered.

Upon occupying the West Bank in 1967, Israel declared all water resources to be its property and instituted a strict system of licensing the construction of new wells and pipes. Israeli settlement of the West Bank started in 1968. A steady increase in the number of settlements and settlers has been studded by sudden surges. The general trend of increase seemed to be interrupted for a moment in 2005 when settlers were forced to leave Gaza by the Israeli army. But only 'seemed', for while 8,500 settlers vacated 19 square miles in Gaza, 14,000 settlers were occupying 23 new square miles on the West Bank.

The settlements started out small. Some have grown to urban centres of more than 20,000 inhabitants. The construction of the settlements and the lives of the settlers consume water that is thereby denied to Palestinians. Israel controls how much water can be used by Palestinians and does not hide the fact that more water goes to the Jewish settlements in the Occupied Territories than to the ordinary Palestinian residents.

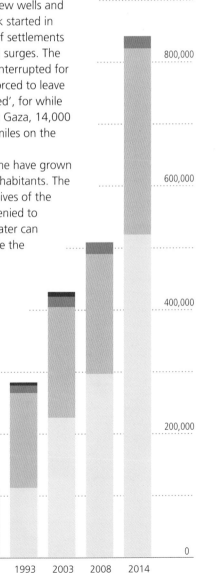

THE SETTLEMENTS
Number of Israeli settlers
1967–2014

- Gaza
- Golan Heights
- East Jerusalem
- West Bank (excl. East Jerusalem)

900,000
800,000
600,000
400,000
200,000
0

1967   1972   1983   1993   2003   2008   2014

The case for the settlements has been tested in law. The Fourth Geneva Protocol of 1949 – part of what was formerly called the Law of War and is now known as International Humanitarian Law – bans a state from moving civilians into occupied territory. Everything that is done to that end is also illegal, including anything done to perpetuate the situation. This was the basis of the International Court of Justice ruling in 2004 that the wall being built as a security barrier between Israel and the West Bank is illegal.

In 1988, the Palestine National Council – the law-making body for the Palestine Liberation Organization (PLO) – was persuaded by its leader Yasser Arafat to recognize Israel within its 1949 boundaries. This entailed accepting that Palestinians had no claim to govern 78 per cent of historic Palestine. Israelis were entitled to question the firmness of the change in position, for no action was taken to amend the Palestine National Charter accordingly, but the PLO's focus since then has indeed been on Gaza and the West Bank. The Islamic Resistance Movement, Hamas, has not recognized Israel as a legal state and said in 2006 that whether to do so should be settled by referendum.

Land: for Israel, it is about securing its continued existence; for Palestinians, it is about Israel's control of the territory and the water. Because of land and water, it is also about Israel's control of Palestine's economic prospects. On top of that, it is about how the occupying forces treat Palestinians. So it is also about the feeling that dignity and hope are permanently under attack. Out of this comes the urge to fight back and take the war to the Israeli civilians. And the measures Israel takes to blunt the threat of Palestinian violence, even when they enhance Israel's short-term security, also serve to exacerbate the underlying problem.

OVERALL POPULATION
2014

Israeli settlers
520,000

2.7m Palestinians

West Bank
3.22 million

1.7m Palestinians

Gaza

350,000 others

1.7m Palestinians

6.2m Jews

Israel
8.2 million

Total Israeli population:
6,720,000

Total Palestinian population:
6,100,000

OCCUPATION
Territory taken by Israel during conflicts *1967–82*

- taken in 1967 and restored in 1979
- taken in 1967 war and still held
- taken in 1982 and held until 1985
- taken in 1982 and held until withdrawal from Lebanon in 2000

WATER
2014 or date shown

72 litres average daily water consumption of a Palestinian

100 litres average minimum daily consumption recommended by the WHO

80% of water from the West Bank mountain aquifer is taken by Israelis

26% of diseases in Gaza are estimated to be water related

300 litres average daily water consumption of an Israeli

90%–95% of the Coastal Aquifer, on which Gaza inhabitants depend for water, is contaminated due to over-extraction and sewage contamination

30km of water networks were damaged or destroyed by the Israeli military in addition to 11 wells operated by the water authorities in Gaza during Operation Cast Lead in 2008

2006 Israel bombed Gaza's only power plant, responsible for the supply of a third of the Strip's energy needs. The plant has never been fully repaired yet electricity is essential to run pumps that distribute water as well as for operating wastewater-treatment plants.

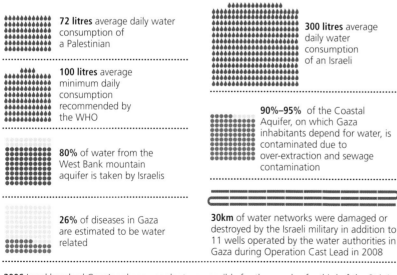

Uprising

The first *intifada* began in 1987 as a people's movement that pitted stone-throwing youths against Israeli armed forces. The images it generated won international sympathy. Israel's standing had been diminished by intervention in Lebanon in 1982 and it now faced the risk of international isolation. The US administration pushed it into the Madrid Peace Conference in 1991, but the conference quickly got bogged down. A quiet Norwegian initiative in 1993 was more productive. Israel wanted a way out of the *intifada*, while the PLO wanted to get back to Palestine from its Tunisian exile. They agreed on a phased peace process, gradually giving Palestinians more autonomy.

The PLO came home but there was no real peace. The Oslo agreement deferred the difficult issues. Militants on both sides opposed it. The West Bank settlements started to expand again from 1996, and there were insecurity and killings on both sides. More Israelis died in the six years after Oslo than in the six before it. Further talks made slow progress though the level of violence subsided in 1998–99.

The second *intifada* was triggered by Likud party leader Ariel Sharon's visit to the area known to Israelis as Temple Mount and to Palestinians as Haram al-Sharif – the site of the al-Aqsa mosque. Sharon was a distinguished soldier, former defence minister, a security hard-liner, and a forthright supporter of the settlements. Whether the motive for the visit was provocative and aimed at winning the next elections, or innocent, the result was an explosion of protest. Initially, the second *intifada* was like the first, but escalated as Islamic Jihad, Hamas and the al-Aqsa Martyrs Brigades mobilized suicide bombers. In response, Israel reoccupied parts of the West Bank, placing Yasser Arafat's headquarters in Ramallah under siege. Both

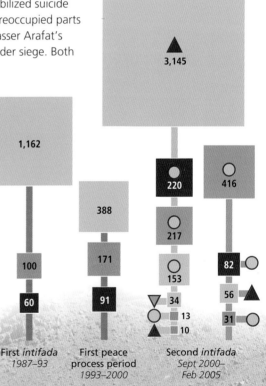

THE DEATH TOLL
1987–2014

People killed:

- Palestinians
- Israeli civilians
- Israeli security forces
- foreign citizens
- other israelis

Killed by, (where known):

- ○ Palestinians
- ▽ Israeli civilians
- ▲ Israeli security forces

Killed in:

- Palestinian territories
- Israel
- unknown

3,145

1,162

100

60

388

171

91

220

217

153

34

13

10

416

82

56

31

First *intifada*
1987–93

First peace
process period
1993–2000

Second *intifada*
Sept 2000–
Feb 2005

sides took the war to the civilians on the other side and each side justified itself by the actions of the other.

During the Oslo years, the PA had little chance to establish good governance in the West Bank and Gaza; it was dependent on international aid, which was transferred via Israel, whose security forces were omnipresent. But what little chance the PA had, it wasted through nepotism, corruption, incompetence and abuse of human rights. When the second *intifada* started, Israel attacked and weakened the PA's security forces so that even if the PA had wanted to act decisively against the suicide bombers, it could not have done so.

In Palestine, disillusion with the PA led to support for Hamas, founded in 1988 out of a social welfare movement that originally started as an offshoot from the Muslim Brotherhood. Where the PA seemed weak against Israel, incompetent and corrupt, Hamas looked strong, competent and clean. Arafat's death in 2004 released Palestinian public opinion from its loyalty to his movement; in January 2006 Hamas won the PA elections.

Israel is as politically divided as Palestine. The gulf between supporters and opponents of the 1993 agreement with the PLO was deep, wide and bitter. In the 1990s, as in the 1980s, electoral fortunes swung between Likud and Labour. As the second *intifada* wore on, many Israelis no longer saw the settlers as heroes, but rather as part of Israel's problem. Recognition that there would have to be some withdrawal from the Occupied Territories grew, even among the settlers' strongest supporters, including Sharon. A tactical withdrawal in Gaza was implemented against furious opposition from the settlers. In the political fall-out, Sharon quit Likud and formed a new party, Kadima ('Forward'). Though successive strokes removed him from politics, his party came out in front in the March 2006 election.

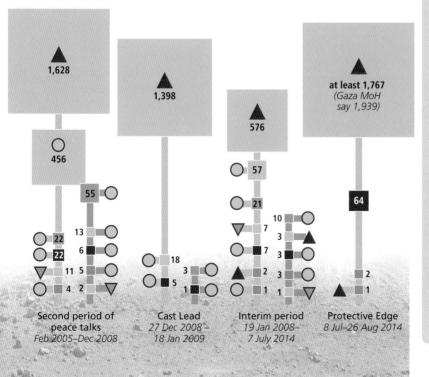

| Second period of peace talks Feb 2005–Dec 2008 | Cast Lead 27 Dec 2008– 18 Jan 2009 | Interim period 19 Jan 2008– 7 July 2014 | Protective Edge 8 Jul–26 Aug 2014 |

CHRONOLOGY *continued*

2002 Israeli tanks move into Bethlehem. 39 Palestinian militants take refuge in the Church of the Nativity. Israel begins to construct security barrier. International discussions held on 'roadmap' for a two-state solution.
2003 *Apr* Roadmap presented to Israeli and Palestinian leaders.
2004 *July* The International Court of Justice rules that Israel's security wall violates international law.
Oct Knesset endorses Sharon's plan to withdraw all settlers from Gaza and some small West Bank settlements.
Nov Arafat dies.
2005 *Jan* Mahmoud Abbas new PA Chair.
Aug Jewish settlers leave Gaza.
Sept Israeli troops pull out of Gaza.
Nov Sharon forms Kadima party.
2006 *Jan* Sharon in coma. Hamas wins Palestinian elections.
Feb Acting PM Ehud Olmert unveils plan for partial unilateral withdrawal from the West Bank.
Mar Olmert wins Israeli elections.
May Hamas announces the formation of The Executive Force security service.
2009 *Mar* Ehud Olmert resigns; Netanyahu becomes PM.
June Endorses two-state solution.
Sept Israel Defense Forces and Palestinian militants accused of war crimes against civilians by Goldstone report.
Nov Netanyahu offers 10-month pause in West Bank settlement construction.
2010 *Jan* Palestinian elections postponed.
May Turkish supply ship to Gaza is boarded by Israeli forces; nine civilians die in ensuing fight.
2012 *Oct* Hamas boycotts West Bank elections; Fatah win only 40% of seats. No elections in Gaza.
Nov UN General Assembly upgrades status of Palestinians to that of a 'non-member observer state'.
2013 *Jan* Netanyahu re-elected Israeli PM.
July US Secretary of State John Kerry announces resumption of Israeli– Palestinian negotiations.
2014 *Apr* Hamas and Fatah intention to agree reconciliation becomes public; Israel terminates peace talks.
June Fatah and Hamas form government.

The occupied territories

As prime minister Ariel Sharon decided the PLO was not a worthwhile counterpart for negotiations and imposed a unilateral peace plan. Announced in 2004, it involved withdrawing all settlements from Gaza and some from the West Bank. It also proposed building a physical barrier to cut the West Bank and Israel off from each other.

Despite settlers' resistance, the Gaza withdrawal was accomplished in 2005. But during the subsequent decade, the number of Israeli settlers and new towns in the West Bank increased significantly, and a substantial section of a barrier with a final projected length of 700 kilometres has been erected. The route of the security 'wall' ensures that many settlements – and areas of projected settlements – are now physically connected to Israel. In the process, Israel has taken over more West Bank land, cutting many Palestinians off from their farmlands and other means of making a living.

For a future Palestinian state, the result is a patchwork. There are four areas under Palestinian control (to the north of Nablus, around Salfit, around Jericho and south of Hebron) and a fifth area, from Ramallah through Jerusalem to Bethlehem, where Israeli and Palestinian control are interspersed. These are islands of limited Palestinian autonomy, for the Palestinian Authority does not have control over its own economic policies or its land borders. Each island is criss-crossed by Israeli roads that are primarily for settlers and the military. It is

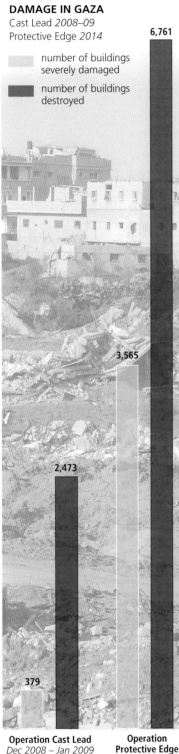

DAMAGE IN GAZA
Cast Lead *2008–09*
Protective Edge *2014*

number of buildings severely damaged

number of buildings destroyed

6,761

3,565

2,473

379

Operation Cast Lead
Dec 2008 – Jan 2009

Operation Protective Edge
July – Aug 2014

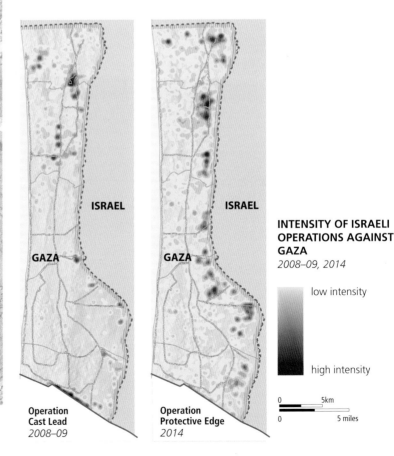

ISRAEL

GAZA

ISRAEL

GAZA

INTENSITY OF ISRAELI OPERATIONS AGAINST GAZA
2008–09, 2014

low intensity

high intensity

0   5km
0   5 miles

Operation Cast Lead
2008–09

Operation Protective Edge
2014

only possible for Palestinians to cross these roads at checkpoints. No farming, building or other development is permitted near the roads.

Gaza, meanwhile, is economically isolated, not only by Israel but also because in 2010 Egypt joined Israel in blockading Gaza.

Israel justifies its actions as necessary for its own security, but the consequence is to make daily life harder for Palestinians and commerce more difficult, thus weakening the economy. Experience shows that these conditions feed sufficient resentment and a strong enough urge to strike back that many Palestinians support or sympathize with violence against Israel and Israelis, even if they know that reprisals are almost certain.

WEST BANK ARCHIPELAGO

Area A: Palestinian control

Palestinian settlement

Area B: Joint Israeli–Palestinian security control

Area C: Israeli control

Israeli settlement

land cut off by the wall

.... 1949 Green Line

——— wall already constructed

.... wall under construction or planned route

===== road accessible to both Israelis and Palestinians

===== road not accessible to Palestinians

--o-- road with restricted access to Palestinians

o check points

Force and peace

The second *intifada* petered out in 2005. In the following decade, Israel found neither peace nor security and nor did the Palestinians. In 2014, Israel launched its heaviest bombardment yet against Gaza – Operation Protective Edge – firing more missiles and killing more people than in previous similar operations. Just as previous assaults had failed to suppress the lower-level violence launched by Hamas from Gaza, so did that of 2014. And so, predictably, will the next one and the one after that.

In Jerusalem at the same time, violence escalated, with retaliatory murders of Israelis and Palestinians and random attacks by individual Palestinians – a car ramming a crowd, an axe attack at a synagogue. By late 2014 many analysts concluded that a new, 'silent *intifada*' had started.

Peace talks came and went without result and in mid-2014 the latest effort ended as a year-long US initiative to bring the parties to the table for a new peace agreement collapsed. The long-sustained goal of a two-state solution, with Palestine controlling some of what are now the Occupied Territories, has come to look less and less likely. Though repeated opinion polls once showed majorities of both Israelis and Palestinians supporting a two-state solution, the details were always unclear and contested, the right political moment never came, and on-the-ground realities have made a future Palestinian state increasingly impracticable.

As if to drive this political reality home, five days after Protective Edge ended in August 2014, Israel took over almost 1,000 acres of land in the West Bank for a further expansion of the settlements.

Israel's forces can mobilize more people with superior equipment and better training than its Palestinian adversaries can. Unlike in earlier wars against the Arab states, Israel no longer has an advantage in morale and commitment. But in technical terms its superiority is unquestionable.

Yet Israel's willingness to use its force superiority does not stop many Palestinians from wanting to fight. Therefore, it does not generate security for Israelis. There are some Israelis, especially the more militant among the settlers in the West Bank and their supporters, for whom the lack of security for ordinary Israelis does not matter. Living with danger is accepted as part of

PEACE TALKS CHRONOLOGY

1991 The Madrid Conference
1993 Oslo
1995 Oslo II
2000 Camp David
2001 Taba
2002 Arab Peace Initiative
2003 Roadmap & Geneva Accord
2007 Annapolis
2010 Washington

COMPARATIVE MILITARY POWER
2013

PALESTINIAN TERRITORIES

Force	Personnel	Strength
The Palestinian Authority's National Security Force The NSF only has real authority within the West Bank	56,000	including: **3,000** presidential security **1,200** special forces **9,000** police **1,000** civil defence
al-Aqsa Martyrs Brigades Loyal to the Fatah group, it has dominated the Palestinian Authority		unknown
Executive force Hamas internal-security grouping	10,000–12,000 (est.)	Major equipment includes artillery rockets, mortars, small and light weapons
al-Qassam Brigades Hamas's military wing, seen as its best trained and most disciplined force	10,000 (est.)	Major equipment includes mines and IEDs (improvised explosive devices), artillery rockets, mortars, small and light weapons

fulfilling what they see to be their mission, just as the prospect of death does not put off the suicide bomber.

For those on both sides who care about their own and their families' safety and security, however, the future looks bleak. There is no evidence to suggest Israel's well-established combination of no compromise with Palestine and readiness to use force will ever bring security and safety. What Israel's militant leaders have counted on is that eventually the Palestinian will to resist must break. That eventuality cannot be ruled out but nothing indicates that Palestinian surrender is more likely now than in any previous decade of Israel's existence.

With all this, Israel's international reputation has suffered. Of the United Nations' 193 member states, 135 recognize Palestine as a state. The UN General Assembly in 2012 accorded it the status of 'non-member observer state', with the last word of the tag representing an important diplomatic victory for the Palestinian cause. Though Israel still has many supporters worldwide, it was symptomatic of its declining international credibility that in late 2014, parliaments in Europe – including the UK, France, Ireland, Portugal and Spain – called on their governments to recognize Palestine. The European parliament also voted for recognition and Sweden formally recognized Palestine.

So far, the USA has been steadfast, even if its diplomatic efforts have failed and its initiatives been rebuffed by Israel. Were that support to falter, Israel might find it has to change its long-standing but evidently flawed policy of trying to achieve peace by force.

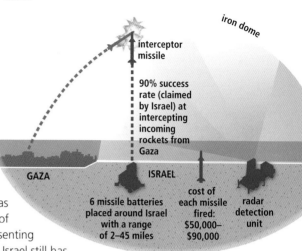

IRON DOME
Short-range rocket interceptor in service since 2011

ISRAEL

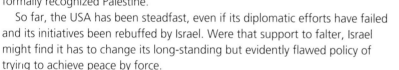

Force	Personnel		
Army	133,000		
	plus 400,000 reserves		
Navy	9,500	plus 10,000 reserves	
Air Force	34,000	plus 55,000 reserves	
Paramilitary	8,000		
Strength			
Land systems	3,870 tanks 9,436 armoured fighting vehicles	706 self-propelled guns 350 towed artillery	88 multiple-launch rocket systems
Air power	680 total aircraft 243 fighters / interceptors	243 fixed-wing attack aircraft 48 attack helicopters	
Naval power	3 destroyers	14 submarines	66 coastal defence craft

LEBANON

Peace in Lebanon faces two core problems: its faith-based political system and its neighbours – Israel and Syria.

Lebanon's diversity includes Shi'a and Sunni Muslims, as well as Druze – an offshoot at least 1,000 years ago from the Ismaili branch of Shi'ism – and Christians of various denominations. Of these, the most numerous are Maronites, with origins in a schism in the Byzantine Church in the first millennium CE. Both Druze and Maronites faced pressures over centuries to conform religiously and politically. Their resistance produced a militant, martial tradition of self-defence.

As elsewhere in the Ottoman Empire, identity became the basis of politics and power. When France received the League of Nations' Mandate for Lebanon and Syria after World War I, it had already been siding with the Maronites for 50 years. In 1926 it imposed a constitution that favoured them. After World War II, France was forced out by local resistance quietly supported by the British and sectarian rivalry was hard-wired into the newly independent state.

Independence necessitated compromise. In the 1943 National Pact, Maronite parties accepted an Arab identity for Lebanon while Muslim parties accepted a disadvantageous quota of parliamentary seats based on the already out-dated results of the 1932 census. Demographic shifts continued and most observers believed Maronites were a minority by the 1960s; checking this with a new census was politically impossible so the problem of unfair quotas in parliament was allowed to fester.

Rivalries across the basic politico-religious fault lines and murderously among competing Maronite groups kept the Lebanese state weak. In the lead-up to civil war, tensions were exacerbated by the presence of the PLO and the way it behaved. In 1948, 120,000 Palestinian refugees from Israel fled to Lebanon; more followed after the 1967 war. In 1970, the PLO was forced out of Jordan and moved its headquarters to Beirut. There it grew in strength and prestige, becoming effectively a parallel government – well armed and looking after its own affairs and interests, not Lebanon's.

After many warning signs, the explosion came in 1975 – a war that killed 50,000 people by early 1976, with the PLO and its left-wing Druze allies controlling about 80 per cent of the country. The Maronite President asked Syria to send forces to end the fighting; Syrian President Assad did so because, though vehemently anti-Israel, he distrusted the PLO and thought it was becoming too powerful.

The respite was temporary. War revived and Israel invaded. A US-led Multinational Force (MNF) arrived in 1982, quickly oversaw the PLO's departure and withdrew, only to return within weeks following the massacres of Palestinians in the Sabra and Shatila refugee camps. These were carried out by Maronite militias in an area controlled by the Israeli army. Israel denied involvement but it has always seemed unlikely that it could not have prevented the killings.

New forces now arose to drive out first the Americans and then the Israelis. The Shi'a Amal militia formed in 1975 and, among other actions, trained the Iranian Revolutionary Guards, who themselves trained Hezbollah after its formation in 1982, which was openly at war with Amal within a few years.

Suicide bombers launched massive and simultaneous attacks on American and French headquarters in 1983. The MNF departed. There followed six years of mayhem, characterized by brutal fighting and abductions of some of the few foreigners who remained – diplomats, spies, journalists and would-be negotiators. There were further attacks on Palestinian refugees – this time by Muslim militia – and the conditions of life for ordinary people worsened as the Lebanese state disintegrated.

By 1988 Lebanon had two prime ministers. Put differently, there was no legitimate prime minister. Fighting between rival Maronite forces weakened all factions to the point that peace was possible. Syria got everybody round a table in Taif in Saudi Arabia. The Accord amended the 1926 constitution to weaken the Maronite grip on power. Parliament and Cabinet were to divide seats equally between Christians and Muslims and Parliament was to choose the prime minister. The faith-based core of the constitution remained intact and Syria took a direct role in Lebanese government.

After that, there was one further spasm of violence and then the war was finally over.

PARTNERS IN CHAOS
Combatants in Lebanon *mid-1980s*

Lebanon
- Government
- Christian forces: Phalange and rival militias; Republic of Southern Lebanon
- Muslim forces:
  - Druze militia
  - Shi'a groups: Hezbollah, Amal, Jundallah (Soldiers of God), Huseyn Suicide Commandos, the Dawah (Call) Party
  - Sunni groups: Tawhid Movement, Al-Mourabitoun, Sixth of February Movement

Palestinian
- PLO
- Popular Front for the Liberation of Palestine
- General Command
- Abu Musa faction
- Palestinian Liberation Army

Iran
- Iranian Revolutionary Guards

Israel

Syria

Multinational Force
- USA
- France
- Italy

Other
- Syrian Social Nationalist Party
- Lebanese Communist Party
- Al-Saiqa (Syrian proxy group)

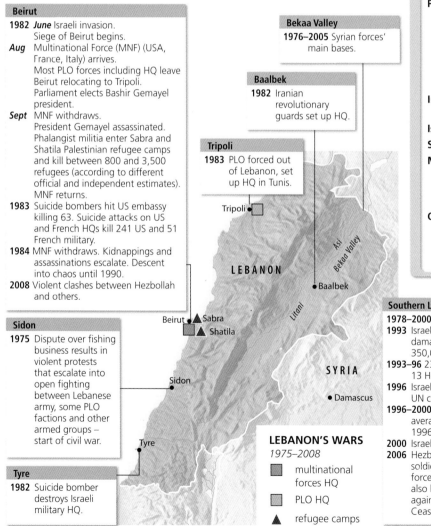

Beirut
1982 *June* Israeli invasion. Siege of Beirut begins.
Aug Multinational Force (MNF) (USA, France, Italy) arrives.
Most PLO forces including HQ leave Beirut relocating to Tripoli.
Parliament elects Bashir Gemayel president.
Sept MNF withdraws.
President Gemayel assassinated. Phalangist militia enter Sabra and Shatila Palestinian refugee camps and kill between 800 and 3,500 refugees (according to different official and independent estimates). MNF returns.
1983 Suicide bombers hit US embassy killing 63. Suicide attacks on US and French HQs kill 241 US and 51 French military.
1984 MNF withdraws. Kidnappings and assassinations escalate. Descent into chaos until 1990.
2008 Violent clashes between Hezbollah and others.

Bekaa Valley
1976–2005 Syrian forces' main bases.

Baalbek
1982 Iranian revolutionary guards set up HQ.

Tripoli
1983 PLO forced out of Lebanon, set up HQ in Tunis.

Sidon
1975 Dispute over fishing business results in violent protests that escalate into open fighting between Lebanese army, some PLO factions and other armed groups – start of civil war.

Tyre
1982 Suicide bomber destroys Israeli military HQ.

LEBANON'S WARS
1975–2008

- ⬛ multinational forces HQ
- ⬜ PLO HQ
- ▲ refugee camps

Southern Lebanon
1978–2000 Under control by Israel and local allies.
1993 Israeli forces attack and destroy or severely damage 70 villages, killing 140 civilians while 350,000 flee north.
1993–96 231 Israeli attacks on civilians, killing 45; 13 Hezbollah rockets fired at Israel, killing 3.
1996 Israeli shelling kills 106 Lebanese civilians in UN camp.
1996–2000 Hezbollah escalates activity from an average of 200 operations annually before 1996 to 1,000 annually thereafter.
2000 Israel withdraws from Lebanon.
2006 Hezbollah militia kills 3 and abducts 2 Israeli soldiers on patrol in Israel. Israel invades but forces are pushed back by Hezbollah, who also launch almost 4,000 Katyusha rockets against Israel, at least 1,000 at urban areas. Ceasefire agreed after 34 days.

Peace and occupation

After Taif, Lebanon was in ruins and Syria was in occupation. Peace was a massive relief and the security imposed by Syria's military presence was understood to be part of that. However, the occupation soon became controversial and viewed by many as burdensome, not least because of the 1 million Syrian migrant workers in Lebanon during the reconstruction period.

Israel remained in control of a zone in southern Lebanon. Its invasion in 1982 had brought no peace either to Lebanon or itself. It ultimately acknowledged its complicity in the Sabra and Shatila massacres, which shocked and alienated much international public opinion and many Israelis and tarnished then Defence Minister Ariel Sharon. He had to resign that position and was later named by an Israeli official enquiry as partially responsible along with other politicians, officials and officers. The occupation of southern Lebanon continued to be controversial, courting conflict and occasional condemnation when retaliation led to seemingly random killing. And still the depth and extent of Shi'a resistance ensured there were no clear security gains for Israel. It finally pulled out in 2000, not exactly defeated by its 22-year intervention in Lebanon, but not successful either.

In 2004, Syria attempted to orchestrate a modification of the constitution to keep the President in power. Some Lebanese politicians responded by quietly getting the UN to pass a resolution urging Syria to pull out of Lebanon. When the architect of this diplomatic success, ex-PM Rafik Hariri, was killed by a car bomb, Syria was universally accused despite its protestations of innocence. Whether the murder was a government decision or the work of a faction within the Syrian secret services, the political fall-out was quick and Syrian forces pulled out within months.

With this, Lebanese politics came more under the control of the Lebanese themselves, though cynics have persistently remarked that the basic division within Lebanon is between the Saudis, Israelis and Americans on one side and the Syrians and Iranians on the other.

Armed action by Hezbollah against Israel continued after Israel's withdrawal, culminating in the 2006 war when Israel bombed and invaded but its forces were held back by Hezbollah's well-organized resistance. It was the first time Israeli forces had been bested on the battlefield since independence. Hezbollah by now was a political party and a social movement as well as an armed force. It had become a well-organized political machine and was widely regarded as broadly uncorrupted by its power and influence. After 2006 it grew in both national and international prestige as well as self-confidence. The result was inevitably that rivalries sharpened and in 2008 Lebanon came close to the brink of a renewed civil war. A government move to shut down Hezbollah's communications network and to remove the head of security at Beirut airport because of his alleged Hezbollah ties resulted in civil unrest and open fighting, leading to 81 deaths. Qatar brokered an agreement that ended the fighting and gave Hezbollah veto power in the Cabinet.

International investigations of the murder of Rafik Hariri remained an explosive issue in the decade following his death, but were largely overshadowed from 2011 onwards by Hezbollah's involvement in the Syrian civil war. For a time, it seemed to many analysts as if Hezbollah's intervention was critical to the survival of the Assad regime. At the same time, the Sunni militias that opposed Assad were recruiting in Lebanon as hard as they could, especially in rural areas.

The spillover of war from Syria to Lebanon took many forms: the arrival of 1 million refugees, fighting on the borders, explosions in Beirut, armed combat in Tripoli. And all this against the backdrop of political crisis as the parliament deferred national elections in 2013 and re-deferred them late in 2014, while also proving unable to elect a new president even months after the previous one ended his term of office. As for so much of its life as an independent state, Lebanon was permanently on the brink of a worse and further explosion that, with a few fanatical exceptions, none of its people or politicians want.

CHRONOLOGY *continued*

May Parliament votes to put off elections until Nov 2014 because of security concerns over conflict in Syria.

July European Union lists military wing of Hezbollah as a terrorist organization.

Aug Twin attacks in Tripoli.

Nov Suicide bombing outside Iranian embassy in Beirut kills at least 22.

2014 *May* President Suleiman ends his term of office; Parliament unable to appoint a successor.

Nov Parliamentary elections deferred again.

NUMBER AND ORIGIN OF SYRIAN REFUGEES IN LEBANON
March 2014

TURKEY

21,700 Hassakeh

175,710 Aleppo

35,930 Raqqah

3,620 Latakia

129,250 Idlib

SYRIA

15,810 Deir ez Zor

2,640 Tartus

66,880 Hama

217,740 Homs

LEBANON

Beirut

119,080 rural Damascus

IRAQ

Damascus

45,880

5,680 Quneitra

450 Suwaida

ISRAEL

61,370 Dara'a

JORDAN

1 million

TOTAL NUMBER OF SYRIAN REFUGEES IN LEBANON
2011–14

2011	2012	2013	2014
2,058	17,817	355,719	(1 million)

ASSASSINATIONS
Political killings in Lebanon *2005 onwards*

In February 2005, Rafik Hariri, former prime minister and 22 others were killed by a one-ton truck bomb. The attack became the focal point of a popular mobilization against Syrian influence, known as the Cedar Revolution. Syria was forced to end its post-civil war occupation of Lebanon. But since then, political assassinations have continued.

2005 *June* **Samir Kassir**, journalist, killed by a bomb in his car in Beirut.
George Hawi, Communist politician: car bomb.
Dec **Gebran Tueni**, journalist and politician, booby trap.

2006 *Nov* **Pierre Gemayel**, Maronite cabinet minister: shot dead (his uncle, President-elect Bachir Gemayel, was assassinated in 1982).

2007 *June* **Walid Eido**, parliamentarian, his son and 8 others: car bomb.
Sept **Antoine Ghanem**, parliamentarian and 6 others: car bomb.
Dec **Brig. Gen. François al-Hajj**, next in line to be army chief: car bomb.

2008 *Jan* **Wissam Eid**, security official investigating the Hariri assassination, and 4 others: roadside bomb.
Feb **Imad Mughniyah**, a senior Hezbollah member: car bomb in Damascus.

Sept **Sheik Saleh al-Aridi**, Lebanese Democratic Party politician: booby-trap.

2009 *Mar* **Kamal Naji (Medhat)**, PLO official: roadside bomb.

2012 *Oct* **General Wissam al-Hassan**, head of Internal Security Forces: car bomb.

2013 *Dec* **Mohamad Chatah**, former finance minister, critic of Syria and Hezbollah: car bomb.
Dec **Hassan Howlo al-Laqqis**, a Hezbollah commander: shot dead.

ALGERIA

Algeria's present and how its citizens think about the future are dominated by the memory of the civil war of 1992 to 2003 in which 150,000 people died. The insurgents were militant Islamists but it was not a religious war. It originated in the political and economic flaws of Algeria's development since independence.

Democracy did not survive long after independence. After two years, the elected President was deposed, placed under house arrest (for 14 years) and replaced by the army Chief of Staff. Algeria was both a one-party state and dominated by the military, a system that combined two rigid forms of government. When rising oil prices made the economy strong in the 1970s, the system worked. When oil revenues fell in the mid-1980s, dissatisfaction rose and the system was too rigid to cope. Unrest culminated in four days of rioting in 1988 with hundreds killed.

Uncertain what to do, in 1989 the government permitted independent political parties to form. The most popular of the new parties took aim at the wealth of the leaders of the once revolutionary FLN. Protests about the economy were driven by moral outrage as well as hardship, and the moral clarity of a political party that urged a return to the basic values of Islam had a broad appeal. In 1990, the Islamic Salvation Front (FIS) won over half the votes in local elections.

The government had a delicate problem: how to have democracy without letting the majority win. In June 1991 it announced parliamentary elections, changed the rules in a way that disadvantaged FIS, and arrested its two most prominent leaders. Even so, FIS dominated the first election round and was clearly heading for victory in the second. Almost inevitably, in early 1992, the military cancelled the second round of elections, replaced the president and suspended political rights.

There was now no avenue for peaceful change. Western governments regarded anything as better than the Islamists taking power, and quietly backed the military, as did most Arab governments. But FIS resisted. Initial

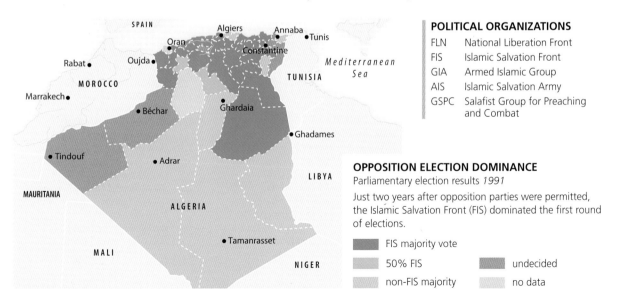

POLITICAL ORGANIZATIONS

FLN	National Liberation Front
FIS	Islamic Salvation Front
GIA	Armed Islamic Group
AIS	Islamic Salvation Army
GSPC	Salafist Group for Preaching and Combat

OPPOSITION ELECTION DOMINANCE
Parliamentary election results *1991*

Just two years after opposition parties were permitted, the Islamic Salvation Front (FIS) dominated the first round of elections.

- FIS majority vote
- 50% FIS
- non-FIS majority
- undecided
- no data

attacks targeted security forces. In 1993 the GIA was formed by veterans of the war in Afghanistan to oppose not only the government but also FIS. Late in 1994, guerrilla groups loyal to FIS but hitherto divided among themselves agreed to bury their differences and formed the AIS.

Though the new president, Liamine Zéroual, supported a hard line in army operations, he held talks with FIS in 1994. In 1995, he won the presidential election with 60 per cent of the vote on a 76 per cent turn out – remarkably high given the boycott by FIS and the GIA's threat to kill anybody who voted.

In 1997, foreshadowing the violence in Iraq and Syria some 17 years later, the GIA launched and openly claimed credit for a series of massacres of civilians targeted in particular at areas near Algiers that had voted for FIS in 1990 and 1991. Their justification appears to have been that those who were not actively fighting the government were corrupt beyond redemption. GIA killers used makeshift weapons such as mattocks and shovels as well as guns and knives. They dismembered men one limb at a time, sliced open pregnant women, dashed children against walls and kidnapped young women for sexual slavery.

In some of the worst of the GIA massacres in 1997–98, government forces stationed nearby did nothing to save the victims. Throughout the war they were also responsible for serious abuses of human rights. An official report later estimated the number of 'disappeared' at 6,000, many of them flung into mass graves.

The majority of Algerians had shown with their votes that they preferred order to war. The sickening effect of the GIA's massacres only emphasized the preference. When Zéroual stepped down as president in 1999, the army supported Abdelaziz Bouteflika, who stood unopposed because of other candidates' and parties' concerns about the high risk of electoral fraud. Bouteflika opened negotiations with the AIS, leading to an agreement on amnesty. The AIS disbanded the following year. The army concentrated on destroying the GIA and, from several thousand fighters in the mid-1990s, the group was down to about 60 by 2003. The number of war-deaths each year fell from over 10,000 in the 1990s, to 1,900 in 2001, 1,400 in 2002 and 900 in 2003. Slowly but not always steadily, there was a sense of some normality returning, even though the 2002 elections were marred by violence.

CIVILIAN MASSACRES

Incidents in which more than 50 people were killed
by Armed Islamic Group (GIA)
1997–98

▼ 1997

▼ 1998

Mediterranean Sea

Algiers
Beni-Messous • Bentalha
Rais • Sidi-Hamed
Si-Zerrouk
Haouch Khemisti
Tadjena
Souhane
Beni-Ali
Guelb el-Kebir
Sahnoun
Qued el-Had
Ouled-Tayeb
El-Abadel
Ramka
Kherarba
Thalit
ALGERIA
Sidi el-Antri
Dairat Labguer
Oued-Bouaicha
Baloul

CHRONOLOGY *continued*

1990 FIS wins 55% of vote in local elections.

1991 Law changed to restrict campaigning in mosques. FIS leaders jailed but party dominates first round of national elections.

1992 Second round of national elections cancelled, State of Emergency imposed and FIS declared illegal. War starts.

1993 Formation of the GIA.

1994 Armed groups loyal to FIS form AIS. Newly appointed President Liamine Zéroual begins negotiations with FIS.

1995 Presidential elections confirm Zéroual in office. GIA and AIS fight each other.

1997 Pro-Zéroual party wins national elections. AIS declares unilateral ceasefire. GIA takes up strategy of massacring civilians.

1998 Formation of GSPC – a breakaway group from GIA.

1999 Former foreign minister Abdelaziz Bouteflika elected president with no opposition. Thousands of Islamist fighters pardoned.

2000 AIS disbands.

2001 Berber Black Spring. 120 civilians die demanding Berber autonomy.

2002 Government recognizes Berber language, Tamazight, as a national language.

2004 President Bouteflika is re-elected to a second term.

2005 Government-commissioned report acknowledges security forces were responsible for disappearances of over 6,000 people during the war.

2006 GSPC joins al-Qaeda.

2007 GSPC renamed Al-Qaeda in the Islamic Maghreb.

2008 *Nov* Constitutional amendments passed to abolish two-term limit, allowing President Bouteflika to run for a third term.

2009 *Apr* Bouteflika wins a third term at the polls, taking 90% of the votes amid widespread accusations of fraud.

Struggling out of war

2011 Jan Rioting triggered by rising food prices. Man dies after setting himself on fire.

Feb President Bouteflika lifts 19-year state of emergency – a key demand of anti-government protesters.

Sept President ends state monopoly over radio and TV.

Nov New law requires 33% of parties' election candidates to be women.

2012 May Ruling FLN wins 220 of 463 parliamentary seats; women win almost one-third of seats.

2013 Jan Hostage-taking incident in In Amenas gas complex by al-Qaeda-affiliated group, 40 employees killed.

2014 Apr Bouteflika wins fourth term as president; opposition condemns elections as flawed. After stroke, is hospitalized for 3 months in France.

June Algerian opposition rallies and calls for real democracy.

Algeria is the world's third largest exporter of natural gas, which ought to be the basis for a reasonable degree of prosperity. The system of power and privilege against which FIS stood in 1990 and 1991 has never allowed a general well-being to flourish, however, and that did not change significantly with the end of the war. Though the GIA had been largely crushed, the GSPC that had broken away from it survived, numbering some 300 fighters by 2005. In January 2007 it announced that it had become Al-Qaeda in the Islamic Maghreb (AQIM). Armed incidents and acts of terror have persisted thereafter. The fall of the Qaddafi regime in neighbouring Libya in 2011 is believed to be responsible for large numbers of weapons being available in the region, contributing to Algeria's security problems.

Meanwhile, President Bouteflika, elected unopposed in 1999 for the first of a constitutionally defined maximum of two terms in office, won his fourth term in April 2014, thanks to a constitutional amendment passed in 2008 ending the term limit. And in further evidence of business as usual, rising food prices triggered protests in 2011 at the same time as pressures for democratic change were surging in Tunisia and Egypt and about to begin in Libya. These protests did not bring major change to Algeria, but nor did they escalate into war or a massive surge in state repression. In 2014, after Bouteflika's re-election, renewed protests called for a shift to a genuine, open democracy in Algeria.

AL-QAEDA IN THE ISLAMIC MAGHREB (AQIM) *2007–14*

AQIM is descended from the GSPC, which was a breakaway from the GIA. It operates in Algeria, Mauritania, Mali and Niger. The history of breakaways has continued. By 2011, AQIM had split into two groups, with the northern cells sticking to their *jihadi* origins while the southern cells turned to criminal activity. In 2012 a group variously known as Those Who Signed in Blood and as The Masked Men Brigade broke away from AQIM and the following year attacked the gas complex at In Amenas. It may have pledged itself to ISIS, as has another AQIM breakaway – The Soldiers of the Caliphate – who announced themselves in September 2014 with a video showing the execution of a French guide.

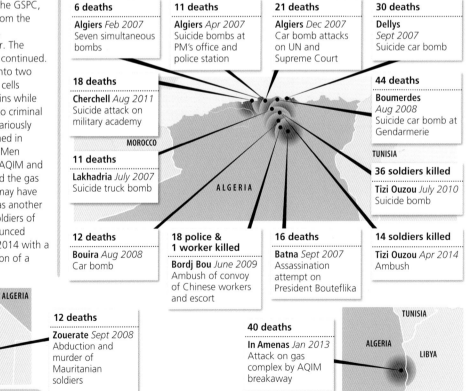

6 deaths
Algiers *Feb 2007*
Seven simultaneous bombs

11 deaths
Algiers *Apr 2007*
Suicide bombs at PM's office and police station

21 deaths
Algiers *Dec 2007*
Car bomb attacks on UN and Supreme Court

30 deaths
Dellys
Sept 2007
Suicide car bomb

18 deaths
Cherchell *Aug 2011*
Suicide attack on military academy

44 deaths
Boumerdes
Aug 2008
Suicide car bomb at Gendarmerie

11 deaths
Lakhadria *July 2007*
Suicide truck bomb

36 soldiers killed
Tizi Ouzou *July 2010*
Suicide bomb

12 deaths
Bouira *Aug 2008*
Car bomb

18 police & 1 worker killed
Bordj Bou *June 2009*
Ambush of convoy of Chinese workers and escort

16 deaths
Batna *Sept 2007*
Assassination attempt on President Bouteflika

14 soldiers killed
Tizi Ouzou *Apr 2014*
Ambush

12 deaths
Zouerate *Sept 2008*
Abduction and murder of Mauritanian soldiers

40 deaths
In Amenas *Jan 2013*
Attack on gas complex by AQIM breakaway

MOROCCO

ALGERIA

TUNISIA

WESTERN SAHARA

ALGERIA

MAURITANIA

TUNISIA

ALGERIA

LIBYA

The Berbers in Algeria

As far back as there are records of North Africa, there is evidence of Berbers. They comprise several ethnic groups, which official statistics often treat as an indistinguishable part of an Arab–Berber population. Most Berbers are Muslims, their forbears having converted at the time of the Arab conquests, but many Berber customs survive and they remain an identifiably separate group.

The Berber languages – collectively known as Tamazight – are spoken by some 25 million people, of whom about 20 million live in Morocco and Algeria. There are 7 to 10 million Berbers in Algeria, who comprise about 20 to 30 per cent of the population.

In the 19th and 20th centuries, Berbers were the main source of resistance to French colonialism. The heart of the guerrilla struggle in the first phase of the war of independence from 1954 was in Berber areas, and in 1957 four out of nine FLN leaders were Berbers.

Many politically active Berbers concluded that independence in 1962 did not bring them the rewards they anticipated, which were instead monopolized by the urban Arab elite that dominated the FLN at that time. A Berber uprising demanding improved rights started in 1963 and lasted for two years. In 1980, in events that came to be known as the 'Berber Spring', the authorities banned a lecture on ancient Berber poetry, sparking protests, mainly by students. The government's harsh response led to a death toll variously reported as between 30 and 100. There was more campus unrest on the anniversary of the 'Spring' in 1981 and 1985. The demand was for Tamazight to be an official national language. The FLN, however, demanded cultural and political uniformity and in 1981 codified Algerian identity as a product of Arab and Islamic civilization, thus denying the acknowledgement and, by implication, the rights that Berbers sought.

In the midst of civil war in 1995, the Rome-based Sant' Egidio Community facilitated an agreement between most Algerian opposition groups – excluding the GIA – which expressed a shared view of the Algeria they hoped for after the war.

As well as an emphasis on democracy, a key element of the agreement was tolerance of diversity. The document treated Berbers and Arabs, and the Islamic faith as essential aspects of Algerian national identity.

As the civil war tailed off, there was renewed Berber activism. Violent confrontation in 2001, around the anniversary of the 1980 Berber Spring, was this time known as 'Black Spring', as 120 people died and 2,000 were injured in protests demanding autonomy in the Berber area of Kabylia. The following year, President Bouteflika announced that Tamazight would be recognized as a national language. Since then it has been taught in schools and there have been promises of more support for economic development in Berber areas.

Complaints remain among Berbers, however, about widespread discrimination, reflected in high unemployment rates. And in both 2011 and 2014, as the call for increased democracy found voice in Algeria again, Berbers were prominent among the activists.

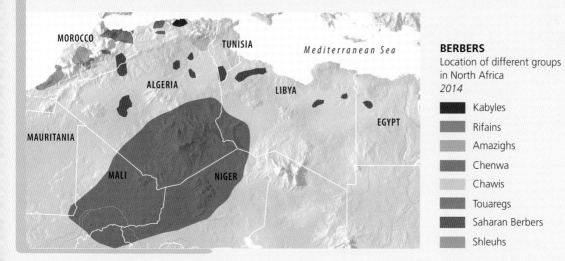

BERBERS
Location of different groups
in North Africa
2014

- Kabyles
- Rifains
- Amazighs
- Chenwa
- Chawis
- Touaregs
- Saharan Berbers
- Shleuhs

THE KURDS

The international system is not going to permit the formation of a unified Kurdish state, the dream of some Kurdish leaders. But as a group, Iraqi Kurds and their political leaders benefited from the invasion of Iraq by the USA and allies in 2003 and the subsequent occupation.

Though the war and mayhem that the invasion of Iraq unleashed have brought suffering to many Kurds, for many others it has brought a sense that at last their culture and identity are receiving appropriate respect, the reality of political autonomy and the prospect of independence. They have even been able to benefit from the oil in their homeland. These are all things that had previously been systematically denied them. Yet Kurdish progress in Iraq has meant, if anything, further pressure on Kurds in Iran, Syria and Turkey, where governments oppose and fear increased Kurdish autonomy.

There are over 30 million Kurds in the area traditionally known as Kurdistan and a further 5 million living outside it. They are united by geography and a common history that is believed to go back more than two millennia and can certainly be dated to the time of the founding of Islam. But there appears to have been little, if any, common sense of Kurdish identity until the declining years of the Ottoman Empire. In the wake of World War I, as the remains of the Ottoman realm were shared out, the formation of a state of Kurdistan was a promise that was made and quickly forgotten (see map on p 29).

As the new states of Turkey and Iraq were being formed, Kurdish tribes continued a centuries-long tradition of rejecting subjugation. To suppress Kurdish identity, the new states utilized law, education, exhortation and force, and treated Kurdish people's rights with such raw contempt that they consistently fed new rounds of resistance. Any attempt to acknowledge Kurdish culture or even language was treated, especially in Turkey, as an act of dangerous political dissidence. For several decades, Turkish law denied that there was such a group of people as the Kurds, and in the 1980s laws were passed to prevent both people and places from having Kurdish names. Similarly in Syria, each decade from the 1960s saw the government bring in new measures to discriminate a bit more, to make difficult lives even harder (see p 93).

The reason there is no single state of Kurdistan, however, is not only explained by the arbitrary and cruel behaviour of governments and the enormous odds faced by Kurdish nationalists. It also results from internal differences. Kurds are divided by many factors: by differences of dialect that, in some respects, are as significant as the differences between, say, English and German; by the difficulties of travel and communication in their mountainous region; by their tribal social structure and by ensuing political differences. These divisions and differences have inevitably weakened Kurdish uprisings against the central authorities of Iran, Iraq and Turkey.

So deep did the divisions go that all Kurdish uprisings in Iraq from the 1920s until into the 1990s met armed opposition from Kurds, sometimes fighting in tribal Kurdish forces and sometimes in government units. From 1960 until just before the US invasion of Iraq in 2003, Kurdish politics in Iraq was characterized by deep division between two leaders – Mullah Mustafa Barzani, followed by his son, and Jalal Talabani. There was a sense of unity only in times of extreme danger, and usually only briefly.

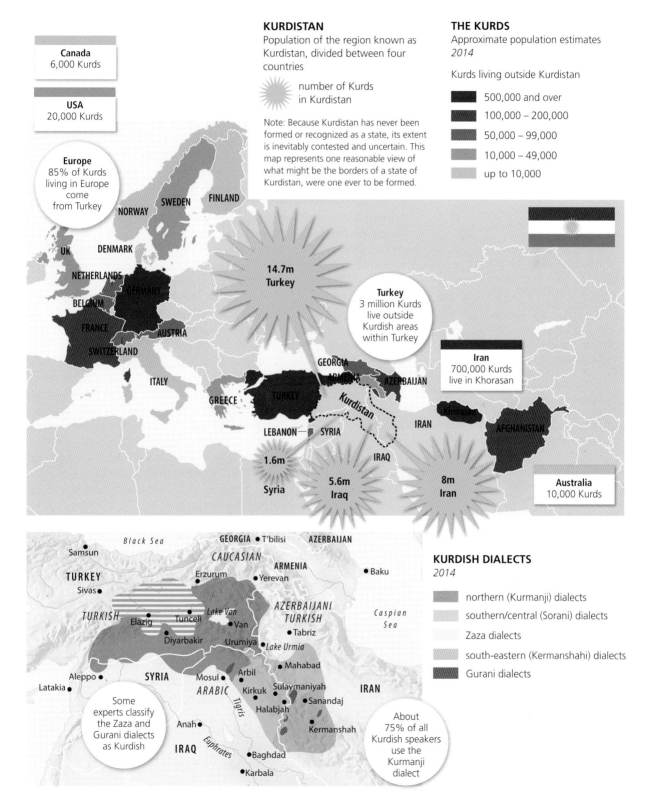

KURDISTAN
Population of the region known as Kurdistan, divided between four countries

number of Kurds in Kurdistan

Note: Because Kurdistan has never been formed or recognized as a state, its extent is inevitably contested and uncertain. This map represents one reasonable view of what might be the borders of a state of Kurdistan, were one ever to be formed.

THE KURDS
Approximate population estimates *2014*

Kurds living outside Kurdistan

500,000 and over
100,000 – 200,000
50,000 – 99,000
10,000 – 49,000
up to 10,000

Canada
6,000 Kurds

USA
20,000 Kurds

Europe
85% of Kurds living in Europe come from Turkey

14.7m Turkey

Turkey
3 million Kurds live outside Kurdish areas within Turkey

Iran
700,000 Kurds live in Khorasan

1.6m Syria

5.6m Iraq

8m Iran

Australia
10,000 Kurds

NORWAY SWEDEN FINLAND
UK DENMARK
NETHERLANDS
BELGIUM GERMANY
FRANCE AUSTRIA
SWITZERLAND
ITALY
GREECE TURKEY
GEORGIA ARMENIA AZERBAIJAN
Kurdistan
LEBANON SYRIA IRAN Khorasan AFGHANISTAN
IRAQ

KURDISH DIALECTS
2014

northern (Kurmanji) dialects
southern/central (Sorani) dialects
Zaza dialects
south-eastern (Kermanshahi) dialects
Gurani dialects

Black Sea
Samsun
GEORGIA ● T'bilisi AZERBAIJAN
CAUCASIAN
TURKEY Erzurum ARMENIA ● Baku
Sivas ● Yerevan ●
TURKISH Lake Van AZERBAIJANI TURKISH Caspian Sea
Elazig Tunceli Van ● Tabriz ●
Diyarbakir Urumiya Lake Urmia
Aleppo ● Arbil ● Mahabad ●
Latakia ● SYRIA Mosul ● Kirkuk ● Sulaymaniyah ● IRAN
ARABIC Sanandaj ●
Halabjah ●
Anah ● Kermanshah ●
IRAQ Baghdad ●
Karbala ●

Some experts classify the Zaza and Gurani dialects as Kurdish

About 75% of all Kurdish speakers use the Kurmanji dialect

The fight for freedom

By the 1990s, there was open warfare between Barzani's KDP and Talabani's PUK. The KDP even allied with Saddam Hussein's Iraq against the PUK. It likewise supported Turkish military forays into northern Iraq against the Kurdistan Workers Party (known usually by its Turkish initials of PKK), which had been at war with the Turkish government since 1984.

The PKK was leftist and nationalist. It had strong support because of the experience of discrimination and used terror tactics against opponents – the Turkish government, Kurds who worked with it, and rich Kurdish landowners.

Antagonism between Syria and Turkey meant the PKK could base its headquarters in Syria, but security measures along that border meant they also needed bases in northern Iraq. Syria turned against the PKK in 1998 and forced its leader Abdullah Ocalan to leave the country. Arrested in Kenya where he had been hiding in the Greek Embassy, he was tried, convicted and sentenced to life imprisonment (the death sentence has not been used in Turkey for a long time). This created a moment of opportunity for the Turkish government to take a new course with the Kurds. From 2002 the constitution and laws allowed greater rights for Kurds. The path of liberalization is not smooth, for the attempt to suppress Kurdish identity had become a deeply ingrained reflex in the Turkish military, judiciary and some political parties. Even so, there was some progress and in the 2015 elections the Kurdish party emerged as a major parliamentary force.

In Iraq, in the aftermath of the 1991 war, the USA encouraged Kurds to rise up against Saddam but then denied them direct assistance. Saddam's assault on the uprising was overwhelming. About 1.5 million Kurds fled from the Iraqi advance. But in Turkey the government of the time (10 years before liberalization) was wary of their potential impact in the south-east and would not give them refuge. The creation of a 'safe haven' on the Iraqi side of the border was a first for the UN: the Security Council set a precedent by deciding that barbaric behaviour by sovereign states within their own borders was an international concern. Many commentators interpreted the decision as the basis for a new era of international law and concern for human security.

The invasion of Iraq in 2003, by contrast, was widely seen as ending a short-lived era of respect for international law, yet it produced improved rights and freedoms for Iraqi Kurds. For a while at least, the PUK and KDP came together to reap the political harvest, with the establishment of a Kurdish zone in which there is considerable autonomy, and with a role in the national politics of Iraq – indeed, a Kurdish president. There were enough political goods available for Barzani and Talabani to be able to share.

In 2014, as ISIS occupied half of Syria and swathes of northern Iraq, Kurdish militias in both countries became prominent as reliable forces opposing it. Further gains in political rights for Kurds could be available on the back of success against ISIS. Barzani even raised the prospect of turning the Kurdish region of Iraq into an autonomous state. For any such gains to be achieved, and if achieved to be durable, however, Kurdish leaders will have to avoid the strategic divisions that have dogged Kurdish aspirations for decades.

EVENTS IN KURDISH HOMELANDS
1995–2014

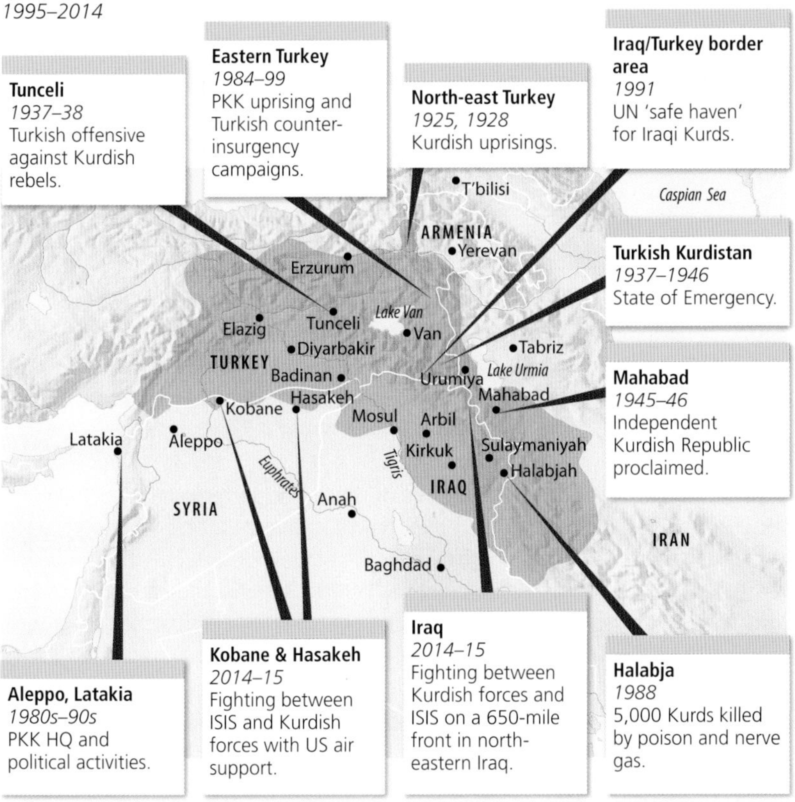

Tunceli
1937–38
Turkish offensive against Kurdish rebels.

Eastern Turkey
1984–99
PKK uprising and Turkish counter-insurgency campaigns.

North-east Turkey
1925, 1928
Kurdish uprisings.

Iraq/Turkey border area
1991
UN 'safe haven' for Iraqi Kurds.

Turkish Kurdistan
1937–1946
State of Emergency.

Mahabad
1945–46
Independent Kurdish Republic proclaimed.

Map labels: T'bilisi · Caspian Sea · ARMENIA · Yerevan · Erzurum · Lake Van · Elazig · Tunceli · Van · TURKEY · Diyarbakir · Tabriz · Badinan · Urumiya · Lake Urmia · Hasakeh · Mahabad · Kobane · Mosul · Arbil · Latakia · Aleppo · Kirkuk · Sulaymaniyah · Euphrates · Tigris · Halabjah · Anah · IRAQ · SYRIA · IRAN · Baghdad

Aleppo, Latakia
1980s–90s
PKK HQ and political activities.

Kobane & Hasakeh
2014–15
Fighting between ISIS and Kurdish forces with US air support.

Iraq
2014–15
Fighting between Kurdish forces and ISIS on a 650-mile front in north-eastern Iraq.

Halabja
1988
5,000 Kurds killed by poison and nerve gas.

DISCRIMINATION IN SYRIA
1963–2008

1962
Decree 93 removes voting and property rights from 120,000 Kurds and their offspring.
It takes all civic rights from 75,000 more (and their offspring).

1963
Plans made to expropriate and internally deport Kurds from 1,200 square miles of oil-rich borderlands with Turkey and replace them with Arabs (implementation started 1973, suspended 1976).

1967
Schoolbooks start to omit mention of Kurds in Syria.

1977
Kurdish place names expunged.

1989
Use of Kurdish language banned in workplaces, at weddings and other ceremonies.

1992
Registration of Kurdish names for new-born children banned.

2000
Ban on Kurdish cultural centres, bookshops, sale of Kurdish cassettes, videos and discs.

2008
Further restrictions on Kurdish right to own property.

CHRONOLOGY *continued*

1991 *Apr* UN 'safe haven' in northern Iraq.

July Kurdish forces take Arbil and Sulaymaniyah.

1992 Iraqi Kurdish elections give KDP 50.8% of vote and PUK 49.2%. Coalition government forms. 20,000 Turkish troops enter 'safe haven' in anti-PKK operation.

1994 Armed conflict starts between KDP and PUK in Iraqi Kurdistan.

1995 Turkish troops attack PKK in northern Iraq aided by KDP.

1996 KDP allies with Iraq government to take Arbil and Sulaymaniyah. PUK takes back Sulaymaniyah a month later.

1998 KDP–PUK peace agreement. Rival governments remain.

1999 Syria expels PKK. In Kenya PKK leader Abdullah Ocalan captured by Turkish agents. Death sentence commuted to life imprisonment. PKK ceasefire.

2003 On the eve of US offensive against Iraq, PUK and KDP create joint leadership in the north. Turkish constitution amended to permit use of Kurdish language.

2004 PKK claims attacks by Turkish forces on Kurds in south-east Turkey, ends ceasefire. Turkish state television broadcasts first Kurdish language programme.

2004–05 Turkish government accuses PKK of bomb attacks.

2005 Alliance of Kurdish parties comes second in Iraqi national election. PUK leader Talabani elected interim president. KDP's Massoud Barzani is president of Kurdish autonomous region.

2012 President Talabani reportedly suffers stroke.

2014 Talabani (now 81 years old) steps down as Iraq's president. Kurdish forces fight ISIS forces in northern Iraq and on Syrian–Turkish border. Barzani announces (but does not carry out) plan for referendum on full independence for Kurdish region of Iraq.

2015 Turkey bombs PKK in Iraq.

IRAN

Iran is a major regional power that the West has consistently failed to understand and in the 21st century has come to fear for its suspected nuclear ambitions.

Seen by the West in the 1960s and 1970s as an island of stability in a volatile region, Iran was a revolution waiting to happen. Opposition to foreign influence and control of the country's oil resources always ran deep. In the 1940s, Mohammad Mossadeq led a movement demanding national ownership and control of the oil. He became prime minister and successfully challenged the Shah, whose rule would have been over had the USA not stepped in with a coup, backed by the UK.

After the 1953 coup, the Shah centralized power and built up the state's repressive apparatus. As well as using coercion, he sought to win support through economic development and reforms, but his efforts were hampered by corruption, inefficiency and his own unpopularity. The country was changing in the 1950s and 1960s, becoming better educated and more urbanized.

Urbanization helped change the role of mullahs in society, bringing them closer to the people, who wanted their advice to handle problems arising from changes in the basic terms of daily life. In the early 1960s, Ruhollah Khomeini emerged as one of the foremost religious leaders. In 1962, he was arrested for criticizing a proposal to give US military personnel immunity from prosecution (a standard US requirement for its forces in foreign countries). The following year he was imprisoned for several months. There were huge demonstrations in his support, which were violently suppressed, with 600 people killed and 2,000 injured. He was exiled in 1964 but not silenced. In Najaf, southern Iraq, from 1965 until 1978, he taught in a theological college, to which many young Iranian mullahs came; his sermons were taped and distributed on cassettes to large audiences in Iran.

Iran's oil income rose 17-fold from 1970 to 1974. The Shah's extravagance grew commensurately. In 1971, he spent $300 million celebrating what he claimed was 2,500 years of monarchy in Iran; the same year, Khomeini published a manifesto for Islamic government. Through the 1970s, the Shah used the increased oil money to buy sophisticated American weaponry. Alongside that, in 1976, shortages of basic foodstuffs started. These quickly hit the middle class as well as the poor and further undermined the Shah's remaining legitimacy. As protests built up, so did repression.

By 1978, the recipe for revolution was clear: hardship amid plenty, a harsh and extravagant regime, a history of resisting injustice and a cultural preference for fairness and equality – and in the exiled Khomeini, a moral leader who voiced the people's complaints and an alternative vision of government. Violent response to massive public demonstrations ignited cycles of renewed protest. In each protest, people were killed by the state security forces so each was followed by a 40-day mourning period. Then came a new protest and more killings. The Shah offered compromises but to no avail. Ill with cancer, he seemed to lose the will to rule and left the country in 1979. A few days later, Khomeini returned.

It was a revolution – but not freedom. A new clampdown soon started. The Revolutionary Guards broke up meetings of groups that did not accept

Khomeini's leadership, and arrested those who would not be quickly silenced. Many were executed. The US Embassy was invaded and the diplomats taken hostage, breaking the laws of inter-state relations.

Iran promised to spread Islamic revolution, and sent Revolutionary Guards to Lebanon. But exporting revolution largely had to wait. In 1980, Iraq seized on what seemed a moment of Iranian weakness and invaded (see pp 98–99). The USA paid Iran back by supporting Iraq. Eight years of war killed at least 300,000 Iranians, slashed oil exports and shattered the economy. Eventually, war fatigue pushed Iran into a ceasefire.

Khomeini had previously refused all calls for compromise and made no secret that not defeating Iraq was a bitter pill. To ensure this did not weaken the regime more profoundly, Khomeini ordered wholesale execution of political prisoners. One estimate of the death toll by an Ayatollah who opposed the executions is 30,000.

ETHNIC DIVERSITY
Estimated location of ethnic groups
2013

- Persian
- Azeri
- Kurd
- Arab
- Lur
- Baloch
- Qashqai
- Turkoman
- Gilaki
- Mazandarani
- Talysh
- other
- sparse population

RELIGION
2008

90% of the Iranian population are Shi'a

- areas with statistically significant Sunni populations

Security barrier

700km (435 mile) security barrier with a 3m (10ft) high wall divides the Baloch people in Iran from those in Pakistan

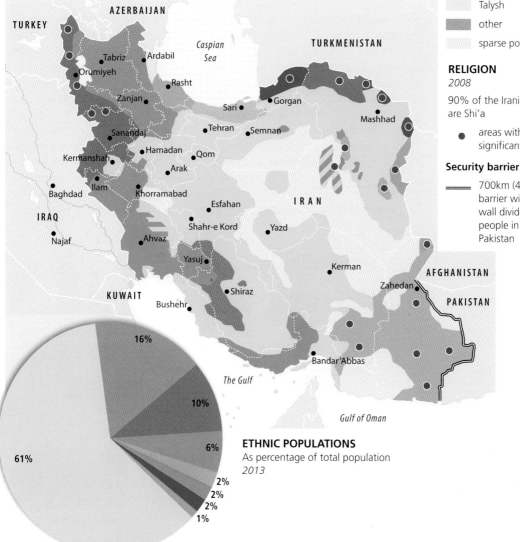

ETHNIC POPULATIONS
As percentage of total population
2013

61%, 16%, 10%, 6%, 2%, 2%, 2%, 1%

Revolutionary cycles

In the febrile post-war atmosphere of 1989, Iran broke international rules again when Supreme Leader Khomeini authorized the murder of British writer, Salman Rushdie, claiming his novel *The Satanic Verses* was blasphemous. It seemed Iran was stable only if it kept fighting battles at home and abroad.

In successive parliamentary elections, though all candidates are vetted by the Council of Guardians, the balance has swung between parties that seek continuing Islamic revolution and those who want less fervour and more personal freedom. The more moderate group won in 1992 and 2000, the revolutionaries in 1996 and 2004. And for two terms, 1997 to 2005, there was a reforming president in Mohammed Khatami. His inability to deliver economic improvement, and the continuing restrictions on political freedoms, led to harshly repressed demonstrations in 2003. In 2005, Mahmoud Ahmadinejad was elected president, with policies of limited economic liberalization, social conservatism and international militancy – and a hard line on freedom at home.

Internationally, Ahmadinejad refreshed Iran's insurgent energy by advocating Israel's destruction, denying the Holocaust and accelerating Iran's controversial nuclear programme. He started up enrichment again, insisting it was wanted only for nuclear energy. Enrichment is the process by which uranium is turned into fuel for nuclear reactors or, by further enrichment, into material for nuclear weapons. So the claim of peaceful purposes is credible, but the suspicion of weaponizing intentions is not unfounded.

Ahmadinejad's presidency was an economic disaster, not only because of the US and EU sanctions. A reserve fund established under Khatami in 2000 had, according to reports, reached $160 billion at its peak; by 2013 it stood at zero. Socially and culturally, Iran is full of paradoxes. Some observers argue that religious militancy has alienated many people, leading to a society significantly more secular than elsewhere in the Middle East. And Iran faces other pressures.

CONSTITUTION OF THE ISLAMIC REPUBLIC

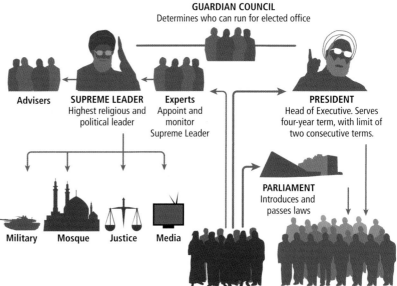

GUARDIAN COUNCIL
Determines who can run for elected office

Advisers

SUPREME LEADER
Highest religious and political leader

Experts
Appoint and monitor Supreme Leader

PRESIDENT
Head of Executive. Serves four-year term, with limit of two consecutive terms.

Military   Mosque   Justice   Media

PARLIAMENT
Introduces and passes laws

VOTERS

Cabinet 22 ministers

For example, 40 per cent of Afghanistan's opium production is exported through Iran, and the UN estimates that about 1.2 million Iranians are addicted to hard drugs.

In 2013, the balance swung again and Hassan Rouhani was elected president on promises to engage in international dialogue and improve the economy for ordinary Iranians. Contact with the USA was quickly re-opened and negotiations with the USA, Russia and EU set out the broad terms for agreement on the nuclear programme. Meanwhile in Iraq, Iran and Western powers made some degree of common cause against the ISIS *jihadis* who threatened to topple the US-created, Iran-backed, Shi'a-led government. Further progress was slow. It seemed Rouhani had limited room for manoeuvre on the nuclear issue, with Supreme Ruler Khamenei in charge of the big decisions. And in Syria, Iran and the West remained at odds, with Iran still backing Assad while the West was increasingly unsure of what to do and whom to back.

Agreement came eventually in July 2015. Inevitably controversial and attacked by Israel's government and US Republicans, the deal limits (but does not end) Iran's nuclear programme, facilities and materials. In return, it lifts economic sanctions and releases over $100 billion of frozen assets back to Iran.

Much of the criticism of the agreement centred on what Iran could do with that cash. In Iran, the answer appeared straightforward: strengthen the economy. But communication between Iran and the West has been full of mutual mistrust and incomprehension. Most Western governments seem not to understand why there was a revolution and have denied its legitimacy ever since. Some Iranian leaders seem not to care about regional stability. In these circumstances, it takes a lot of effort to avoid confrontation and escalation – the kind of effort that led to the nuclear deal.

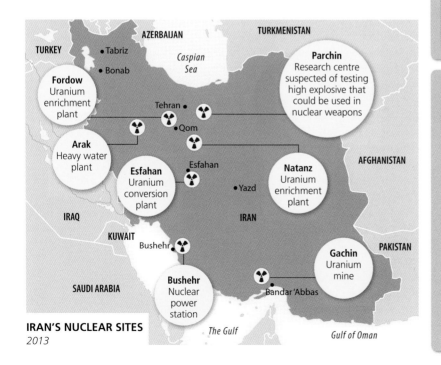

IRAN'S NUCLEAR SITES
2013

IRAN'S NUCLEAR PROGRAMME

1950s Iran starts a civilian nuclear programme with US support.

1968 Iran signs Nuclear Non-Proliferation Treaty.

1979 Revolution: Khomeini ignores nuclear programme. Many nuclear experts leave.

1984 The Iran–Iraq war persuades Khomeini to restart the programme.

2002 US intelligence identifies nuclear plants.

2004 Iran voluntarily suspends enrichment.

2005 Ahmadinejad elected president and accelerates and expands nuclear research programme.

2008 Iran test-fires Shahab-3 missile it says can hit Israel. US and Israel start collaboration (code-named 'Olympic Games') for cyberattacks on Iranian facilities.

2009 Iran says the uranium enrichment plant it is building near Qom is for peaceful purposes.

2013 First direct talks between US and Iran since 1979 lead to outline agreement that Iran's nuclear programme can proceed. Deadline for final agreement Nov 2014.

2014 *Nov* Deadline extended to July 2015.

2015 *July* Agreement reached.

ATTACKS ON IRANIAN NUCLEAR SCIENTISTS

2007 *Jan* 1 death is reported as accidental 'gas poisoning'.

2010 *Jan* Tehran physics professor killed by motorcycle bomb.

2010 *Nov* Head of Iran's Atomic Energy Organization wounded in bomb attack. Physicist killed by car bomb.

2011 *Jan* Chemical scientist killed by car bomb.

2011 *July* Electronics expert shot dead.

2011 *Nov* Head of Iran's ballistic missile program killed in explosion at a military base.

2012 *Jan* Deputy Head of Natanz enrichment plant killed by car bomb.

THE IRAN–IRAQ WAR

Iraq's invasion of Iran in September 1980 set in train a series of events that killed millions and hit both countries' economies hard. It led to further rounds of war that brought American and other foreign forces to the region and turned Iraq itself into the site of mayhem and chaos.

At the outset, Saddam Hussein probably had a double motive. First, to deal a pre-emptive blow to the new Islamic Republic of Iran to stop it from exporting its Shi'a revolution to Iraq's large Shi'a population. Second, to gain more power and influence in the region.

Iraq seemed set to win, with an army of 190,000 soldiers and 2,200 tanks; though Iran's air force still had the latest US combat aircraft, bought before the revolution, its army was weakened by purges of officers. Iraq's initial offensive seized Iranian territory near the border, but 200,000 Iranian volunteers strengthened the front lines and Iraq's gains were consequently limited.

Saddam was responsible for starting the war but Ayatollah Khomeini kept it going. Iran's Supreme Leader turned down successive ceasefire proposals and offers of negotiations. Once the initial offensive had been held back, his objective was not defensive – he aimed for the overthrow of Saddam Hussein.

Tactics were brutal. Both sides attacked cities. Iran compensated for a lack of tanks by throwing 'human waves' into its offensives. To begin with, they were volunteers, but one account from March 1984 tells of thousands of boys tied together with ropes and forced to attack through a minefield. And Iraq used chemical weapons (CW) – both mustard gas and nerve gas according to irrefutable, independent evidence.

The war extended to attacks on shipping in the Gulf. Although Iraq began the 'tanker war' and carried out most of the attacks, it was often Iran that was blamed by the West. By early 1988, 8 navies from the region and 10 from outside it were deployed in the Gulf to protect commercial shipping.

Iraq was supplied by France, the USSR and the USA. In February 1982, the Reagan administration removed Iraq from the list of terrorist countries and in November 1983 decided to work to prevent an Iraqi defeat. Its main assistance was economic – about $5 billion in commercial loans for agriculture and oil pipeline construction. The State Department knew Iraq was using CW routinely and US intelligence was given to Iraq to aid its military operations, including CW use. At the same time, the USA made overtures to Iran and secretly supplied it with weapons, hoping to make contact with less adamantly anti-US factions in the leadership, and to get Iranian assistance in tracing US hostages held by Shi'a groups in Lebanon. Some observers believe the US aim was to weaken both combatants equally, but in practice its assistance to Iraq far outweighed the scale and significance of its help for Iran.

By the end of 1987 Iran's forces were seriously depleted while Iraq had been able to re-equip and its army had shown new levels of effectiveness. Further offensives in 1988 took the war back onto Iranian territory and Iraqi missile attacks on Tehran caused 30 per cent of the city's population to flee. In August, Khomeini took a decision he described as 'a cup of poison' and agreed at last to a ceasefire.

In terms of territory, there were no losses, no gains. In terms of people, at least half a million died, probably a million, and perhaps as many as 1,500,000. And the economy of both countries was devastated.

THE IRAN-IRAQ WAR
1980–88

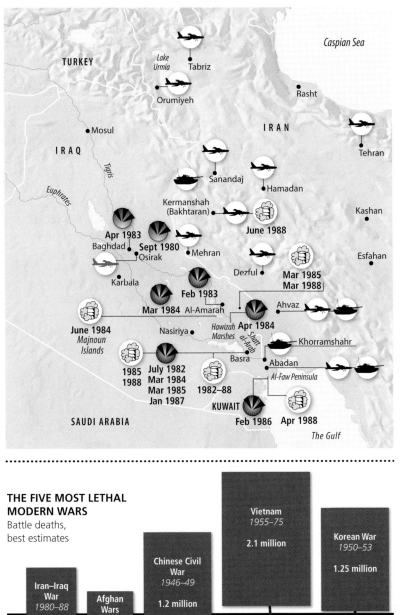

 Iraqi air raids *September 1980*

 Israeli air attack *June 1981*

Iraqi ground attacks
September 1980

Iranian offensives
date as shown

Iraqi use of chemical weapons
in major offensives
date as shown

THE FIVE MOST LETHAL MODERN WARS
Battle deaths,
best estimates

War	Period	Battle deaths
Iran–Iraq War	1980–88	650,000
Afghan Wars	1978–2002	560,000
Chinese Civil War	1946–49	1.2 million
Vietnam	1955–75	2.1 million
Korean War	1950–53	1.25 million

Data on war casualties are extremely uncertain. Competing propaganda claims, combined with the difficulty of getting reliable and comprehensive information when those recording the death toll are themselves in mortal danger, make hard facts rare. The data get further confused by mixing up direct battle deaths and the indirect effects of war, such as increased disease when health facilities have been destroyed. A common and reasonable estimate is that the total death toll in a war may be four times as high as the battle deaths.

Amid the uncertainties, the Iran–Iraq War emerges as one of the most deadly since the end of World War II.

IRAQ

With about 9 per cent of the world's oil reserves and a population of 30 million, Iraq has the basic requirements for both prosperity and regional prominence. Its history since independence has, however, been marked by dictatorship and wars, culminating in the chaos of the 21st century.

Upon the demise of the Ottoman Empire, Iraq was formed as a dependent British territory. It was made up of three imperial provinces. British control continued until after World War II, despite formal independence in 1932. Though there were elections as early as 1925, Iraq was never a democracy until after the 2003 intervention by the USA (see pp 106–109). Real power was always in the hands of other states, various army factions or, for 35 years from 1968 to 2003, the Ba'ath Party.

Each of the three old Ottoman provinces that made up Iraq had its own history and identity. Broadly, the north was Kurdish with large Assyrian and Turkoman minorities, while the centre was Sunni Arab and the south-east was Shi'a Arab. Into this patchwork, in 1921, the British brought an outsider to be king – Faisal, son of the Sharif of Mecca, commander in the Arab uprising against the Ottomans from 1916. The name al-Iraq that the British gave to the new mandate territory had previously been used for an area near Basra in the south. There was little basis for regarding Iraq as a unified country.

The lack of a common history and a unifying national consciousness did not make control by an outside power popular. In Iraq's first decade Britain held the country together by holding it down. In 1920, before Faisal was placed on the throne, there was an uprising against British domination by about 100,000 fighters. The British responded by bombing and strafing rebel villages. They have been widely accused of using poison gas weapons (not banned by treaty until 1925); though the evidence about this is not clear, there is no doubt that commanders in Iraq and the authorities in London considered the option.

The early years of Iraq's formal independence from 1932 were marked by political instability. The military moved onto the political stage in 1936 with a coup inspired by the model of Turkey under Kemal Atatürk. The monarchy remained in place through a succession of upheavals. In 1941, Britain re-exerted complete control after a pro-German faction in the army had staged a coup. Finally in 1958 the monarchy was overthrown in a violent coup. This time the coup-makers were inspired by the Free Officers' Movement in Egypt that had overthrown King Farouk six years earlier and, indeed, referred to themselves as the Free Officers.

Its leader Brigadier Qassem, became president. The coup had mass support but there was disunity about Iraq's position in the Arab world. The choice lay between the pan-Arab unity of Nasserism and an Iraq-first approach. Some officers wanted to join the United Arab Republic, newly formed by Egypt and Syria (see pp 34–35).

But Iraq-first had strong support, including from the Iraqi Communist Party, which had flourished despite being banned under the monarchy, and could mobilize 500,000 supporters in demonstrations. For them, much of the point of the revolution was to be free of the influence of foreign leaders and outside powers, whoever they were.

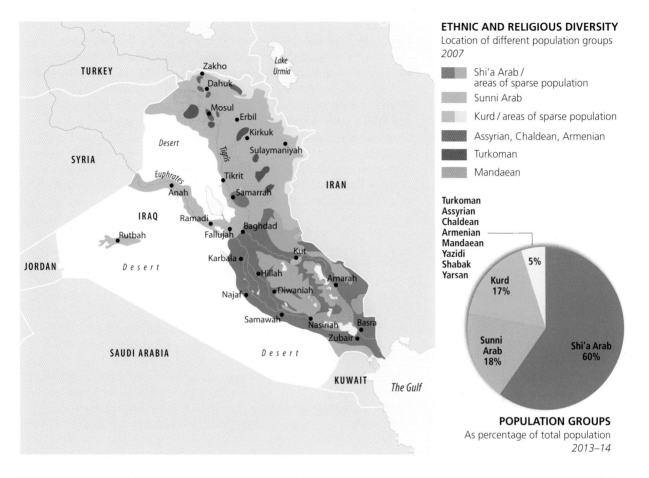

ETHNIC AND RELIGIOUS DIVERSITY
Location of different population groups
2007

- Shi'a Arab / areas of sparse population
- Sunni Arab
- Kurd / areas of sparse population
- Assyrian, Chaldean, Armenian
- Turkoman
- Mandaean

Turkoman
Assyrian
Chaldean
Armenian
Mandaean
Yazidi
Shabak
Yarsan — 5%

Kurd 17%

Sunni Arab 18%

Shi'a Arab 60%

POPULATION GROUPS
As percentage of total population
2013–14

IRAQ'S DIMINISHING DIVERSITY

Information on minority groups in Iraq is patchy and inconsistent but all accounts concur that Iraq's ethnic diversity has declined sharply since the country was first formed, and sharply again since US intervention in 2003.

Jews Jews were prominent in establishing the post-Ottoman state under the British mandate and the first minister of finance was Jewish. Anti-Jewish pressure started in the 1930s and escalated when Israel was formed. Over 120,000 Jews migrated to Israel. Most of the remainder left by the early 1970s. Estimates of Jewish population in the 21st century range from five to eight individuals.

Mandaeans Followers of a Gnostic religion, largely living in southern Iraq, Mandaeans faced pressure to assimilate to Arab ways in the 1950s and 1960s. There remained a Mandaean community estimated at 70,000 in 2003. Persecution led to migration of an estimated 90 per cent of the community.

Yazidis Gaining international notice and sympathy only when persecuted by ISIS, the Yazidi religion has elements of several faiths. Estimates of numbers pre-ISIS range from 70,000 to half a million and more.

Yarsani Yarsanism is a Kurdish syncretic religion founded in the late 14th century. There are no generally accepted estimates of the population.

Shabaks The Shabak people are an ethnic group speaking their own language, which is in the same language group as the Zaza-Gurani variants in Kurdish. About 70 per cent are thought to be Shi'a, the rest being Yarsani or Sunni. Numbers were estimated at 15,000 in the 1970s.

Christians Estimates of Iraq's Christian population in 2003 ranged from half a million to 1.5 million. Many have fled to neighbouring countries. The estimated Christian population ten years after intervention is about 200,000.

The Ba'ath Party

The Ba'ath Party was a bastion of pan-Arabism (see pp 34–35). Formed originally in Syria, the party's name means 'renaissance'. A party merger in 1952 had made it the Arab Ba'ath Socialist Party. The Ba'athists in Iraq lacked the Communists' numbers on the streets but were influential in the military. As it became clear that Qassem would keep Iraq out of any unification with other Arab states, the Ba'athists turned against him. In 1959, only one year after the revolution, they attempted an insurrection and sent an assassination team against Qassem. It failed. One of its members was Saddam Hussein, then aged 23.

In 1963, the CIA backed a coup against Qassem because of his pro-Soviet policies. Ba'athists were prominent among the military faction that now came to power. Several days of severe fighting were followed by several months of arrests and executions of Qassem's supporters, especially the Communists. The same year, the Ba'ath Party adopted a programme of collective ownership of agriculture, central planning and a one-party state. Ba'athists in the army opposed this new radicalism and pushed the radical Ba'athists out of power in late 1963; in street fighting, the army crushed the Ba'athist militia.

The catastrophic Arab defeat by Israel in 1967 inspired a distrust of military regimes that helped pave the way to the 1968 revolution in Iraq. This time Ba'athists acted in unity and alone. The president and chair of the Revolutionary Command Council (RCC) was Ahmad Hassan al-Bakr, once a member of the Free Officers. A close relative of his was deputy chair and responsible for internal security – Saddam Hussein, aged 31.

All the influential players in the new regime had military backgrounds except Saddam. Family and clan connections helped him get over that handicap; political skill and ruthlessness took him the rest of the way to the top.

Long before he became president, Saddam was customarily described as the regime's 'strong man'. The regime distinguished itself for both the efficiency and the refinements of its system of repression. It began with the public execution of 14 alleged conspirators in 1969, to which hundreds of thousands of people came to bear witness at the behest of the regime and, though it was not said openly, to become a little complicit.

Like many other repressive regimes, Ba'athist Iraq maintained a momentum of discovering plots and putting the plotters on trial. People could disappear – for a time or permanently – for uttering the mildest doubts about the state of the country. Families sometimes only learned that a son or father had been executed when the authorities required them to pay the funeral costs. Others were imprisoned for years without trial. Torture was commonplace and extreme. And through the widespread system of informers, reaching into every part of social and working life, the regime ensured millions of ordinary people were complicit with repression; those who refused to help the authorities knew they put themselves and their families at risk.

The Ba'athist years constructed a new elite in Iraq, with Sunni Arabs receiving a disproportionate share of government posts. Among Sunnis, in the rise to higher levels, clan loyalties were critical; like both al-Bakr and Saddam many senior figures came from the area of Tikrit. At the same time, leftist and nationalist ideology survived and guided aspects of government policy. There was considerable and successful investment in health, education and in basic infrastructure, such as clean water supplies and good transport. One side of the Ba'athist regime was repression, cruelty and denial of rights for Kurds, for the Shi'a and for anybody who voiced disagreement with the state; the other side was that a significant part of the new oil wealth was spent on measures that would benefit ordinary people. Those Sunni Arabs who did not challenge the regime did not fare badly.

In 1979 Saddam Hussein took control of the state. Al-Bakr was placed under house arrest and at least 500 senior party officials were executed, including one-third of the RCC. Those RCC members who were not denounced proved their loyalty by joining the firing squads; once again, the Iraqi system of repression sought complicity from those – in this case, members of the political elite – who were themselves at risk.

Saddam Hussein now set out on a course that brought one disaster after another. In 1980 he ordered the invasion of Iran, launching a war in which more than half a million people died and which was economically ruinous (see pp 98–99). When it ended in 1988, its consequences became the prelude to the next war. Heavy borrowing had been necessary to finance the war, and Saddam needed a way to avoid paying. His argument that Iraq had fought the war on behalf of all Arabs was not one that played any part in his strategic calculations when he launched the war, then expecting a quick victory.

In the first half of 1990, Saddam made a series of speeches warning that he would take action if he did not receive satisfaction on his grievances against Kuwait. It is impossible to know what Saddam would have done had he faced a strong negative reaction from other Arab states or from the USA. But the fact that he did not face clear indications of not only disagreement but of willingness to use force to oppose him may have encouraged him to think he could get away with invading Kuwait.

Saddam Hussein set out on a course that brought one disaster after another

---

At the end of the Iran–Iraq war, despite using chemical weapons against Iran and against the Kurds, Iraq had been seen by the USA as a factor for regional stability. The revolutionary nature of Iran, and in particular the experience of the embassy hostages in 1979–81 made Iraq seem moderate in US eyes. US economic assistance during the war meant that by 1988 the Iraqi economy was more closely linked to the West than at any time since the Qassem years. Up until mid-1990, the USA persuaded itself that, tough as he was, Saddam Hussein was a leader with whom they could do business.

The US administration therefore soft-pedalled its reactions to his speeches in the first half of 1990. They were not alone in doing so. It seemed nobody took Saddam Hussein at his word.

SADDAM'S GRIEVANCES

The war with Iran left Iraq heavily in debt, especially to Kuwait:

$14 billion debt.

Saddam Hussein argued that Iraq had fought as defender of the Arabs against the old Persian enemy.

Therefore, the debt should be waived or eased. But by 1990, Kuwait was pressing for repayment.

In OPEC, Iraq argued for overall cuts in production to drive up prices.

Iraq also wanted a larger production quota for itself to increase revenue even more.

Kuwait was among those who said no.

Iraq accused Kuwait of slant drilling into neighbouring Iraqi oil fields – stealing Iraq's oil.

THE GULF WARS

Despite Iraq's long list of loudly voiced grievances against Kuwait, the invasion in August 1990 genuinely surprised other Arab states and the West. Reaction was quick, with both the Arab League and the UN condemning the invasion. Within a week, US forces started to deploy to Saudi Arabia to ensure Iraq would not make an even more ambitious military move, though there was no clear evidence that this was the intention.

A major diplomatic effort led by the Bush (Snr) administration in the USA and supported by its Western European allies and the Arab monarchies in the Gulf put together a 34-country coalition to enforce the UN demand for Iraq to quit Kuwait, with the legal backing of UN Security Council resolutions. When Saddam Hussein refused to pull his forces back, a one-month air offensive and a week-long ground war inflicted a decisive defeat and forced Iraq out of Kuwait. There are no firm data on war deaths in Iraq resulting from the US-led offensive. Generally accepted estimates for military deaths are in the region of 10,000 during the air offensive and 10,000 during the ground war, while the civilian death toll is usually put at 2,500–3,500.

The speed and ease of the US coalition's victory were another surprise. The Bush administration discussed going further – all the way to Baghdad – but decided against exceeding the mandate from the UN. The USA, in short, did what it had legal authority to do and no more.

Resisting the temptation to which his son later succumbed, President Bush decided to avoid the responsibility of trying to run Iraq. Instead, he made

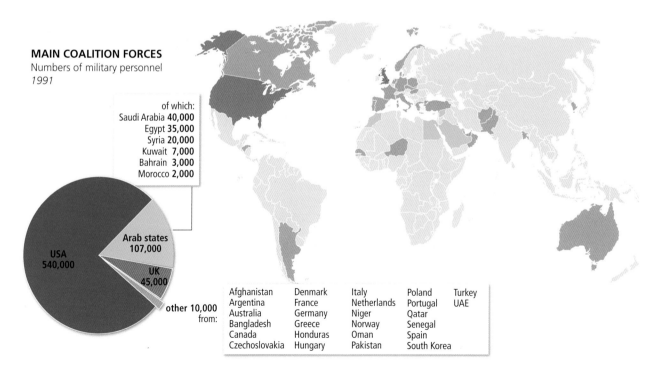

MAIN COALITION FORCES
Numbers of military personnel
1991

of which:
Saudi Arabia **40,000**
Egypt **35,000**
Syria **20,000**
Kuwait **7,000**
Bahrain **3,000**
Morocco **2,000**

Arab states 107,000

USA 540,000

UK 45,000

other 10,000 from:

Afghanistan	Denmark	Italy	Poland	Turkey
Argentina	France	Netherlands	Portugal	UAE
Australia	Germany	Niger	Qatar	
Bangladesh	Greece	Norway	Senegal	
Canada	Honduras	Oman	Spain	
Czechoslovakia	Hungary	Pakistan	South Korea	

speeches urging Iraqis to take matters into their own hands. The result was two uprisings – one in the south, primarily involving Shi'a groups, and one by Kurds in the north. It began in Basra where an army officer spontaneously led an attack on government buildings and prisons and a majority of the population rallied to back him. In other towns and cities – and most of Iraq's major cities were in rebel hands at some point in the following weeks – reports spoke of mass mobilizations, with armed insurgents moving in as the authority of the state's local representatives and forces crumbled.

Despite what some thought Bush said, the US coalition gave no direct assistance to either uprising, except for humanitarian aid in the north when the uprising was quashed. In the south, Iran gave some practical support. In the north, the USA, Britain and France imposed a no-fly zone (but exempted helicopter flights); in the south, the no-fly zone was only imposed the following year. Saddam Hussein's elite Republican Guard struck back. Some tens of thousands of people died and two million at least were displaced from their homes. In the aftermath, the Baghdad Government accelerated a programme of draining the Mesopotamian Marshes in the Tigris-Euphrates river system, driving Shi'a Arabs out of the area. In the north, the Kurdish Autonomous Republic was established.

Saddam Hussein's regime emerged with its internal grip intact, despite defeat in Kuwait and international isolation.

CHRONOLOGY continued

1991 15 Jan UN deadline elapses with Iraqi forces still in Kuwait.

17 Jan US-led forces open air offensive on Iraq (Operation Desert Storm).

23–27 Feb Ground offensive forces Iraqi troops out of Kuwait.

28 Feb Ceasefire agreed.

Mar Shi'a and Kurdish uprisings. Northern 'no-fly zone' established.

Apr UN orders Iraq to disarm weapons of mass destruction.

May British Prime Minister John Major and US Secretary of State James Baker declare economic sanctions remain on Iraq while Saddam Hussein is in power.

1992 Aug Southern no-fly zone established.

1993 June US missile attack on Baghdad follows discovery of plot to assassinate ex-president George Bush during visit to Kuwait.

UN SECURITY COUNCIL RESOLUTIONS ON IRAQ-KUWAIT CRISIS 1990–91

1990 2 Aug UNSCR 660 Condemns invasion of Kuwait and urges Iraqi withdrawal.

6 Aug UNSCR 661 Imposes economic sanctions against Iraq.

9 Aug UNSCR 662 Declares Iraq's annexation of Kuwait 'null and void'.

25 Aug UNSCR 665 Imposes a shipping blockade.

29 Nov UNSCR 678 Authorizes use of 'all necessary means' if Iraq fails to withdraw by 15 January 1991.

1991 3 Apr UNSCR 687 Establishes ceasefire, requires Iraqi disposal of WMD and sets up UN Special Commission (UNSCOM) to monitor compliance on WMD.

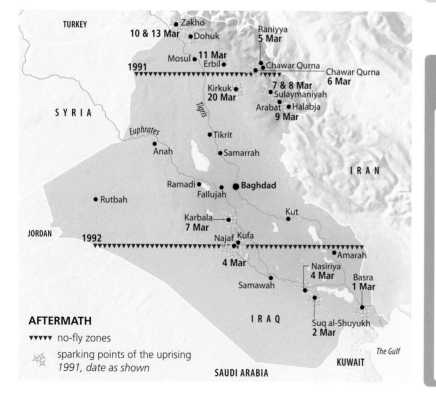

AFTERMATH

▼▼▼▼▼ no-fly zones

sparking points of the uprising 1991, date as shown

Sanctions and the second war

After the war of 1991, there followed a decade in which the West slowly bled Iraq and occasionally attacked it. Economic sanctions, imposed when Iraq invaded Kuwait in August 1990, were left in place after the war. The UN resolution establishing the ceasefire in April 1991 made the removal of sanctions dependent on Iraq abandoning weapons of mass destruction (WMD) and the capacity to make them.

The UN Special Commission (UNSCOM) was set up to make sure it happened. Its inspectors faced constant harassment from Iraq. They nonetheless identified and eliminated 40,000 munitions for chemical weapons, 3,000 tonnes of chemical warfare agents and the ingredients for making them, and dismantled weapons programme facilities. During 1991, nuclear bomb material was removed from Iraq and, by the end of 1992, most facilities used in Iraq's nuclear programme had been destroyed. The inspectors saw no grounds for believing that Iraq still had any nuclear capability, though total certainty is impossible when trying to prove a negative in a large country where information is so tightly controlled.

Economic sanctions, meanwhile, were hurting the ordinary people of Iraq. Despite a UN programme set up in 1995 to sell Iraqi oil to pay for meeting humanitarian need, independent studies suggest that sanctions to the end of 2000 led to approximately 350,000 deaths of children under the age of five. Some of these deaths can be traced also to the after-effects of the war and its destruction of basic infrastructure, including clean water supplies.

The US and UK governments both announced that sanctions would stay till Saddam left, which was not the basis on which the UN had imposed sanctions. The sanctions made the Iraqi people pay for the actions of their leader, over whom they had no control or influence, and by whom they were repressed and beaten down. Both the moral and the political logic of this were hard to fathom.

Sanctions were not enough for some American opinion-makers who wrote to President Clinton in 1998 calling for Saddam's overthrow. When the second President Bush took office in 2001, they were closer to power. When al-Qaeda militants attacked the World Trade Center and the Pentagon in September 2001, their opportunity arrived. The attacks were so spectacular that the WMD

WAR FROM THE AIR
US and UK air attacks *1992–2003*

When	Target	Rationale
Dec 1992	Mig-25 aircraft	Iraqi incursion into no-fly zone
Jan 1993	Radar and surface-to-air missile sites. Nuclear research facility	Iraqi attacks, radar lock-ons. Iraqi non-cooperation with UNSCOM
June 1993	Intelligence HQ, Baghdad	Retaliation for assassination attempt on ex-President Bush
Apr 1994	Various military targets	Iraqi radar lock-ons
Dec 1998	Biological, chemical and nuclear facilities. Air defence battery	Iraqi non-cooperation with UNSCOM. Radar lock-ons
Apr 2002 – early 2003	Various military targets	General threat from Iraqi terrorism/WMD
Mar 2003	Nationwide	Full scale war

issue got a new dimension – the possibility of terrorists such as al-Qaeda getting WMD from a source such as Iraq.

Tales of links between al-Qaeda and Iraq never seemed credible. The religious piety and militancy of Osama bin Laden and al-Qaeda contrasted sharply with the secularism of the Ba'athist state of Iraq. There was no hard evidence and the supposed linkage always looked more like the work of an opportunistic publicist, fusing two enemies in the public imagination, rather than the work of a careful intelligence analyst.

It was widely believed in Western intelligence that Iraq had active WMD programmes. Some evidence existed – most notably, items that UNSCOM had calculated Iraq possessed at some time but had never been found. It seemed credible because Saddam Hussein had used chemical warfare against both Iran and the Kurds, and had always been uncooperative with UNSCOM. As US political pressure on Iraq increased, the UN Security Council sent a new monitoring mission into Iraq at the end of 2002, to check. There were threats of serious consequences if Iraq did not cooperate. As ever, cooperation was grudging and slow. But once the inspectors were there, it was logical to let them finish the job. When the USA and Britain refused to accept that logic, most observers concluded they were never serious about inspections and were using them only as a means to get international support for a war they had long since decided upon.

The impatience of the Bush administration, in particular with the UN, was a striking feature of the build-up to war. The price of this impatience was that the war was fought without the legitimacy that a UN resolution would have given, and with little international support. It was efficiently fought and quickly won.

And when US inspectors were then given the run of the country, they could find no WMD of any kind. It turned out UNSCOM had been successful. Amid the genuine shock of many politicians and commentators, it became clear that the WMD justification of the war was ultimately fake. With that, the last chance that the war against Iraq would generally be seen as legitimate had evaporated.

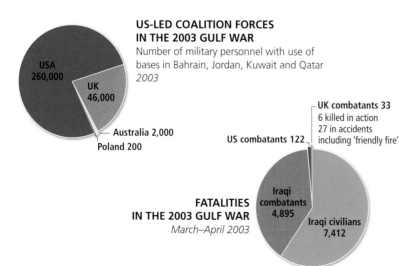

US-LED COALITION FORCES IN THE 2003 GULF WAR
Number of military personnel with use of bases in Bahrain, Jordan, Kuwait and Qatar
2003

USA 260,000
UK 46,000
Australia 2,000
Poland 200

FATALITIES IN THE 2003 GULF WAR
March–April 2003

UK combatants 33
6 killed in action
27 in accidents
including 'friendly fire'

US combatants 122
Iraqi combatants 4,895
Iraqi civilians 7,412

CHRONOLOGY *continued*

2003 *7 Mar* USA, Britain and Spain sponsor UN Security Council resolution for war against Iraq but find too little support to get it passed.
17 Mar President Bush ends diplomatic process giving Saddam Hussein 48 hours to leave Iraq.
19 Mar War begins.
5 Apr US troops enter Baghdad.
7 Apr British forces take Basra.
9 Apr Baghdad falls – statue of Iraqi president pulled down.
1 May President Bush declares end of 'major combat operations'.
22 May UN ends sanctions against Iraq and provides mandate for US-led coalition's presence.

UN SECURITY COUNCIL RESOLUTIONS ON IRAQ *1991–2002*

1991 *3 Apr* UNSCR 687
Establishes ceasefire and requires Iraqi disposal of WMD.
15 Aug UNSCR 707 Urges Iraq to comply with the terms of UNSCR 687.
1996 *12 June* UNSCR 1060 Ditto
1997 *21 June* UNSCR 1115 Ditto
23 Oct UNSCR 1134 Ditto
12 Nov UNSCR 1137 Ditto
1998 *2 Mar* UNSCR 1154 Ditto – and warns of severe consequences of non-compliance.
9 Sept UNSCR 1194 Urges Iraq to comply with 687.
1999 *17 Dec* UNSCR 1284 Sets up UN Monitoring & Verification Mission (UNMOVIC) to replace UNSCOM.
2002 *8 Nov* UNSCR 1441 Declares Iraq in breach of 687 and requires Iraq's accurate accounting of WMD in 30 days, with serious consequences for non-compliance.
2003 *22 May* UNSCR 1483 Lifts sanctions against Iraq and establishes mandate for international forces' presence in Iraq.

War after war

The war was all brutal efficiency; organizing for peace proved much more difficult. In May 2003, a memo by a senior British official described the office of General Garner, installed by the US as head of the Coalition Provisional Authority (CPA), as 'an unbelievable mess'. Soon, that judgement would be applicable to more than the bureaucracy.

There had been no real planning for the peace. The US State Department had worked away on it for several months but a couple of months before the war started the Defense Department took over and ignored all the work done until then. The deeper problem was the issue of legitimacy. The lack of it was barely an inconvenience during the war itself but in the effort to build peace, it became a serious and practical problem. British doctrine for peace operations emphasizes that legitimacy and popular acceptance of the mission are fundamental components of success. By sacrificing legitimacy, the US administration got the war it wanted, and Britain backed it, but took the first step towards losing the peace.

Insurgents exploited those deficiencies. Ba'athists had multiple reasons for fighting the occupation – ideological, nationalistic, and because they had all lost their public-sector jobs. Al-Qaeda and associated groups were soon active too. By the first half of 2006, insurgents were thought to number 15,000–20,000. They targeted water, oil and power, as well as police recruits, the occupying forces and Iraqis who worked with them, religious sites, and qualified professionals such as doctors and lawyers. They also made apparently random attacks on civilians, especially the Shi'a. So well-organized Shi'a militia groups mobilized. By mid-2006 they were blamed for hundreds of killings and kidnappings each month. Moreover, Shi'a joined the police in large numbers and there was evidence they used their positions to maltreat and murder Sunnis.

Facing all this, the US Army routinely employed massive force, in line with its Soldier's Credo, which is not merely to defeat but to destroy the enemy. It works intimidatingly well in war but is less

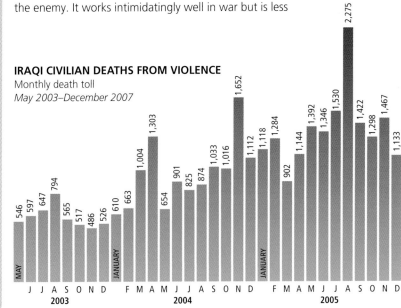

IRAQI CIVILIAN DEATHS FROM VIOLENCE
Monthly death toll
May 2003–December 2007

effective for winning the peace. The destruction unleashed on Fallujah shocked even hardened war reporters while the abuse of Iraqi prisoners in Abu Ghraib and elsewhere was on a scale that indicates it was deliberate policy.

Despite the mayhem, there were some gains. Three years after the overthrow of Saddam Hussein, he was on trial for crimes against humanity. A parliament had been elected. New Iraqi police and security forces existed. British forces were starting to leave. Both Kurds and Shi'a could believe in a future in which their rights are acknowledged.

But every achievement had a downside. Voters in the December 2005 election divided on ethnic and religious lines, revealing the potential for a profound fracturing of the country. Every gain for the Shi'a seemed to mean a loss for the Sunnis. The risks were illustrated by lethal attacks on Shi'a religious sites in 2005 and early 2006.

By early 2007, there was less clean water, sewage control and energy supply compared to pre-2003. Oil output was down. Crime was rampant and unemployment was about 50 per cent. President Bush responded with a 'surge' of force – a relatively small increase in US troop numbers combined with finding new allies among Iraq's armed groups. Judged by fatalities, the strategy worked. The daily death toll fell from a peak of 100 to just 30. But Iraq's future would ultimately be defined not by military action but by how fairly and effectively the new state could be run.

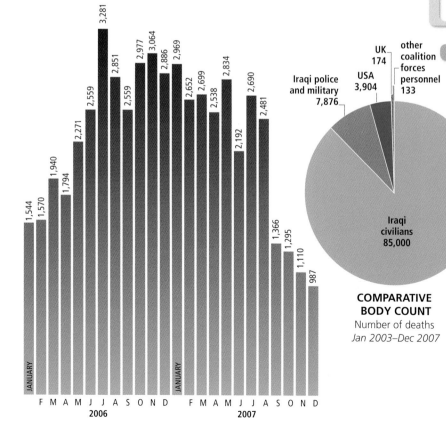

COMPARATIVE BODY COUNT
Number of deaths
Jan 2003–Dec 2007

There is considerable controversy about how many civilians have been killed in Iraq since the end of the six-week war in 2003. Estimates go as high as a million, with one widely reported study producing a figure of 655,000 deaths by mid-2006, based on surveys of households in locations chosen as representative. These figures imply that in some months there have been almost 1,000 violent deaths per day, with nobody reporting or registering the fact. The figures shown here are from the organization Iraq Body Count, whose method is to count deaths reported by two separate media sources. On this reckoning the total civilian toll by the end of 2007 was about 85,000 deaths. It must be regarded as the minimum estimate.

THE NEW IRAQ

CHRONOLOGY

2006 *June* Al-Qaeda in Iraq (AQI) leader Musab Al-Zarqawi is killed in a US strike. Abu Ayyub al-Masri, also known as Abu Hamza al-Muhajir, takes his place as leader of AQI.

Oct Ayyub al-Masri announces the creation of Islamic State in Iraq (ISI), with Omar al-Baghdadi as its leader.

2007 *Feb* A bomb in Baghdad's Sadriya market kills more than 130 people. It is the worst single bombing since 2003.

Mar Insurgents detonate three truckloads of chlorine gas in Fallujah and Ramadi, injuring hundreds.

Apr Bombings in Baghdad kill nearly 200 people.

Aug Truck and car bombs hit two villages of Yazidi Kurds, killing at least 250 people – the deadliest attack since 2003. Kurdish and Shi'a leaders form an alliance to support Prime Minister Maliki's government but fail to bring in Sunni leaders.

Sept Blackwater security guards fire at civilians in Baghdad, killing 17 and injuring 20.

Dec Britain hands over security of Basra province to Iraqi forces.

2008 *Jan* Parliament passes legislation allowing former officials from Saddam Hussein's Ba'ath Party to return to public life.

Mar Prime Minister Maliki orders crackdown on militia in Basra, sparking pitched battles with Muqtada al-Sadr's Mehdi Army. Hundreds are killed.

Sept US forces hand over control of Anbar – once an insurgent and al-Qaeda stronghold – to the Iraqi government. It is the first Sunni province to be returned to the Shi'a-led government.

Nov Agreement reached for all US troops to leave the country by the end of 2011.

2009 *Jan* Iraq takes control of security in Baghdad's fortified Green Zone and assumes more powers over foreign troops based in the country.

The invasion of Iraq by the US-led 'coalition of the willing' in March and April 2003 set in motion a chain of events its prime movers neither wanted nor predicted. Justified as a strike against dictatorship and against terrorism, it helped unleash more terror and a new kind of tyranny.

Chaos mounted in Iraq and the death toll kept rising even after the country's first ever democratically elected government had been formed. The US 'surge' that was announced in January 2007 by President Bush successfully paved the way for his successor Barack Obama to prepare to withdraw US forces. Shrewdly allying with local Sunni leaders, the US strategy started to cut the ground from under the militants of al-Qaeda and associated groups; it did not touch their *jihadi* ardour but it made the militants' operating environment less and less accommodating. After several months during which casualties remained high, by the end of 2007 it started to look as if a corner had been turned. Though attacks on civilian targets and sectarian murders continued, the death toll started to decline. It fell by 60 per cent over the course of 2008 and a further 50 per cent during 2009.

But the surge did not bring real peace. After 2007, two separate parallel processes were playing out, almost disconnected from each other. One was the preparation for withdrawal by US and other forces. The war had been swift and popular back home; what came after was anything but. The Bush administration wanted out but could not say so; the new Obama administration wanted to withdraw and had no trouble in saying so. To prepare the way, it was important that the Iraq mission, though difficult, though not achieved by 1 May 2003 when President Bush spoke in front of a banner declaring 'Mission Accomplished', could nonetheless be seen as ultimately successful. To this end, the official narrative emphasized the building of a new Iraqi state, based on democratic elections and the rule of law, with a new police force and a new army, offering new freedoms for Kurds, with the oilfields starting to crank up production again so the country would be prosperous as well as free.

IRAQI CIVILIAN DEATHS FROM VIOLENCE
Monthly death toll
January 2007–February 2015

There was some truth in parts of this narrative. But beneath the surface, the reality was very different. The government was notoriously corrupt, too many parts of it were effectively non-functioning, and the country was dangerously divided against itself. The Shi'a had been silenced under the previous regimes but now they were in the majority and the Shi'a political leaders were the country's national leaders. They were far from united in a single bloc, as was graphically revealed when Prime Minister al-Maliki unleashed the new Iraqi army against Shi'a militias in Basra province in 2008, Even so, the Shi'a parties could make a coalition of convenience to ensure power was not in Sunni hands. In vain, the Americans encouraged al-Maliki to run a government that was consistently of and for all Iraqis. The sectarianism ran too deep. Sunni politicians felt excluded and marginalized while all too many members of the increasingly Shi'a police force continued in their anti-Sunni ways.

When the moment of truth came in June and July 2014 as ISIS declared the Islamic State, many ordinary Sunnis decided the *jihadis* were more likely to safeguard the conditions for ordinary life than the increasingly Shi'a state would ever be. As Shi'a militias were mobilized to fight ISIS, and increasingly took revenge on ordinary Sunnis for ISIS atrocities, that view did not seem far-fetched. And the Kurds resurrected their goal of independence.

CHRONOLOGY *continued*

2009 *June* US troops withdraw from towns and cities in Iraq, having formally handed over security duties to new Iraqi forces.

Oct Two car bombs near the Green Zone in Baghdad kill at least 155 people – deadliest attack since April 2007.

Dec The ISI claims responsibility for attacks killing 370 people.

2010 *Mar* Parliamentary elections. Nine months pass before a new government is approved. Abu Bakr al-Baghdadi becomes leader of ISI when its previous leader and the head of AQI are killed in a US strike.

Aug The last US combat brigade leaves.

Oct More than 50 Christians killed in attack on Baghdad church.

Nov/Dec Jalal Talabani and Nouri al-Maliki reappointed as president and prime minister respectively.

2011 *Aug* Violence escalates, with more than 40 apparently co-ordinated nationwide attacks in one day.

IRAQI DEATHS IN OCCUPATION AND INSURGENCIES
May 2003–February 2015

Total: approx. 210,000

Over 200,000 Iraqis and at least 5,000 non-Iraqis have died in the fighting since President Bush declared the end of the war.

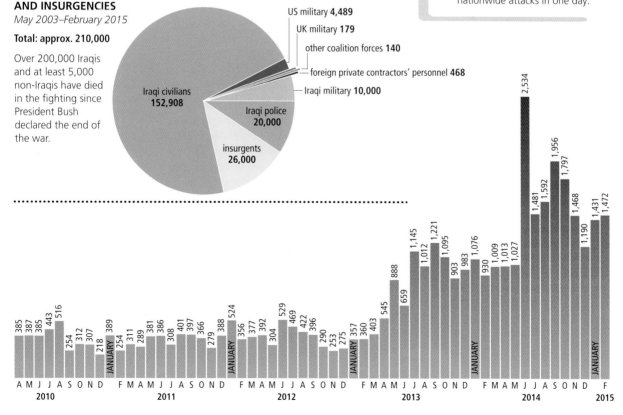

US military **4,489**
UK military **179**
other coalition forces **140**
foreign private contractors' personnel **468**
Iraqi military **10,000**
Iraqi civilians **152,908**
Iraqi police **20,000**
insurgents **26,000**

Old enemies, new allies

In mid-2014, ISIS, a breakaway group from al-Qaeda that was founded in Iraq in 2006 and in 2013 had spread across the border to fight and seize territory in Syria, struck in Iraq. Its forces rolled forward, threatening strategic targets such as dams and oilfields as well as towns, sowing fear through atrocity and massacre. The weight of these blows seemed likely at one point to break apart the fractured state of Iraq. The army failed to hold off ISIS. Shi'a militias were mobilized and sent to the front. The president of the Kurdish Region, Masoud Barzani, announced plans (later put on hold) for an independence referendum, declaring that the country was already effectively partitioned.

By the end of 2014, more than 10 per cent of Iraqis had fled their homes, many finding temporary shelter in mosques and public buildings – a 'temporary' that stretched on for months on end. The advance of ISIS was stopped in the autumn and early winter – or, at least, the resistance to it started to be effective enough that its advance was no longer inexorable. The longer-term outcome remained unclear.

ISIS is the most militant and uncompromising of Sunni *jihadi* groups, yet attempts to characterize its growth, offensive and its successes purely in terms of the sectarian divide between Sunni and Shi'a fall flat in the face of persistent evidence of the close collaboration between the deeply religious (in their way) militants who are the core of ISIS and the secular Ba'athists with whom they are allied, in particular the General Military Council for Iraqi Revolutionaries. While ISIS grows out of a long line of Sunni politico-religious movements and militancy, it has been reported that it was a former colonel of air force intelligence under Saddam Hussein who devised the ISIS strategy in Syria. The long-term aims of these Ba'athists have little in common with those of the *jihadis* but in the short term they have common enemies and can make common cause.

The insurgency against the Iraqi government in the middle of 2014 was not confined to ISIS and its Ba'athist allies. There were other Ba'athists in the Naqshbandi Army, alongside Kurds and, so it is reported, some Shi'a, and there were other Sunni in Ansar al-Islam (Supporters or Helpers of Islam). All Shi'a were by no means united in support of the Iraqi government, even if the vast majority were united in anxiety and fear of ISIS.

But opposition to ISIS was enough of a unifying factor to bring some odd-looking alliances together. Not only did Kurdish forces fight with the army of the Baghdad government, they also fought alongside Iranian forces. And not only did the USA and its allies carry out air operations against ISIS, but so did the Syrian air force of President Bashar Assad.

Crisis often brings strange bedfellows together. The big question is what happens after the crisis. Experts and commentators wonder, if ISIS were to prevail over the Baghdad government, how long it would be before open fighting would break out with the Military Council for Iraqi Revolutionaries. And equally if the government prevails over ISIS, the question is whether it would be able to bring real peace to Iraq.

The crisis of mid-2014 was the occasion for the demise of the al-Maliki government, though, roundly condemned as he was by most Western opinion for corruption and sectarianism and for centring all power on himself and his close circle of loyalists, he nonetheless stayed on as vice-president.

Unfortunately, the initial actions of the new government under Haidar al-Abadi gave little grounds for believing that here was a political strategist prepared to unite the country across religious and ethnic divisions. No more than al-Maliki did al-Abadi show in his first six months in office that he would oppose and prevent Shi'a violence against Sunnis.

Part of the thinking behind the US 'surge' in 2007 was that the development of an Iraqi state based on the rule of law was held back by widespread violence and the ambience of insecurity and fear. The violence never ended but it did reduce. Yet the development of the institutions of a law-abiding state did not ensue. The consequence of that was the powerlessness of Iraq's security forces in the face of the ISIS advance in 2014. The consequence was the preference of ordinary Sunni citizens for a force that is famous for beheading, burning and indiscriminately massacring its opponents over the elected government. And the consequence was also that an unusual alliance of the USA and Iran came together in the effort to prevent the whole country falling prey to ISIS.

THE STRUGGLE FOR CONTROL OF IRAQ
2014–15

Approximate territorial control

- ISIS & its allies
- Kurdish Peshmerga
- Iraqi government
- mixed or unclear control
- □ taken by ISIS *date as shown*
- ✹ areas of fighting *date as shown*
- ⚒ dams

113

TUNISIA

The 'Arab Spring' was triggered by the self-sacrifice of a Tunisian. Four years later it was the only country where political change was unfolding relatively peacefully, though it faced extreme *jihadi* pressure.

Tunisia's history has a gentler tone than its neighbours. It was part of the Ottoman Empire, yet with significant autonomy. Then it was under French control, yet never as tightly as neighbouring Algeria. And the war of independence, compared to Algeria's, was shorter, with fewer casualties, and less trauma for both Tunisia and France.

Under Habib Bourguiba, the politics of Tunisia's independence was populist and nationalist rather than about socialist or pan-Arab ideological purism. He took control of the Neo-Destour Party machine before independence and the machinery of early statehood immediately after. Discussion about the new constitution was restricted to a small circle within the party. Political rivals were marginalized or arrested. This authoritarianism had a modernizing agenda: the creation of a secular republic, with equal rights for women and men, and with limited privileges for Islamic institutions.

Despite the authoritarianism, independence provided distinct gains for ordinary citizens in education and the economy. Generally, if not comprehensively, living conditions improved. Over time, however, progress stalled. Expectations were raised and then disappointed, so frustration grew. And after Zine Ben Ali pushed Bourguiba aside in a bloodless coup, little changed.

Mohamed Bouazizi was a university graduate; with no jobs available, he became a street vendor, facing constant police harassment and humiliation. One last incident pushed him to breaking point and he set fire to himself. His suicide over his economic dead end triggered political protests in early 2011 that brought down President Ben Ali within weeks.

Part of what now kept Tunisia on a relatively peaceful track compared to Egypt, Libya and Syria was that the army was not an important political player.

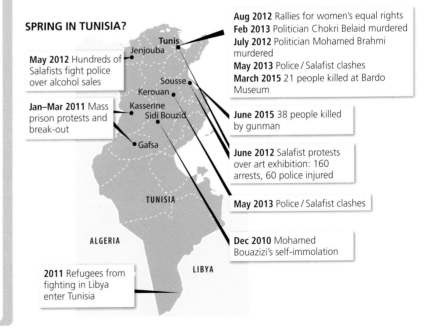

SPRING IN TUNISIA?

May 2012 Hundreds of Salafists fight police over alcohol sales

Jan–Mar 2011 Mass prison protests and break-out

2011 Refugees from fighting in Libya enter Tunisia

Aug 2012 Rallies for women's equal rights
Feb 2013 Politician Chokri Belaid murdered
July 2012 Politician Mohamed Brahmi murdered
May 2013 Police / Salafist clashes
March 2015 21 people killed at Bardo Museum

June 2015 38 people killed by gunman

June 2012 Salafist protests over art exhibition: 160 arrests, 60 police injured

May 2013 Police / Salafist clashes

Dec 2010 Mohamed Bouazizi's self-immolation

Tunis
Jenjouba
Sousse
Kerouan
Kasserine
Sidi Bouzid
Gafsa
TUNISIA
ALGERIA
LIBYA

Similarly, unlike some other countries, while the Salafist tradition in Tunisia is strong, it is not dominated by political militancy. The leadership of the Ennahda movement, the Islamists who took power in 2011, is cautious and pragmatic. Though the movement includes more militant and impatient groups, and despite inconsistencies in policy and action, the Ennahda government avoided the error that the Islamists committed in Egypt of pressing forward with a narrow agenda that would please only the movement's supporters.

In 2014, under a new constitution, there were new elections, won by the secular Nidaa Tounes party, also a coalition of disparate forces including some leading figures from the days of Bourguiba and Ben Ali. Following an election campaign in which Nidaa Tounes used extreme language about the threat to freedom if Ennahda won, the new government will need a calmer tone and an inclusive approach to maintain peace.

Tunisia lives in a dangerous neighbourhood with war to its east and *jihadis* on all sides. The country has faced plenty of *jihadi* violence and in 2015 the tempo and scale of the attacks began to increase. With growing alienation among young men and a feeling of being left out of the benefits of revolution, recruitment from Tunisia for ISIS in Syria has been disproportionately high. Many Tunisian *jihadi*s are also training in Libya.

Within Tunisia, the felt need for reform as promised by Nidaa Tounes is strongest in the metropolitan north; in the rural south there is a widespread feeling of being left out. And political reform is yet to deliver the economic goods. The underprivileged remain so and youth unemployment was heading towards 40 per cent in early 2015. Meanwhile, many observers comment that politics today is done just as it was under Bourguiba and Ben Ali. If progress stalls, whether because the government cannot deliver, or because the pressure from the *jihadis* takes the country to the edge of war, it is an open question whether and when Tunisia will get another chance for peaceful change.

NORTH AND SOUTH

Parliamentary Elections
October 2014

Second round of Presidential Elections
December 2014

Governorates of Tunisia in which the plurality of voters supported:

 Nidaa Tounes ('Call for Tunisia', secular)

Ennahda ('Renaissance Party', Islamist)

Governorates of Tunisia in which the plurality of voters supported:

Béji Caïd Essebsi (Nidaa Tounes)

Moncef Marzouki (independent and secularist backed by Ennahda)

CHRONOLOGY *continued*

2010 *Dec* Mohamed Bouazizi sets himself on fire in protest at harassment by government officials. Dies the following month.

2011 *Jan* State of Emergency declared. Over 200 die in violent protests. President Ben Ali flees to Saudi Arabia. Interim government formed.

June Exiled ex-president Ben Ali is convicted of theft and sentenced to 35 years.

Oct Parliamentary elections. Islamist Ennahda party wins but without outright majority.

Dec Parliament elects human rights activist Moncef Marzouki president, with Hamadi Jebali of Ennahda as prime minister.

2012 *May* Clashes between Salafists and police over alcohol sales.

June Government imposes an overnight curfew in eight areas following riots by Islamists against an art exhibition.

Aug Thousands protest in Tunis against government moves to reduce women's rights.

2013 *Feb* Political crisis after murder of left-wing leader Chokri Belaid. Prime Minister Jebali resigns.

July Assassination of left-wing leader Mohamed Brahmi prompts general strike.

Aug Government labels the Salafist Ansar al-Sharia movement a 'terrorist group'.

2014 *Jan* Parliament passes new constitution. Ennahda hands over power to caretaker government.

Mar President Marzouki lifts the state of emergency imposed in 2011.

May Tunisia's interim parliament approves a new electoral law.

Oct Secular Nidaa Tounes party wins most seats in parliamentary elections.

Dec Béji Caïd Essebsi (Nidaa Tounes) elected president.

2015 *Mar* 21 people killed in attack in Bardo Museum, Tunis.

June 38 people killed by gunman in Sousse resort.

EGYPT

Egypt is the most populous Arab country. Its size, strategic location, cultural and intellectual output and history combine to make it the traditional centre of the Arab world.

For most Arabs, Egyptian leadership of the Arab cause was fitting in the 1950s and Nasser's success in the Suez crisis underlined Egypt's credentials. He was a complex combination of Arab pan-nationalist and Egyptian nationalist. His war in Yemen and willingness to use chemical warfare showed the limits of his Arab solidarity yet it was his over-riding commitment and it trapped him into the 1967 war with Israel (see p 72). His successor, Sadat, sought a wholly new direction and set out to balance the opposition this would generate among other Arab leaders by finding new friends in the West.

The 1973 war was launched by Sadat to strengthen his position against Israel and buy diplomatic room for manoeuvre to undertake an epochal change. Paradoxically, the war was the start of his peace initiative. Though it did not seem so at the time, it was actually the beginning of a process of aligning Egypt with the West, making peace with Israel along the way, and opening economic doors to Western trade and investment in order to boost development. At the same time he shifted economic policy away from Nasser's reliance on central planning

This generated stiffening opposition from the left, who were only partially

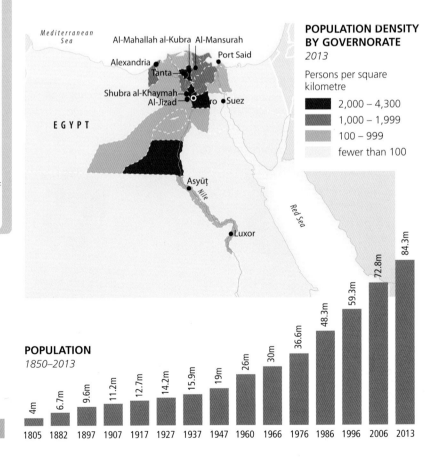

POPULATION DENSITY BY GOVERNORATE
2013

Persons per square kilometre

- 2,000 – 4,300
- 1,000 – 1,999
- 100 – 999
- fewer than 100

EGYPT – A YOUNG COUNTRY

Percentage of population in each age group
2006 (date of last census)

Age group	Percentage
60 and above	3.9
45–59	9.6
30–44	17.1
15–29	26.1
0–14	43.5

POPULATION
1850–2013

Year	Population
1805	4m
1882	6.7m
1897	9.6m
1907	11.2m
1917	12.7m
1927	14.2m
1937	15.9m
1947	19m
1960	26m
1966	30m
1976	36.6m
1986	48.3m
1996	59.3m
2006	72.8m
2013	84.3m

won over by Egypt's relative success in the 1973 war – or, less charitably and more precisely, the lesser degree of failure compared to 1967. To weaken the socialist opposition, Sadat took the fateful step of quietly providing practical support and semi-official tolerance to the Muslim Brotherhood and newer Islamist groups.

The Muslim Brotherhood began in the 1920s. It became a major force, providing welfare services for ordinary people and challenging the nationalists for political support in the 1940s. It assisted in the Free Officers' revolution in 1952 but, as a potential rival for popular allegiance, it was banned in 1954. Even so, it remained a dynamic social force. In response to the Brotherhood's partial suppression, more radical groups – often more willing to use violence – attracted growing numbers of recruits.

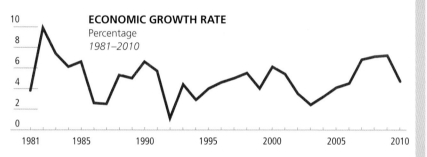

ECONOMIC GROWTH RATE
Percentage
1981–2010

In the wake of the 1967 war, influential Arab writers noted that what they saw as a religious state – Israel – had humiliated the secular Arab states. For these writers, the Arabs could turn the tide by reconnecting their religion with their politics. At the same time, in the long Arab discussion about how best to relate to the West – by copying it, or by borrowing from it what is compatible with Islam, or by rejecting it – the increasingly Islamist tone of political debate leaned towards rejection, leavened by selectively exploiting the West's technological accomplishments.

Sadat's tactical encouragement of the Islamists in the late 1970s thus helped strengthen the position of a movement that was already strong and self-confident. It was a movement that rejected root and branch every item of his economic and political agenda, the legitimacy of the state he led, and its growing accommodation with Israel and the USA.

The state of emergency that Hosni Mubarak declared when he took over the presidency – after Sadat's assassination by Islamic militants in 1981 – remained in place until Mubarak himself left office 30 years later. Islamic political organizations were banned and secular political parties could not operate without being officially approved. Economic growth was often impressive through the Mubarak years but not enough to meet the needs and expectations of a growing population.

Egypt's young and increasingly well-educated population developed a thirst for change that its political system was consciously designed to frustrate. It was the guile and determination of political leaders and security forces that provided stability, not solid social and economic foundations. It was an inherently fragile kind of stability.

CHRONOLOGY *continued*

1954 Nasser becomes prime minister.
1955 British troops leave Egypt.
1956 Nasser becomes president. Nationalization of the Suez Canal. Suez crisis and war with Britain, France and Israel.
1958–61 The United Arab Republic of Egypt and Syria.
1962–67 Yemen War. Egypt deploys 55,000 troops and uses chemical warfare.
1967 Six Day War.
1969–70 The Israeli–Egyptian War of Attrition.
1970 Death of Nasser. Anwar al-Sadat becomes president.
1973 Yom Kippur War.
1977 Sadat addresses Israeli Knesset.
1978 Camp David Accords for peace between Israel and Egypt.
1979 Egyptian–Israeli Peace Treaty. Egypt excluded from the Arab League.
1981 Assassination of Sadat by members of the Jihad Organization. Hosni Mubarak becomes president.
1989 Egypt rejoins Arab League.
1991 Egyptian forces in combat in US-led anti-Iraq coalition.
1992 Internal conflict. Main opposition group is al-Jama'a al-Islamiyyah (the Islamic Group). Attacks on tourists a common tactic.
1997 Luxor massacre, 58 tourists killed. Security forces clamp down hard on Islamists. Al-Jama'a al-Islamiyyah accepts ceasefire.
2002 Egypt downgrades relations with Israel, citing Israeli treatment of the Palestinians during the *intifada*.
2004 Bomb attacks target tourist areas in Sinai, killing 34 people. Other attacks on tourists in Cairo.
2005 88 people die in a bomb attack in Sharm el-Sheikh.
2006 Bomb at Dahab resort kills 23.
2009 US President Obama makes major speech at Cairo University calling for a new beginning for the US and Muslim world.
2010 In elections to consultative assembly, Muslim Brotherhood wins no seats and alleges vote-rigging.

Pressure for change

2011 17 Jan Echoing Tunisia, a man sets himself on fire near Egyptian parliament in protest against poor living standards. Egypt's media report six similar acts in following days.

25 Jan Day of Revolt. The day after Pres Ben Ali steps down in Tunisia, tens of thousands of protestors against the Mubarak government occupy Cairo's Tahrir Square. Simultaneous protests in Ismailiya, Alexandria and Suez (where at least two demonstrators are killed). Government curtails access to internet to stop communication between protesters.

28 Jan Friday of Anger. Hundreds of thousands demonstrate. Mass prison break-out, with rumours that government organized it. At least 13 people killed.

29 Jan Mubarak sacks Cabinet. Army ordered into Cairo to restore order.

1 Feb March of Millions. Over 250,000 people demonstrate against Mubarak in Cairo. The pyramids in Giza are closed for business. Thousands of holiday-makers gather at the airport trying to leave. Mubarak promises political reforms.

2 Feb Mubarak supporters ride camels and horses into Tahrir Square, clashing violently with anti-government protestors.

4 Feb Day of Departure. Tens of thousands form a human chain to blockade the building where people go to get official paperwork processed.

8 Feb Though Egypt's transition government claims to be developing a plan for a peaceful transfer of power, hundreds of thousands of people join protests in Tahrir Square.

9 Feb Access to parliament building is blocked by increasing numbers of demonstrators. Workers go on strike at the Suez Canal. Pyramids of Giza reopen for business but tourists are few.

Much changed in Egypt in the six decades between the Free Officers' revolution against King Farouk and the events of 2011. But much stayed the same. In 1952, the Free Officers overthrew the old regime to end corruption, inequality and the power of a small elite, and to assert national pride against British hegemony and the existence of Israel. In 2011 when the people rather than the army were the prime mover of change, only the British had departed the scene. The other drivers of political upheaval persisted, combined with something new.

Egypt's population has grown dramatically. As in other countries, this is a sign of successful development as living conditions and basic standards of health improved. It creates extra demands on the state and on resources but with a dynamic economy and a reasonably well-run government, it is not necessarily a problem. The difficulty is that the Egyptian economy has never been quite dynamic enough and government has been well run only in some ways. The repressive apparatus of the Egyptian state has been remarkably efficient, but the same state's ability to deliver welfare to the people has been quite patchy, which is one big reason why the Muslim Brotherhood became so popular – not only because of what it stands for but because of what it does for the people.

To smooth out underlying problems in securing the conditions for a decent life, the Egyptian government used food subsidies, especially for bread, for which it is a massive wheat importer. When prices rise on the world market to a point where the state no longer has the economic capacity to keep prices low

THE GLOBAL CLIMATE, FOOD PRICES AND REVOLUTION IN EGYPT

In Nov 2010 China suffered a once-in-a-century drought in its wheat growing eastern region.

There were also drought and wildfires in Russia and Ukraine…

…cool, wet weather in Canada…

…and heavy rain in Australia.

These factors led to **reduced** global wheat **supply.** Global wheat price **doubled.**

This had a serious economic impact on Egypt – the world's **largest wheat importer**…

$ $

June 2010   February 2011

2.8 million tons

1.6 million tons

2009   2010

Wheat imports to Egypt

for the consumer, the non-functional nature of the system becomes clear. Inevitably, popular anger turns against the state. Because of climate change, these kinds of pressures are increasing. Interacting with the rest of the causes of stagnation and grievance, in 2011 the result was explosive.

Part of what stood in the way of change was the military. A revolutionary force in 1952, it became deeply embedded in the system of government Nasser developed. It built on that to become a major economic force. Military personnel number about 460,000, which is not excessive as a percentage of population, and military spending accounts for about two per cent of the national economy, which is similar to the European average. But the military as an institution is much more than that.

The military already had an industrial role in the 19th century, producing guns and uniforms to meet its own needs. The scale of production grew in the 1950s under Nasser but it seems to have been after the 1979 peace agreement with Israel that the big jump was made, partly because the military had to shrink and there was a large number of potentially unemployed soldiers to look after. Military-run firms today trade in food, cement and gasoline, produce vehicles, and are big in construction, using conscripts in the last six months of their service. Estimates of the military's economic scale vary widely; a reasonable estimate that some researchers would regard as modest is about 10–15 per cent of GDP.

One reason why the military may have been willing to let Mubarak lose power was that in his last decade he had been cultivating an alternative power base among civilian entrepreneurs and laying the groundwork for handing power to his son, which was reportedly unpopular with senior officers.

CHRONOLOGY continued

10 Feb Amid rumours that President Mubarak intends to resign, thousands gather in Tahrir Square to watch televised speech. When he expresses determination to stay celebrations quickly turn to anger.

11 Feb Friday of Departure. Demonstrators block offices of state TV. Others march on the Presidential Palace. Mubarak steps down and transfers executive and legislative powers to the Supreme Council for the Armed Forces (SCARF). Celebrations.

13 Feb SCARF dissolves parliament and suspends constitutions, as protestors demanded.

Mar New constitution adopted by referendum.

Apr Mubarak and sons are arrested on suspicion of corruption.

Aug Mubarak goes on trial charged with ordering the killing of demonstrators.

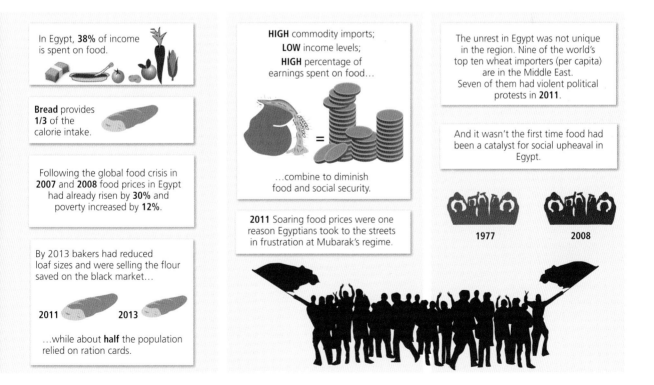

In Egypt, **38%** of income is spent on food.

Bread provides **1/3** of the calorie intake.

Following the global food crisis in **2007** and **2008** food prices in Egypt had already risen by **30%** and poverty increased by **12%**.

By 2013 bakers had reduced loaf sizes and were selling the flour saved on the black market…

2011   2013

…while about **half** the population relied on ration cards.

HIGH commodity imports;
LOW income levels;
HIGH percentage of earnings spent on food…

…combine to diminish food and social security.

2011 Soaring food prices were one reason Egyptians took to the streets in frustration at Mubarak's regime.

The unrest in Egypt was not unique in the region. Nine of the world's top ten wheat importers (per capita) are in the Middle East. Seven of them had violent political protests in **2011**.

And it wasn't the first time food had been a catalyst for social upheaval in Egypt.

1977   2008

After the revolution

2011 Oct At Cairo protest against destruction of a Coptic Church in Aswan, army uses live ammunition: 28 are killed and 212 injured, mostly Copts.

Nov Protesters clash with police and army: 90 dead and thousands injured.

Dec Further protests, 15 dead and hundreds injured.

2012 Jan Islamist parties claim victory in parliamentary elections.

May Military leaders announce end of the state of emergency.

June Muslim Brotherhood candidate Mohamed Morsi narrowly wins presidential election.

Aug President Morsi transfers to himself powers the military assumed after Mubarak's ousting.

Nov Morsi issues interim constitution giving himself far-reaching powers. Protests follow. Morsi responds by withdrawing some clauses.

2013 Jan Over 50 people are killed in street protests. Army chief General Abdel Fattah al-Sisi warns of risk of state collapse.

July The military removes President Morsi amid mass demonstrations calling for him to quit.

Aug Over 1,100 are killed as security forces storm protest camps in Cairo set up by Morsi supporters. Some 40 Coptic churches are destroyed in a wave of attacks.

Nov New law passed restricting public protests.

Dec Government labels the Muslim Brotherhood a terrorist organization after bomb blast in Mansoura kills 12.

2014 Jan New constitution approved by referendum – includes ban on religiously-based parties.

Mar 529 people are sentenced to death – most *in absentia* – by a court in Minya.

Apr A further 683 people are sentenced by the same court in Minya.

May An independent report lists 41,163 people arrested and prosecuted for political actions since July 2013.

The 2011 revolution in Egypt grabbed the world's attention and convulsed the region. Change in Tunisia started just a few weeks sooner, but what happened in Egypt, given its central position in the Arab world, reverberated more widely.

The Islamists – and especially the Muslim Brotherhood – were much more organized than the secular liberals who had initiated the Tahrir Square protests. The pay-off for older, better, socially more embedded organizations came in the elections. Islamist parties won elections to an interim assembly in early 2012 and their chosen candidate, Mohamed Morsi of the Brotherhood, won the presidential election. The alliance between the Islamists and the secular liberals had been an informal of-the-moment affair, a coalition of convenience and pragmatism, united by anger and disgust at the Mubarak government and all it stood for.

The events of the following six months after Morsi's election are and always will be mired in controversy and contending interpretations. What seems clear is that one of Morsi's first ambitions was to consolidate power to the elected authorities, away from the military. To do this, he and his inner circle ensured that as many government appointments as possible went to members or supporters of the Muslim Brotherhood. It also seems clear that this alienated liberal opinion just as much as it infuriated the top of the military hierarchy. And finally it seems clear that the government in 2012 was dramatically overspending its resources and building towards a crisis in the national finances.

Among the many aspects of this history that are contested is whether Morsi's focus on consolidating power came at the expense of meeting the needs of the Muslim Brotherhood's traditional constituencies. And equally contested is the motive for consolidating power. It could have been a democratic impulse, to restrict the power of the military. But it could also have been either for personal glorification, which some suspected, or so that the Islamists would never give up power, which many suspected. The escalation of violence against the Coptic Christians was also a bad sign for many liberals, implying that a religiously intolerant regime was emerging.

When President Morsi announced a new draft constitution giving the presidency far-reaching powers in November, large numbers of Egyptians assumed the worst. With that, Morsi forfeited the trust and the tolerance of many liberals and democrats who seemed genuinely to prefer government based on military authority to the risk of leaving the Islamists in power. From January 2013 it became clearer by the week that the Morsi government's days were numbered. As protests against the government escalated, the military moved in and quickly and forcibly cracked down on the Islamists. Hundreds died in armed confrontations while tens of thousands were arrested, with further hundreds condemned to death (though not all those death sentences were confirmed). The following year, a new constitution was put to referendum and Abdel Fattah al-Sisi, who as head of the army had the previous year sounded the warning to a heedless Morsi, was elected president.

By early 2015, the Islamists had been fragmented, fractured and silenced as a political force and, from the point of view of their political weight, the secular opposition to first Mubarak and then Morsi had fared no better. The mainstream political scene in Egypt was showing great life and energy, but primarily fuelled by personal or group rivalries, rather than by competing overall visions of how

Egypt should develop. Some commentators saw remarkable similarities between politics in the first months under Sisi and the last years of Mubarak. It remained to be seen whether the full range of problems and deficiencies that fuelled anger and upheaval in 1952 and 2011 would persist, or whether some might be addressed under the new dispensation. From early evidence, acceptance from above of the need for root-and-branch reform seemed unlikely.

Though so much seemed to remain constant in Egyptian politics and national challenges, there had been change of potentially all-encompassing dimensions. The events set in motion first in Tunisia and then in Egypt have produced a new set of regional security issues. In Egypt, the embers from the violent conflict of the 1990s that culminated in the Luxor massacre of tourists in 1997, which had a brief recrudescence in the mid-00s, flared again after Mubarak was overthrown. Branding itself first as an al-Qaeda affiliate, the *jihadi* group Ansar Beit al-Maqdis (Champions of the Holy House) attacked sporadically, repetitively and then continually in the North Sinai, before rebranding itself as the Sinai Province of the Islamic State. These developments gave a new dimension to Egypt's emergency.

CHRONOLOGY *continued*

May General Abdel Fattah el-Sisi wins presidential election.

Nov *Jihadi* group Ansar Beit al-Maqdis switches allegiance from al-Qaeda to ISIS and changes its name to Sinai Province.

2015 ***Apr*** Ex-president Morsi sentenced to 20 years in prison for inciting violence against anti-government protestors in 2012.

May Ex-president Morsi is one of 106 people sentenced to death over jail breaks in 2011.

THE COPTS

The Coptic Orthodox Church of Alexandria is the largest Christian denomination in the Middle East and Egypt is its centre. Formed in a schism from the Byzantine Church in CE 451, in a dispute over the nature of Christ, the Coptic Church has between 6 and 9 million adherents in Egypt, some 7–10 per cent of the population. Copts were prominent among liberals and nationalists in the independence movement of the 1920s and freely participated in the Wafd (see p 31). Relations with some Muslim groups deteriorated in the 1940s but improved under Nasser. After his death, Sadat's encouragement of Islamist groups so as to restrict leftist influence quickly spilled over into violence against Copts and their religious buildings. Tensions and violence increased thereafter and accelerated after the overthrow of Mubarak in 2011.

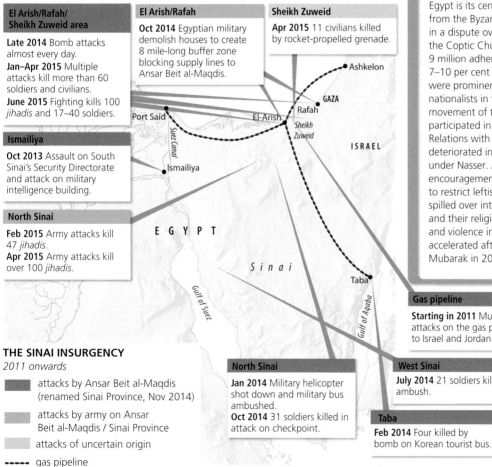

El Arish/Rafah/Sheikh Zuweid area

Late 2014 Bomb attacks almost every day.
Jan–Apr 2015 Multiple attacks kill more than 60 soldiers and civilians.
June 2015 Fighting kills 100 *jihadis* and 17–40 soldiers.

Ismailiya

Oct 2013 Assault on South Sinai's Security Directorate and attack on military intelligence building.

North Sinai

Feb 2015 Army attacks kill 47 *jihadis*.
Apr 2015 Army attacks kill over 100 *jihadis*.

El Arish/Rafah

Oct 2014 Egyptian military demolish houses to create 8 mile-long buffer zone blocking supply lines to Ansar Beit al-Maqdis.

Sheikh Zuweid

Apr 2015 11 civilians killed by rocket-propelled grenade.

Gas pipeline

Starting in 2011 Multiple attacks on the gas pipeline to Israel and Jordan.

North Sinai

Jan 2014 Military helicopter shot down and military bus ambushed.
Oct 2014 31 soldiers killed in attack on checkpoint.

West Sinai

July 2014 21 soldiers killed in ambush.

Taba

Feb 2014 Four killed by bomb on Korean tourist bus.

THE SINAI INSURGENCY
2011 onwards

- attacks by Ansar Beit al-Maqdis (renamed Sinai Province, Nov 2014)
- attacks by army on Ansar Beit al-Maqdis / Sinai Province
- attacks of uncertain origin
- ----- gas pipeline

LIBYA

Libya was the third Arab Spring country. Within months of the overthrow of Muammar Qaddafi after 42 years in power, chaos reigned.

The first two decades of Libya's independence made only a limited break with the colonial past. The Ottomans had been replaced by the Italians and then the British – always the outside power was key. Then Qaddafi, aged just 27, led a coup to overthrow the monarchy. Under Qaddafi Libya became a pariah and an enigma for most outside observers.

At times it seemed that Qaddafi's espousal of a militant pan-Arabism amounted to an attempt to claim the mantle of Egypt's Nasser. Yet, with a population less than one-twelfth of Egypt's, the ambition for leadership in the Arab world would always be greater than the capacity. Qaddafi could never get much more than purely rhetorical support for essentially anachronistic attempts to unify Arab states in the 1970s and later. And his radical anti-US policies and support for violent revolution were not to the taste of most Arab leaders. Nonetheless he was a more serious and important figure than many Western commentators were prepared to acknowledge. His support for the formation of the African Union was particularly influential in Africa, while the secular basis of his politics provided an alternative kind of anti-Americanism to that promoted by the Islamist movements and *jihadis*.

Qaddafi enunciated a political philosophy, encapsulated in his so-called 'Third Universal Theory', of direct democracy and popular control of the state. That never persuaded foreign observers, however, that his four decades in power were attributable to anything but the usual apparatus of personalized state control, which included both the media and direct repression. Nonetheless, there were benefits for ordinary people in Libya from the country's oil wealth in the education system, health service and welfare, even though gross inequalities persisted and, in familiar autocratic style, Qaddafi made sure that he, his family and his inner circle all enjoyed that wealth disproportionately.

Libyan foreign policy focused primarily on the Israeli-Palestinian conflict, in which Qaddafi rejected all compromise; on eliminating outside influence on the Arab world; and on the export of revolution. Support was given not only to the PLO (until it tried to make peace with Israel in the Oslo Accord of 1993), and other groups in the Middle East but also, for example, to the IRA in the form of training and supplies. The policy led to direct confrontation with the USA, culminating in the 1986 bombing of Libya in the wake of a bomb in a Berlin nightclub in which many Americans were wounded. A few years later came international political isolation when evidence linked Libya to the death of 270 people on board PanAm flight 103, which was blown up in mid-air over Lockerbie, Scotland.

The secularism of the Qaddafi regime provoked opposition from militant Islamists, and returning fighters from the war in Afghanistan launched a war in the mid-1990s to overthrow him. Though some of the events, the policies and the thinking that drove them remain unclear to outside observers, it seems that it was the threat from the *jihadis* that led Qaddafi to seek normalization with the West, beginning in the late 1990s.

Handing over the Lockerbie suspects (one was convicted, one acquitted), acknowledging responsibility, agreeing US$2.7 billion compensation and terminating its programme to develop weapons of mass destruction allowed Libya back to international normality. The end of UN sanctions – and of the separate sanctions imposed by the USA – raised the prospect of increased international investment in Libyan oil. US companies returned to Libya in 2005. It seemed pariah status was over.

CHRONOLOGY *continued*

2004 Libya offers compensation for Berlin bombing and other actions. End of US sanctions.

2006 USA restores full diplomatic ties.

2007 Al-Qaeda announces LIFG has joined it.

2008 Libya has presidency of UN Security Council. Qaddafi's son awarded PhD at London School of Economics, US Secretary of State Condoleeza Rice visits Libya.

2009 Qaddafi becomes chair of African Union.

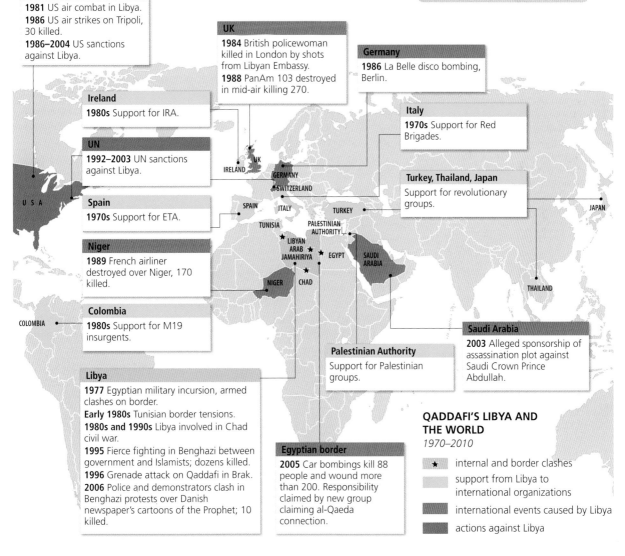

USA
1981 US air combat in Libya.
1986 US air strikes on Tripoli, 30 killed.
1986–2004 US sanctions against Libya.

UK
1984 British policewoman killed in London by shots from Libyan Embassy.
1988 PanAm 103 destroyed in mid-air killing 270.

Germany
1986 La Belle disco bombing, Berlin.

Ireland
1980s Support for IRA.

Italy
1970s Support for Red Brigades.

UN
1992–2003 UN sanctions against Libya.

Turkey, Thailand, Japan
Support for revolutionary groups.

Spain
1970s Support for ETA.

Niger
1989 French airliner destroyed over Niger, 170 killed.

Colombia
1980s Support for M19 insurgents.

Saudi Arabia
2003 Alleged sponsorship of assassination plot against Saudi Crown Prince Abdullah.

Palestinian Authority
Support for Palestinian groups.

Libya
1977 Egyptian military incursion, armed clashes on border.
Early 1980s Tunisian border tensions.
1980s and 1990s Libya involved in Chad civil war.
1995 Fierce fighting in Benghazi between government and Islamists; dozens killed.
1996 Grenade attack on Qaddafi in Brak.
2006 Police and demonstrators clash in Benghazi protests over Danish newspaper's cartoons of the Prophet; 10 killed.

Egyptian border
2005 Car bombings kill 88 people and wound more than 200. Responsibility claimed by new group claiming al-Qaeda connection.

QADDAFI'S LIBYA AND THE WORLD
1970–2010

★ internal and border clashes

support from Libya to international organizations

international events caused by Libya

actions against Libya

Into chaos

Qaddafi's belated pragmatism did not win him international protection when popular protest sprung up in early 2011. Drawing for legitimacy on Qaddafi's stated intransigence and belligerence in February 2011, and with support from many Arab states, France and the UK stepped in with air cover to stop a threatened Qaddafi offensive on Benghazi. Some months later, they supported a ground offensive that drove Qaddafi from his capital and ended with his discovery and death.

Estimates of the death toll in 2011 were initially as high as 30,000. Later government estimates put it at about 10,000 lives lost.

The armed groups that combined to overthrow Qaddafi formed a coalition of convenience only. Conflict soon started. By the end of 2011 and early 2012, the country was in what turned out to be the prelude to chaos. Three years later, there were 1,800 or so mostly local militia groups of varying sizes, capacities and allegiances. Some are idealistic, some criminal, some about self-protection – and some a mixture of all three.

The attempt to build a democratic state based on the rule of law did not get far. Participation in post-Qaddafi elections started low and then plummeted. A large part of the problem is how Qaddafi built and ran his state. He kept the army and police force on a tight rein and focused resources on the elite forces run by his son. The regular army and police force faded away in 2011 while the armed groups that fought in the insurgency largely sought to maintain their autonomy afterwards and stay together but stay out of the regular security sector. So the interim government – the National Transitional Council (NTC) – put the armed groups on its payroll.

This provided contending groups with resources and brought new groups onto the scene – ones that never fought Qaddafi. All were affiliated with the state, yet autonomous from it, with their own interests and agendas. The NTC put Libyan Shield under its authority to quell violent conflicts. Its forces were soon larger and its members better paid than the regular armed forces. But it functions as a collection of militias, not a unified force. Sent to deal with localized conflict, they act not as guardians of security but as partisans in increasingly bitter fighting. The power of the militias has blocked the work of building a law-based state.

As fighting escalated in 2014, casualty figures were unclear but one estimate of 1,500 deaths in some of the main cities implied the total could easily be twice that. Militias held 8,000 prisoners and by early 2015 there were almost 400,000 internal refugees.

In the 2011 insurgency, Qatar and the United Arab Emirates gave support to different groups among the anti-Qaddafi opposition. As the anti-Qaddafi coalition broke into fighting factions, so this transformed into sponsorship of different factions. When the Muslim Brotherhood was forced from power in 2013, Egypt joined as a militantly anti-Islamist factor. At the outset, the rivalries among Libya's armed groups did not conform to a neat polarization between secularists and Islamists. But this is the approximate shape into which international support for competing factions is starting to push Libyan politics. Khalifar Haftar, a Qaddafi-era general who fought against him in 2011 and has emerged as a leader of the Dignity group, opposes all Islamist groups, 'moderates' and 'extremists' alike, without distinction.

Libya has become an arena in which regional rivalries are being fought out as much as local conflicts. It has become in parts a safe haven for human trafficking, a staging post for unregistered migrants to Europe. And inevitably, it has become host to a powerful faction of ISIS-oriented *jihadis*.

VOTER TURNOUT

2012 July
Election for the General National Congress
Turnout: **50%**
1.7 million votes cast

2014 Feb
Election for the constitutional assembly
Turnout: **15%**
498,000 votes cast

2014 June
House of Representatives / Council of Deputies
Turnout: **18.5%**
630,000 votes cast

THE WAR OF ALL AGAINST ALL
Groups contending for power in Libya
2014–15

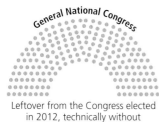

General National Congress

Leftover from the Congress elected in 2012, technically without authority.

House of Representatives / Council of Deputies

The elected government, now in Tobruk. Internationally recognized. Largely powerless. Supports Dignity.

LIBYA

Tripoli
Nafusa Mountains
Benghazi
Derna
Tobruk

Dignity

A coalition of eastern tribes, federalists, secularists, disaffected military units.
National Army Led by Khalifa Haftar, chief of army staff under Qaddafi.
The Libyan Army Most of Qaddafi's army that has remained operational has joined Haftar.
Al-Saiqa Elite unit of the Qaddafi army, Benghazi-based.
Zintan Powerful coalition of militias based on Zintan in the Nafusa mountains.

External supporters of Dignity
United Arab Emirates, Egypt, Saudi Arabia.

Dawn

An alliance of militias and Islamists of various hues.
Libyan Revolutionary Operations Room/Libyan Shield Set up to support General National Congress.
Ansar al-Sharia *Jihadi* group believed to have killed US Ambassador in 2012. Strong in Benghazi area.
Misrata Most powerful militia force in the country, combining 235 fighting brigades – 40,000 fighters, 800 tanks and 2,000 other fighting vehicles.
Seventeenth February Martyrs Brigade Based in eastern Libya, funded by Tripoli government.

External supporters of some, but not all, of the groups that make up Dawn
Qatar, Sudan, Turkey.

Islamic State (ISIS)
Islamic Youth Council, which declares allegiance to ISIS, controls Derna.

SYRIA

In March 2011 Syrian government forces killed four people demonstrating for freedom of expression. Unrest spread. The government proposed limited political reforms to appease the opposition but it was not satisfied. Violence escalated and civil war began.

This is far from the first upheaval in Syria. There was a time when coups were common – three in 1949 alone, the same number in 1963, 12 in all in the first 25 years of independence. In 1958 Syria experimented with giving up statehood by joining Egypt in the United Arab Republic (UAR). The experiment failed. Egypt was by far the larger country, and Nasser's self-confidence and authority as its leader were enhanced by the 1956 Suez crisis and war. Inevitably, Egypt dominated the union – two-thirds of the new Parliament and Cabinet were Egyptian, while Egyptian officials got senior government posts in Syria itself. Syrian resentment grew and it was little surprise when one of the dozen military coups levered Syria out of the UAR.

Even so, the Ba'athist emphasis on Arab unity was influential and in 1963 the Ba'athists came to power. But the party was torn by dispute between those who emphasized pan-Arab unity and those who emphasized the needs and interests of Syria. Steadily, the more nationalist faction, strengthened by support in the armed forces, gained the ascendancy – and then took power in 1966. The new regime was increasingly active against Israel. It intensified the pressure of guerrilla attacks on Israel while its diplomatic and political pressure forced Egypt into ever more confrontational mode with Israel to maintain its leadership within the Arab world. The policy successfully escalated the conflict but culminated in June 1967 in another catastrophic Arab defeat by Israel, which included the loss of Syrian territory in the Golan Heights.

General Hafez al-Assad, minister of defence, managed to avoid the blame. Another military fiasco strengthened his hand further. In the factional maelstrom of Ba'athist politics, Assad controlled the air force but not the army. When open fighting broke out between the PLO and the Jordanian government in September 1970, the Syrian government wanted to intervene on the PLO's side. Assad disagreed and refused to provide air cover when Syrian army tanks went into Jordan; the Jordanian army accordingly was victorious. Less than two months later, in a bloodless coup, Assad assumed power. Confirmed in office by a referendum in 1971, he stayed in power until his death, succeeded by his son.

The durability of the Assad regime until the civil war was due to a number of factors, including many Syrians' relief that the previous period of instability was over. Benefiting from oil revenues, economic growth helped the middle class prosper. A loyal core to run the state has also been crucial. The Assad family is Alawi. This religious group, whose origins are pre-Islamic, makes up about 12 per cent of Syria's population. A weak and impoverished minority for centuries, the community benefited after independence from the rise to prominence of a significant number of Alawis. Assad's assumption of the presidency in 1970 opened the door for many more co-religionists to take important positions.

Ruthlessness has also been fundamental. In 1973 there were demands from some groups that Islam be declared the state religion, an especially pointed demand since many Sunni Muslims refuse to acknowledge that the Alawi faith is in fact Islamic. A surge of violence around this issue in the late 1970s culminated in a major uprising and open fighting in the city of Hama in 1982;

reliable sources indicate that 10,000 or more civilians were killed by the Syrian army.

In the mid-1970s, Lebanon joined Israel as a pre-eminent foreign policy and security issue for Syria. Whereas Israel and the Western multinational forces were forced out of Lebanon, Syria stayed. It defined the terms of the agreement that ended the war in Lebanon and took a dominant role in the shattered country. In early 2005, Rafik Hariri, former Lebanese prime minister and an opponent of Syrian influence, was assassinated. Syria was widely believed to have organized the killing and an independent UN report concluded that senior Syrian officials were behind the murder. The pressure on Syria to end its military presence in Lebanon was overwhelming and it did so in 2005, though it carried on seeking to influence events by other, less visible means.

Another, less tangible component of the Assad-era stability was the regime's intransigence and willingness to take risks. It was always a rejectionist state when it came to any compromise with Israel, always home to militantly and violently anti-Israel groups. It permitted the Kurdistan Workers Party – the PKK – to have its headquarters in Syria as it pursued its war against Turkey. Likewise, Syria and Iraq had an intensely antagonistic relationship, partly because the two regimes emerged from rival wings of Ba'athism. With this background it was not Bashir al-Assad's style to offer concessions to the new democratic opposition in 2011.

CHRONOLOGY *continued*

1980 Muslim Brotherhood tries to kill Assad – organization banned. Start of Iran–Iraq war. Syria backs Iran.
1981 Israel annexes Golan Heights.
1982 Muslim Brotherhood uprising in Hama put down, thousands killed. Syrian forces do badly against Israel in Lebanon.
1984 PKK allowed to run its war against Turkey from Syria.
1990 Syria ends Lebanese civil war.
1990–91 Syrian government supports US against Iraq.
1998 Syria expels PKK leader Abdullah Ocalan.
2000 Assad dies and son Bashar takes over presidency – 600 political prisoners released.
2004 US partial sanctions on Syria for supporting terrorism.
2005 Assassination of Lebanese ex-PM Rafik Hariri. Two UN reports later implicate senior Syrian officials in his murder.
2006 Start of five-year drought affecting 60 per cent of Syrian territory. Iran and Syria restore diplomatic relations.
2007 Bashir Assad wins presidential election with 97.6 per cent of vote.
2008 UN launches appeal for $20 million to assist one million drought-affected Syrians. Syria establishes diplomatic relations with Lebanon.
2011 Peaceful protests seeking political rights are fired on by government forces. State of Emergency is lifted in effort to appease protestors. Clashes continue. Civil war starts. Syria suspended from Arab League.
2012 The Syrian National Coalition is formed as an alternative government.
2013 *Aug* Chemical weapons are used in suburb of Damascus, killing 355 people.

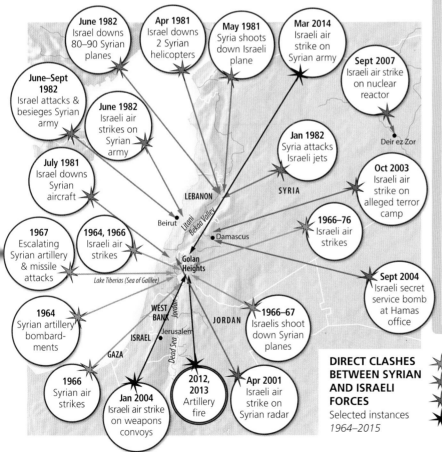

June 1982
Israel downs 80–90 Syrian planes

Apr 1981
Israel downs 2 Syrian helicopters

May 1981
Syria shoots down Israeli plane

Mar 2014
Israeli air strike on Syrian army

Sept 2007
Israeli air strike on nuclear reactor

June–Sept 1982
Israel attacks & besieges Syrian army

June 1982
Israeli air strikes on Syrian army

Jan 1982
Syria attacks Israeli jets

Deir ez Zor

Oct 2003
Israeli air strike on alleged terror camp

July 1981
Israel downs Syrian aircraft

LEBANON

SYRIA

1966–76
Israeli air strikes

Beirut
Litani
Bekaa Valley

1967
Escalating Syrian artillery & missile attacks

1964, 1966
Israeli air strikes

Damascus

Golan Heights

Sept 2004
Israeli secret service bomb at Hamas office

Lake Tiberias (Sea of Galilee)

1964
Syrian artillery bombardments

WEST BANK
Jordan
JORDAN
Jerusalem
ISRAEL
Dead Sea
GAZA

1966–67
Israelis shoot down Syrian planes

1966
Syrian air strikes

Jan 2004
Israeli air strike on weapons convoys

2012, 2013
Artillery fire

Apr 2001
Israeli air strike on Syrian radar

DIRECT CLASHES BETWEEN SYRIAN AND ISRAELI FORCES
Selected instances
1964–2015

✳ pre-1967 War
✳ 1981–82
✳ 2001–07
✳ since 2011 in Syrian Civil War

◯ Israeli action
◯ Syrian action

The civil war

The organization of many groups and coalitions fighting in Syria is fluid, as are the loyalties of some, and a lot of the basic information about them is uncertain.

The Free Syrian Army Fighting under political leadership of Syrian National Coalition. Military wing of the secular opposition to Assad. Fighting strength 2013 estimated as high as 65,000–100,000 – almost certainly a wild exaggeration; total was less than that and declined in 2014–2015.

Kurdish Popular Protection Groups 10,000–15,000 fighters in northern Syria.

Al-Nusra Front / Jabhat al-Nusra Al-Qaeda affiliate. Committed to creating Islamic state in Syria and preparing pathway to new Caliphate. About 10,000 fighters.

Ahrar ash-Sham Salafist force with strong presence in north-west and south. Widely believed to be backed by Gulf Kingdoms and Turkey. Was driving force in formation of **Islamic Front** in 2013, which also had Saudi support. The Front seemed to fragment in 2014 but Ahrar ash-Sham still uses the name and has absorbed other groups in 2014 and 2015.

Tawhid Brigade of Aleppo Close ally of Ahrar ash-Sham.

Ansar ash-Sham Salafist group active mainly in Latakia and Idlib.

ISIS (Islamic State in Iraq and ash-Sham / Islamic State). Formerly an al-Qaeda affiliate, announced Caliphate in June 2014. Holds large tracts of Iraq and Syria. CIA estimated its fighting strength in late 2014 as up to 30,000.

Jaysh al-Muhajirin wal al-Ansar (Army of the Emigrants and Helpers). Unclear whether closer to al-Nusra or ISIS, consists of some hundreds of foreign fighters.

Islam Army of Damascus Formerly part of Islamic Front, allegiance (if any) now unclear.

The Syrian civil war began as a popular uprising against a dictatorship. In its early months, it was widely seen as the next in line for the Arab Spring. Change had come quickly in Tunisia and Egypt and Libya was yet to enter chaos, so there were many outside Syria who expected the uprising soon to be successful. But the state of Bashar al-Assad neither crumbled nor compromised. Offers of a few small concessions were probably meant to buy time and peel off the less committed among the opposition. He stood firm and, as it had in Libya, popular protest became war. And just like Libya, war was the pathway to chaos.

The suppression of militant Sunni Islamism under the Assads meant the war immediately became a sectarian battle. Because of that it simultaneously took on a regional dimension, bringing in Iran, the Shi'a government of Iraq and the Shi'a Hezbollah in Lebanon, to resist a Salafist resurgence in Syria. This brought Saudi Arabia, Qatar and Turkey into the frame as funders and to some degree trainers of the Islamist insurgents, while the US and European allies were more reluctantly engaged in support of the secular insurgents and making common cause for a time with any opponent of Assad. In turn Russia became engaged both diplomatically and with arms supplies in support of Assad and of Iran, as a counterweight to Western influence.

Within Syria, the picture is even more entangled. Within two years of the start of fighting, much of the country was a war zone, contested between militias of often changeable loyalty. Arms delivered to a group of rebels would end up being used to support the regime because the recipients changed sides.

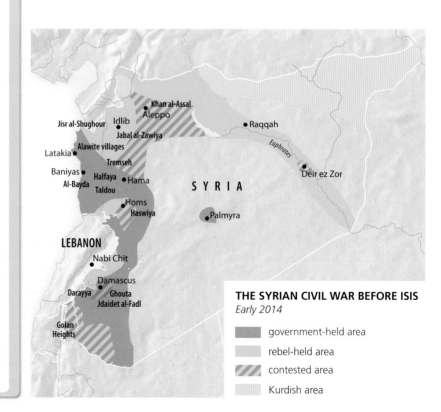

THE SYRIAN CIVIL WAR BEFORE ISIS
Early 2014

- government-held area
- rebel-held area
- contested area
- Kurdish area

And were quite capable of changing back again. The regime's opponents fought each other and often joined with pro-regime forces for temporary tactical advantage.

After four years of war, in a population of 23 million, 3 million had left the country and lived as refugees. Of 20 million people who stayed, 6.5 million had been forced from their homes and a further 4.3 million were in need of humanitarian assistance from the UN. More than half the population was unemployed, more than half the children had no school to go to, more than 75 per cent of people lived in poverty – and 50 per cent in conditions internationally defined as extreme poverty.

Estimates of death varied significantly and were, as in almost every modern war, sharply contested. In early 2015 the UN produced an estimate of 220,000 war deaths. Overall, other sources suggested the death toll was of approximately that scale. One independent count of documented war deaths produced a total of about 257,000 by April 2015 and noted that there could be as many as 86,000 undocumented deaths. A different source identified about 125,000 civilian and insurgent deaths, with the highest rates of killing coming from mid-2012 to early 2014.

CIVIL WAR DEATHS
Documented March 2011 – April 2015

Civilians and insurgents who were not previously soldiers

86,559	7,049
men	women

11,021
children

46,843	Syrian army soldiers and officers
37,336	Syrian rebel and Islamist fighters
31,346	pro-regime Syrian militia
28,253	foreign Islamist fighters
3,162	unidentified dead people (documented by photos and video)
2,844	other pro-regime Shi'a militia
2,512	defectors from Syrian armed forces
682	Lebanese Hezbollah fighters

OPPOSITION AND CIVILIAN DEATHS
March 2011 – December 2014

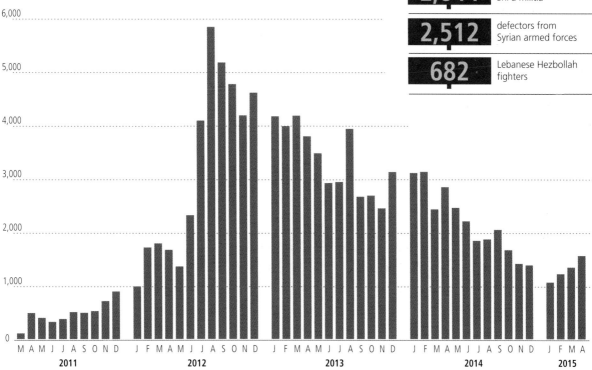

Chemical weapons

2012 July Syria confirms it has CW.

Aug US President Obama says CW deployment and use constitute 'red line' Syria must not cross.

Dec Seven CW deaths reported in Homs.

2013 Mar 25 reported CW deaths and dozens injured, Aleppo; phosphorous kills two in Adra.

June French government confirms nerve gas sarin has been used.

Aug Assad agrees to UN inspections of three alleged CW uses; Damascus: 588–1,429 deaths, and 3,600 injuries from neurotoxic causes.

Sept USA and Russia discuss and agree plan for CW disarmament of Syria, accepted by Assad.

Dec Deadline missed for sending most critical CW out of country. Organisation for the Prohibition of Chemical Weapons receives Nobel Peace Prize.

2014 Jan First CW shipments out of Syria on Danish and Norwegian ships.

Apr–May Chlorine gas used in attacks in Idlib province.

June 19th and final shipment of CW agents out of Syria.

July–Aug Neutralization of Priority 1 CW agents at sea in Mediterranean

Oct OPCW announces 98 per cent of Syrian CW have been safely and irreversibly destroyed with the rest to follow in the next few months.

2015 Apr UN Security Council views video of recent chlorine gas attack in Idlib.

Eliminating a country's arsenal of chemical weapons (CW) in time of war had never been done until the Syrian civil war.

Chemical weapons (CW) have caused less than 1 per cent of the death toll in the Syrian civil war. Barrel bombs have killed far more. But CW evoke special horror that supersedes the arithmetic of death. When details of their use on the rebel-held area of Ghouta, a suburb of Damascus, in August 2013 became public, military action by the West became more likely. The previous year, President Obama had declared that use of CW would cross 'a red line'.

As the debate heated up, and after the UK parliament had decided not to support military strikes without further evidence and argument (a vote that was interpreted by the government and observers as a flat rejection of the military option), US Secretary of State John Kerry was asked if there was anything President Assad could do to avoid military strikes. 'Sure,' he replied, 'he could turn over every single bit of his chemical weapons to the international community in the next week – turn it over, all of it without delay and allow the full and total accounting (of it). But he isn't about to do it and it can't be done.'

Russia took Kerry at his word and came up with a plan, which Assad accepted, and the USA and UN signed up to. If Kerry was wrong about Assad's willingness, he was not wrong to be sceptical about the practicalities. Keeping dangerous chemicals from falling into the wrong hands during transit in time of war would be demanding.

There were delays, deadlines were missed, but the process moved ahead. The whole Syrian stockpile of 1,308 metric tonnes of sulfur mustard agent and precursor chemicals were removed by mid-2014 and destroyed by the end of the year. Yet the larger war also moved ahead and CW continued to be used.

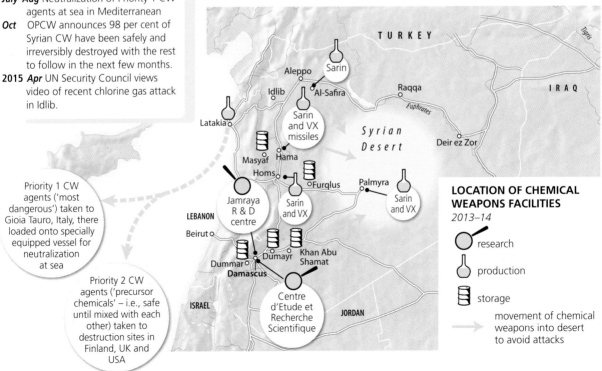

Priority 1 CW agents ('most dangerous') taken to Gioia Tauro, Italy, there loaded onto specially equipped vessel for neutralization at sea

Priority 2 CW agents ('precursor chemicals' – i.e., safe until mixed with each other) taken to destruction sites in Finland, UK and USA

LOCATION OF CHEMICAL WEAPONS FACILITIES
2013–14

research

production

storage

movement of chemical weapons into desert to avoid attacks

The Geneva talks

Talks about peace in Syria have not had even the smallest chance of success in ending the war. That does not make them wrong or a waste of time.

If war is to end by agreement, those who are fighting must agree to stop, but the combatant groups and outside powers in this conflict have ignored this principle. They have approached the task of achieving a peace agreement with conditions that prevented even minimal progress.

The West wanted to discuss peace in Syria without President Assad or his representatives, and did so at the first Geneva Talks in 2012. The war continued. When Assad launched a peace plan based on national dialogue he stipulated that he would not sit down with any group that had betrayed Syria. When the West was ready in late 2013 to agree to new talks in Geneva with Assad's government, significant pressure was needed on the Syrian National Coalition to win its agreement to participate. When, in 2014, the second round of Geneva talks did start, the Islamist opposition was excluded.

Despite the bleak diplomatic prospects, when the Geneva II talks convened they seemed to offer the only path to peace, even though that would involve all the main parties compromising on each other's status after the war, which they showed no sign of doing. Yet, however improbable a diplomatic and peaceful solution was, a decisive military victory for any of the forces looked completely impossible.

Whatever chance Geneva II offered in January and February 2014, it was spurned. After two sessions there was no progress. Fighting continued. In the year that followed, realities on the ground changed dramatically as ISIS declared itself and started to take control of increasing swathes of territory and win the allegiance of increasing numbers of fighting groups. Even with ISIS on the rise, and whatever the outcome of the international military action against it, diplomacy may yet have a part to play. Giving up on diplomacy will only mean more war. If the combatants and the outside powers want some form of political solution, they will need a diplomatic process. And they will have to decide to talk with everybody – not just the few they each like.

GENEVA PEACE TALKS

Nov 2011 – Jan 2012 Arab League monitoring mission established, then abandoned because of escalating violence.

2012 *Jan* Russia and China block UN Security Council resolution calling for set-up of transitional government.

Feb Kofi Annan appointed UN envoy to Syria, announces six-point plan to end the violence – accepted by both Assad and main opposition.

Apr Russia and China veto UN Resolutions to place sanctions on Syria.

June UN observer mission (part of Annan's plan) is scrapped because of risk of working in conflict areas. Geneva I peace talks (without Syrian government) agree on principles for establishing a transitional governing body.

Aug Lakhdar Brahimi replaces Annan as UN envoy to Syria.

Dec Iran proposes six-point plan for a 'diplomatic solution' through national dialogue.

2013 *Jan* President Assad proposes a national reconciliation conference, elections and a new constitution. Brahimi proposes a six-point plan.

May USA and Russia hold talks on Syria without producing agreement. UN General Assembly praises opposition and condemns government.

2014 *Jan* Geneva II peace talks begin, based on the Geneva I proposal of a transitional governing body.

Feb Second session of Geneva II talks take place. Agreement on a 'humanitarian pause' to allow women, children and the elderly to evacuate from The Old City in Homs.

May Brahimi resigns as UN envoy.

July Experienced UN diplomat Staffan de Mistura becomes UN envoy to Syria.

Oct De Mistura presents action plan for local 'freezes' in fighting to allow aid deliveries and pave way to peace talks.

GENEVA PARTICIPANTS

Syrian government delegation	Headed by Walid al-Muallem, foreign minister.
Opposition delegation	15 members headed by Ahmad Jarba, president of the Syrian National Coalition.
	Members include two representatives of the country's ethnic Kurdish minority, four defectors from the Syrian army, some senior members of the SNC, and delegates of armed groups fighting in Syria.
Delegations from 30 countries	Includes the UN, five permanent members of the Security Council (China, France, Russia, UK and USA), the Arab League, EU, and the Organization of Islamic Cooperation, and 26 other countries (including Syria's immediate neighbours – Jordan, Iraq, Lebanon and Turkey).

The state of war

The first four years of civil war brought massive physical destruction, widespread human misery and steep economic decline, and no clear view of how Syria and the Syrians could be dragged out of the pit they were in.

The Assad government proved much more resilient than many observers initially forecast and its regional and international supporters far more shrewd and decisive. The secular rebels proved less proficient than the West first hoped and the West much less willing to support them than they had imagined. Though the *jihadi* insurgents had a bigger resource base than the secular opposition and steadily proved more effective in combat, they proved more divided against themselves than anyone could have believed. And then came ISIS.

Neither the government nor the secular opposition nor the *jihadis* showed either the willingness to compromise in order to end the war by agreement, nor by mid-2015 the capacity to win it. This was as true of ISIS in mid-2015 as it was of the other combatants.

Many things mark ISIS out as different from the other fighting forces, even compared to the *jihadis* of al-Nusra and other groups. First, ISIS is extremely well organized and led, with committed fighters and effective tactics. ISIS is rich thanks to its seizure of the central bank reserves in Mosul, Iraq, and well equipped thanks in part to the amount of American equipment Iraqi soldiers have abandoned to it. Its effectiveness extends to global social media, on which it has thousands of people working to project its messages. These include the

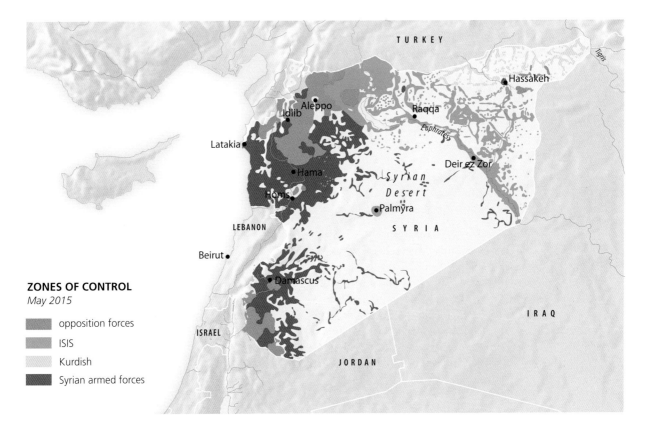

ZONES OF CONTROL
May 2015

- opposition forces
- ISIS
- Kurdish
- Syrian armed forces

depictions of its own brutality with which it has both shocked and fascinated its worldwide audience – the decapitations, the mass murders, the sexual enslavement, perpetrated against Yazidis, Shi'a, foreign journalists, captured fighters and Sunni Muslims who do not accept its authority. On the strength of all this, ISIS has been able to take, control and exploit large tracts of territory in both Syria and Iraq, in the service of its self-declaration as the modern Caliphate – its rule as successor to the Prophet Mohammed.

But no more than the other combatants has ISIS yet shown that it would be able to exert stable authority over the territory it now has, let alone the territory of Syria as a whole and further afield. Nothing can be ruled out but the fortunes of war wane as well as wax and the effectiveness ISIS has shown on the ground is not matched by the kind of external backing that the other major combatants have. In late 2014 and early 2015, ISIS suffered reverses and lost territory under the pressure of Arab and Western bombing – and there was, of course, nobody to bomb the enemies of ISIS.

When ISIS took control of Palmyra (Tadmur) in central Syria in mid-2015, it nominally controlled half the country. But much of the territory is empty; the government continued to control the main population centres. And while the victory at Palmyra was impressive, it was in part the result of a significant strategic shift of government forces to the northern front. Were Assad not hard pressed by *jihadis* in the north, ISIS, the common enemy, would have had an even harder battle at Palmyra.

It is not yet clear if ISIS can exert stable authority over the territory it holds

----

However, if that suggests that ISIS's victories in Syria are not the result of a clear-cut superiority of force and leadership, it also reveals the weakness of the Assad government, increasingly short of both economic resources and troop numbers, with, it has been reported, unsustainably high casualties among the most loyal fighters, the Alawis.

By mid-2015 Syria's most likely destiny seemed to be becoming another Somalia or Lebanon. In Somalia, the dictator Siad Barre was overthrown in 1991, after which came a quarter of a century of war, chaos, gangsterism, international intervention, the rise of the Salafists almost to state power and the breakaway of two-thirds of the country. Lebanon was destroyed in 15 years of civil war and put back together only when peace was forcibly imposed and held in place by an external power – Syria.

Yet there were also amid the destruction some signs of hope. There were places where local ceasefires and arrangements for displaced people to return were negotiated, agreed and implemented. To people desperate for reasons to hope, these were signs that productive negotiations on the ground were possible. Perhaps peace would come to Syria not through high diplomacy and a grand design agreed in Geneva but in a patchwork of locally brokered agreements.

SAUDI ARABIA

CHRONOLOGY

1744 Alliance between Prince Mohammed ibn Saud and Sheikh Mohammed ibn Abdul Wahhab leads to founding of the first Saudi State.

1803 Saudi forces capture Mecca and Medina.

1817 Ottomans drive the Saudis from Mecca and Medina. Saudi leaders are taken to Istanbul and beheaded.

1824–99 Second Saudi State.

1902 Abdul Aziz ibn Saud re-conquers Riyadh.

1913 Ibn Saud gains control of much of the Gulf coast of Arabia.

1925 Ibn Saud captures Mecca.

1932 Founding of Saudi Arabia (the third Saudi State).

1938 Oil discovered. US-controlled Arab-American Oil Company (Aramco) controls production.

1953 King Abdul Aziz dies, succeeded by Crown Prince Saud.

1960 Saudi Arabia becomes a founding member of OPEC.

1964 King Saud is deposed by his brother, Crown Prince Faisal, following complaints by senior princes about financial management.

1972 Saudi Arabia gains 20% share in Aramco.

1973 Saudi Arabia leads oil boycott against countries that supported Israel in the October War.

1975 King Faisal killed by a resentful nephew, succeeded by Crown Prince Khalid.

1979 Islamist militants occupy the Grand Mosque of Mecca for ten days.

1980 Government announces creation of a consultative assembly (*Majlis al-Shura*) but does not convene it. Saudi Arabia gains full ownership (retroactive to 1976) of Aramco.

1982 King Khalid dies, succeeded by Crown Prince Fahd.

1985 UK and Saudi Arabia initiate al-Yamamah arms deal.

1986 'Custodian of the Two Holy Mosques' is added to King's official title.

Saudi Arabia's crude oil reserves are about 16 per cent of the world total, and its oil output is about 8 per cent. Though both these figures are smaller than a decade ago as new oil discoveries and new producers enter the picture, Saudi Arabia's reserves remain the world's largest. Its importance in the world oil industry will not soon diminish.

Abdul Aziz ibn Saud founded the kingdom of Saudi Arabia on the basis of armed strength, monarchical rule and Wahhabism. Oil came later. The Saud family has espoused the puritanical Wahhabist form of Sunni Islam since the mid-18th century. Originally, Prince Mohammed ibn Saud provided Sheikh Wahhab with a vehicle for proselytizing, while Wahhabism, with its focus on cleansing the Islamic faith of distortions, became a source of moral and religious legitimacy for Prince Saud and his successors' rule. The Sauds briefly held Mecca and Medina in the early 19th century but were forced out by the Ottomans and punished. Through the 19th century, the Sauds competed for power in Arabia with two other great families – the Rasheeds and, for long the most powerful of the three, the Hashemites, descendants of the Prophet and guardians of the holy places of Mecca and Medina. It was an alliance with the British that eventually gave the Sauds the upper hand in warfare against first the Rasheeds and then, by the mid-1920s, against those other – disposable and betrayed – British allies, the Hashemites (see p 33).

THE RULING FAMILY
Kings of Saudi Arabia (some dates of birth approximate)

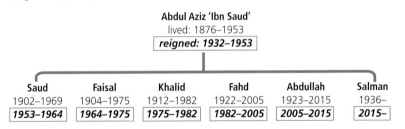

The six kings of Saudi Arabia since Ibn Saud's death have all been his sons. Exact figures on the size of Ibn Saud's family are not available. He is thought to have had 37 sons and about the same number of daughters. The most powerful group of his sons are the seven known as the Sudayri because their mother was Hissa bint Ahmad Al-Sudayri, reputed to have been Ibn Saud's favourite wife.

Six years after the kingdom was established in 1932, oil was discovered. Revenues were modest until after World War II and in the 1950s they began to increase quickly. This wealth of natural resources and, with them, a key place in the world economic system could destine a country, in principle, either to be a prize for others to compete over and take, or to be itself a key player on the world stage. It has taken considerable skill and determination for the Saudi monarchy to be the latter. But oil money has also become a source of potential weakness.

With oil wealth have come allegations of gross extravagance by the royal family and scandals such as over the al-Yamamah deal with British Aerospace in 1985. Lobbied for hard by UK Prime Minister Margaret Thatcher, the two-part deal was reputedly worth over £40 billion and involved the sale of over 200 aircraft. A decade later, media reports surfaced about a special fund connected to the deal, aimed at providing members and associates of the Saudi royal family with luxuries – travel, sports cars, yachts, cash for gambling – as sweeteners to ensure a follow-on contract. In 2004 it was alleged that over time this fund amounted to £60 million but later British police estimated that £6 billion may have been paid out in corrupt commission fees through an array of agents and intermediaries, in order to secure the deal. The police investigation was terminated by the UK government on the grounds that it was not in the public interest. Shortly after, a new and almost equally valuable arms deal was signed between the UK and Saudi Arabia.

Even without corruption, the availability of large sums of money makes it difficult for a monarchy whose legitimacy has a religious basis – both because of its Wahhabist roots and because of its role as guardian of the holy places – to maintain the necessary degree of purity in all its dealings. King Saud was deposed by the family because of reputedly bad financial management and the notorious extravagance of some members of the ruling family is seen by many as undermining the rulers' legitimacy. Beyond that, as the world oil price goes up and down, so does the state's income. The foundation-stone of the Saudi economy is thus inherently unstable.

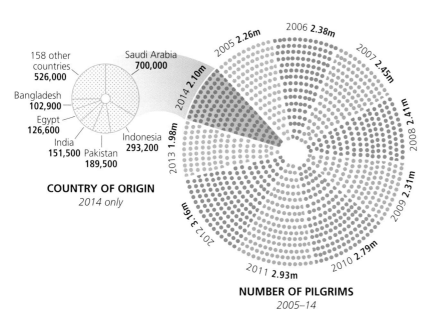

158 other countries
526,000

Saudi Arabia
700,000

Bangladesh
102,900

Egypt
126,600

India
151,500

Pakistan
189,500

Indonesia
293,200

COUNTRY OF ORIGIN
2014 only

2005 **2.26m**
2006 **2.38m**
2007 **2.45m**
2014 **2.10m**
2008 **2.41m**
2013 **1.98m**
2009 **2.31m**
2012 **3.16m**
2010 **2.79m**
2011 **2.93m**

NUMBER OF PILGRIMS
2005–14

THE HAJJ

Pilgrimage to Mecca is, if feasible, one of five core duties ('pillars') of Islam. Hajj occurs in the 8th to 12th days (sometimes the 13th) of the last month of the Islamic lunar calendar. It is the world's largest single gathering of people. Pilgrimage to Mecca outside Hajj is Umrah. Revenues from Hajj and Umrah in 2014 were $19 billion.

Loss of life in the Hajj

1975 Gas explosion causes fire and 200 deaths in pilgrims' camp.
1979 400–500 militants occupy Grand Mosque for 10 days; 250 pilgrims killed.
1987 Iranian pilgrims' demonstration broken up by security forces: 402 killed (of which 275 were Iranian).
1989 Kuwaiti Shi'as detonate bomb. One fatality. 16 suspects caught and beheaded.
1990 Crowd panic: 1,426 pilgrims die in stampede in tunnel.
1994 Crowd panic: 270 pilgrims trampled to death.
1997 Fire: 340 pilgrims killed, 1,500 injured.
1998 Crowd panic: 118 pilgrims trampled to death.
2001 Crowd panic: 35 pilgrims die in stampede.
2004 Crowd panic: 251 pilgrims trampled to death.
2006 Crowd panic: 345 pilgrims trampled to death.

Contrary pressures

Saudi Arabia is a simultaneously modern and traditional society. Pressures for change come from three main, wholly incompatible and irreducibly contradictory sources.

The state was founded in large part on religious principles – a traditionalist form of Sunni Islam that has steadily become, thanks to Saudi wealth, one of the predominant forms of Islam worldwide. The Saudi ruling family has – in the 20th and 21st centuries no less than in the 19th and 18th – allied and worked closely with Wahhabi religious leaders and thinkers not only to establish the basis of legitimacy but to fulfil the everyday functions of the state. Wahhabist principles apply in matters as diverse as personal behaviour, law and order, education and traffic regulations. This is a source of great stability for the Saudi state, yet also a source of challenge.

The state's militant Sunni foundations lead almost inevitably to the exclusion and marginalization of the Shi'a minority, which makes up around 15 per cent of the population, mostly living in the areas where most oil has been discovered. To many Sunni and especially to the Wahhabi, Shi'as are simply a misguided sect, descendants of people who misunderstood the Prophet and erred in the first 50 years of Islam and who have erred persistently since. A senior imam at the Grand Mosque declared in 2009 that Shi'a Muslims were unbelievers who should be hunted down and killed. While that may be a more extreme view than most Saudis and most Sunnis would voice, a former head of Saudi intelligence, a royal prince, has been quoted by a former head of British intelligence as saying, 'The time is not far off in the Middle East when it will be literally "God help the Shi'a". More than a billion Sunnis have simply had enough of them.'

The Iranian revolution in 1979 inspired Shi'a everywhere. The Saudi authorities clamped down hard on expressions of Shi'a identity and demand for a better share of the oil wealth. In 2011, as demands for freedom flowed through the Arab world, there was again an echo in the Shi'a areas of Saudi Arabia. And again there was a hard, unyielding response from the authorities, though information on events is sparse because of restrictions on reporting.

At the same time, there has been a steady pressure for allowing more consultation, freedom of expression and even democracy in the Saudi kingdom, in a way that would take the way of governing away from Wahhabi doctrine. Since the early 1990s, the authorities have conceded some ground to this modernizing constituency, first by convening a consultative assembly, then by allowing voting in local elections, and then by granting some rights to women.

Pressure in the opposite direction – against democracy, equal rights for women, the extravagance of the ruling family, and the rulers' perceived failure fully to uphold Wahhabist principles – comes from Wahhabi purism. Such was the inspiration of some 400–500 militants who seized the Grand Mosque in 1979, holding it for 10 days. At least 255 people were killed and perhaps many more. Though many aspects of modernity outrage Wahhabi militants, the seizure of the Grand Mosque was done for a different reason, guided by a revolutionary religious doctrine that denies the right of a state to control the holy places. Though these militants were executed, many of their demands about education and public standards were quietly accepted. With that, the ruling family has encouraged its potential enemies and is in danger of being burned by the fire it started.

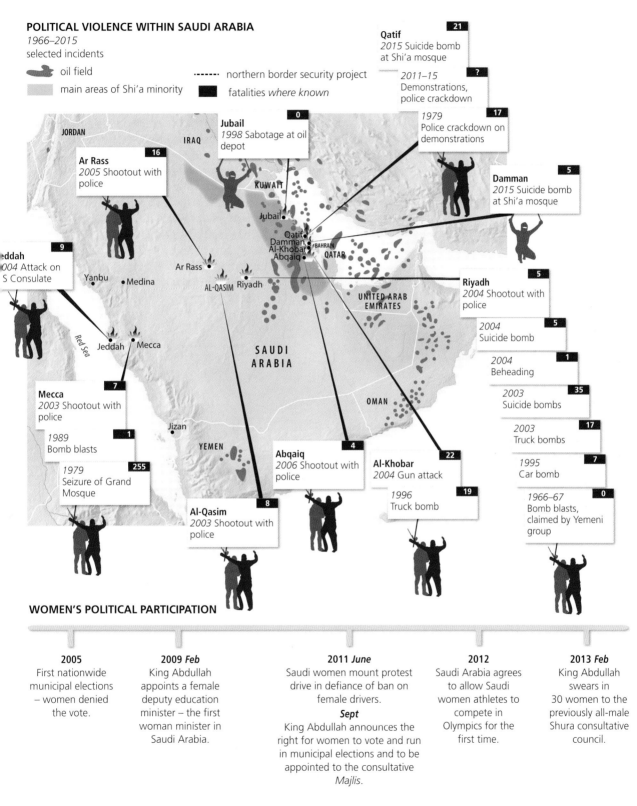

POLITICAL VIOLENCE WITHIN SAUDI ARABIA
1966–2015
selected incidents

- oil field
- main areas of Shi'a minority
- ------ northern border security project
- ■ fatalities *where known*

Qatif `21`
2015 Suicide bomb at Shi'a mosque

2011–15 `?`
Demonstrations, police crackdown

1979 `17`
Police crackdown on demonstrations

Jubail `0`
1998 Sabotage at oil depot

Ar Rass `16`
2005 Shootout with police

Damman `5`
2015 Suicide bomb at Shi'a mosque

eddah `9`
004 Attack on S Consulate

Riyadh `5`
2004 Shootout with police

2004 Suicide bomb `5`

2004 Beheading `1`

2003 Suicide bombs `35`

2003 Truck bombs `17`

1995 Car bomb `7`

1966–67 `0`
Bomb blasts, claimed by Yemeni group

Mecca `7`
2003 Shootout with police

1989 Bomb blasts `1`

1979 `255`
Seizure of Grand Mosque

Abqaiq `4`
2006 Shootout with police

Al-Khobar `22`
2004 Gun attack

1996 Truck bomb `19`

Al-Qasim `8`
2003 Shootout with police

JORDAN, IRAQ, KUWAIT, BAHRAIN, QATAR, UNITED ARAB EMIRATES, OMAN, YEMEN, SAUDI ARABIA
Yanbu, Medina, Jeddah, Mecca, Jizan, Red Sea, Riyadh, AL-QASIM, Ar Rass, Jubail, Qatif, Damman, Al-Khobar, Abqaiq

WOMEN'S POLITICAL PARTICIPATION

2005
First nationwide municipal elections – women denied the vote.

2009 *Feb*
King Abdullah appoints a female deputy education minister – the first woman minister in Saudi Arabia.

2011 *June*
Saudi women mount protest drive in defiance of ban on female drivers.
Sept
King Abdullah announces the right for women to vote and run in municipal elections and to be appointed to the consultative *Majlis*.

2012
Saudi Arabia agrees to allow Saudi women athletes to compete in Olympics for the first time.

2013 *Feb*
King Abdullah swears in 30 women to the previously all-male Shura consultative council.

137

Protecting and projecting power

The Sauds' need to respond to the rising tide of pressure for change, crisis and conflict has steadily led Saudi Arabia's foreign and security policies into an ever more activist shape. In the 1970s and 1980s it was possible to look at the kingdom's expenditure on armaments as if it were a vanity project. No longer. Today its forces are engaged on multiple fronts – in Syria, Yemen and Bahrain.

For many years, there were four focal points of Saudi international policy. Foremost among them, as with many other Arab states, was Israel. And, like the rest of the Arab world, the policy was a failure – neither able to prevent the formation nor the consolidation nor the expansion of the Jewish state. The second and increasingly important focal point was the global oil market. Though Saudi Arabia led the Arab oil producers in identifying the power of the oil weapon, used as a sanction against Western supporters of Israel in 1973, the kingdom has long since recognized that its long-term interest lay in a stable world economy. This implied aiming for relatively stable and predictable prices for oil. This in turn suggested a middle way between pumping the oil as fast as possible and holding the world to ransom to gouge out the maximum possible price. This is what Saudi Arabia came to

CROSS-SECTION OF THE NORTHERN BORDER SECURITY PROJECT DEFENCES

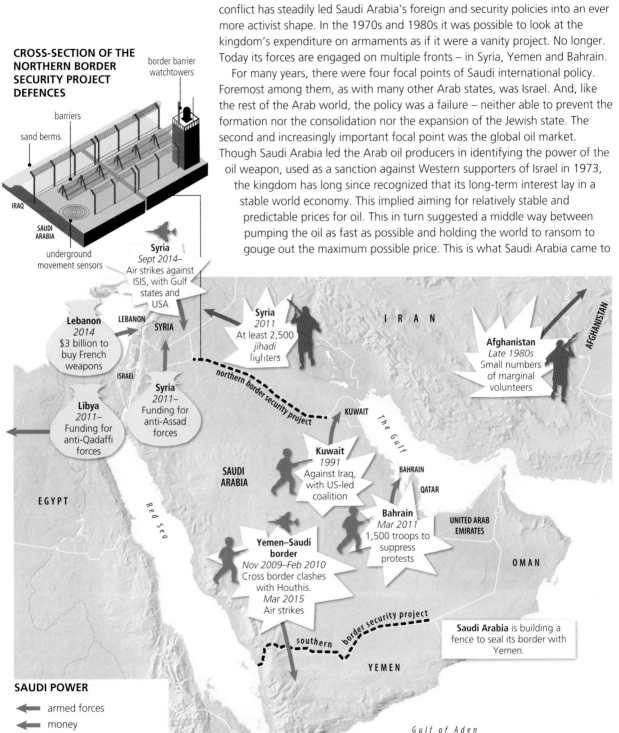

Syria *Sept 2014–* Air strikes against ISIS, with Gulf states and USA

Syria *2011* At least 2,500 *jihadi* fighters

Afghanistan *Late 1980s* Small numbers of marginal volunteers

Lebanon *2014* $3 billion to buy French weapons

Syria *2011–* Funding for anti-Assad forces

Libya *2011–* Funding for anti-Qadaffi forces

Kuwait *1991* Against Iraq, with US-led coalition

Bahrain *Mar 2011* 1,500 troops to suppress protests

Yemen–Saudi border *Nov 2009–Feb 2010* Cross border clashes with Houthis. *Mar 2015* Air strikes

Saudi Arabia is building a fence to seal its border with Yemen.

SAUDI POWER
- armed forces
- money
- non-state

stand for. The third main focus of foreign policy was the regional rivalry with Iran, first under the Shah and then equally, if differently, when the Shah was overthrown. And the fourth was to project the Saudi version of Islam worldwide by funding religious education, Wahhabist translations of the Quran, and the construction of mosques. The Sauds have also allowed rich individuals to provide funding for al-Qaeda, the al-Nusra front in Syria and many other *jihadi* groups.

The relationship with the USA has also been central. The Saudi authorities came to see it as a critical factor of regional stability. Over time, the balance has changed. Oil and the benefits of a well-regulated market have remained central and will for the foreseeable future but the question of Israel has become much less important. Israel is no longer the total outcast; far from it, Israel and Saudi Arabia cooperate tacitly and sometimes openly on a number of regional questions – not least Lebanon and Syria. It is not real friendship but it is a genuine if pragmatic cooperation.

The Sauds' focus is increasingly on the immediate political challenges in the region. Saudi money, influence in Europe and in Washington, and force are all deployed to meet these. The Saudi authorities were understandably nervous about the democratic impulse in 2011 and thereafter, known as the Arab Spring. One immediate priority was to ride it out. Apart from democracy itself, the Saudis quickly saw two great risks: on the one hand, the rise of Sunni militants who would challenge Saudi leadership of the Sunni world and the legitimacy of the Saud family's rule; on the other, a Shi'a resurgence, driven by Iran and bolstered by the power of the Shi'a majority in Iraq.

Protests in Bahrain in 2011 were simultaneously Shi'a in participation and to some degree democratic in tone and substance. Saudi forces were deployed to suppress them. The Assad regime in Syria was closely allied with Shi'a Iran and the Shi'a Hezbollah in Lebanon. Saudi money was put into building the Islamist opposition. In Egypt, the Muslim Brotherhood's accession to power led to fears of instability; Saudi influence was exerted to win international support for bringing down the Morsi presidency and suppressing the Brotherhood. In Iraq and in Syria, the even more militant ISIS grew in power; Saudi aircraft joined in strikes against it. Shi'a Houthi forces took over the Yemeni capital Sanaa; Saudi air strikes against them ensued.

As Saudi Arabia has carved out a more activist foreign policy, so it has also been increasingly critical of US policy when priorities and strategies do not match. The US 'pivot to Asia' in the second Obama administration after 2012 was widely interpreted to mean the USA would be less interested in the Middle East and, from a Saudi perspective, less committed to its version of stability. In turn, this made the Saudi capacity to back itself more important.

Perhaps. Yet what was clear from Saudi use of raw power was not what the outcome would be, but that the stakes and intensity of the battle were escalating all the time. By 2015, the very existence of the Saudi state was on the line as it had never been since its foundation. This was perhaps most clearly advertised by the construction of a security barrier the whole way along its border with Iraq to keep out the threat of militant *jihadis*.

SAUDI ARMED FORCES

$60 billion
Approx. military spending.
4th highest in world.
More than **doubled** in 10 years.

3rd most capable military in region after Israel and Turkey

233,500 active personnel

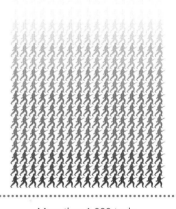

More than 1,000 tanks

More than 6,000 other armoured fighting vehicles

More than 200 fighter jets

More than 200 strike aircraft

YEMEN

Known in antiquity as Arabia Felix because of its green and fertile land, Yemen is the poorest Arab country. Sustained popular protest pushed out the long-time president in 2011 but a prospect of progress has been dashed by civil war and outside intervention.

The Ottoman Empire arrived in the 1540s to ensure the safety of the southern Arabian coastline against threats to the holy cities of Mecca and Medina but never truly controlled the interior of the region. Increasingly they left power in the hands of local rulers and leaders, among whom the hereditary ruling Zaydi Imams were particularly powerful. Leaders of a minority branch of Shi'as, the dynasty was sustained for a thousand years until 1962.

Early in their period the Ottomans had divided Yemen in two and when the British took over the natural harbour of Aden, first to fight the area's pirates and later as a coaling station, it became convenient to formalize the division of North and South Yemen. The Zaydi religious monarchy took power in North Yemen at the end of the Arab Uprising of 1916–1918 and then contested large tracts of what is now Saudi Arabia with the new Saudi kingdom, ending with complete defeat.

British power in the South and the rule of the Zaydi Imams in the North ended at around the same time. Both ends were violent but the overthrow of the northern monarchy particularly so. Egypt's intervention cost it as many as 25,000 lives while estimates of North Yemen's war dead go as high as 200,000.

Politics in both the new Yemens were unstable while economic and social progress was uneven at best. After a period of coups and assassinations in North Yemen that rivalled the chaos preceding the civil war, the next in a line of politically ambitious generals turned out to be not only ruthless when necessary but shrewd, far-sighted and pragmatic. President Saleh took power in 1978 in the North, unified the two Yemens under his authority in the 1990s, stamped out the vestiges of a southern secessionist movement within a few years, and retained power until popular protests proved too much in 2011, the year of regional change.

As elsewhere in the region, protests in Yemen were motivated by the urge for greater freedom and democracy, a distaste for the ruling regime's endemic corruption and a profound social crisis. A growing population had experienced inadequate economic growth for decades and faced shortages of the basics of life. The once-fertile Arabia Felix was experiencing water insecurity to such an extent that the capital Sanaa was close to running out of water.

Al-Qaeda took up residence in Yemen as early as 1992 and one of its showpiece acts of terrorism before the spectacular attacks in the US in September 2001 was the bomb attack on the USS Cole in Aden harbour in 2000. Seeking to strike back against its rising enemy, the USA equipped itself with new weapons and methods. In 2002, the head of al-Qaeda in Yemen was killed in his car with six other people by an armed drone – the USA's first ever use of a drone for assassination. This was far from the end of al-Qaeda in Yemen. It continued to recruit, plot and bomb. At the same time, starting in 2004 a small group of Zaydi Shi'a launched an insurrection. Their leader – Hussein al-Houthi – was killed in the early fighting but the movement steadily grew and by the time of Saleh's overthrow had thousands of fighters.

These two insurgencies meant the president's departure opened the way to new contestations for power. Little changed quickly as Saleh was replaced by the man who had been his vice-president for half his time in office. For ordinary Yemenis, it was a change of face at the top but not much else. The Houthis' insurrection gained pace and in September 2014 they took the capital and drove the still relatively new president out. Meanwhile, al-Qaeda exploited the chaos and the over-stretching of Yemen's military to expand its power base in the eastern part of the country.

Though the Houthis are Shi'a and al-Qaeda are Salafist Sunnis, almost all dispassionate observers of events, both Yemeni and outsider, agree that seeing Yemen's conflicts in terms of a Sunni–Shi'a clash is misleading. It is even further off the mark to see the conflict in Yemen as part of a clash between Iran and Saudi Arabia as the Shi'a and Sunni great powers. Zaydi is a different branch of Shi'a from that followed by Iran's leaders. Tribal leaders who support the Houthis do so not for religious sectarian reasons but because that is where their advantage lies; they will shift allegiance away from the Houthis, if they do, for the same reason. And ex-president Saleh is back in the game, seeming to make common cause with the Houthis against both ex-president Hadi's forces and al-Qaeda.

But Saudi Arabia seems determined to view its southern neighbour through the simplistic sectarian lens. In early 2015, a bombing campaign against the Houthis augmented by a naval blockade was the latest step in Saudi power projection. Within weeks the situation of large numbers of ordinary Yemenis was becoming desperate. In June 2015 aid agencies were reporting that 80 per cent of the population was in urgent need of food, water and medical supplies.

CHRONOLOGY continued

2007 & 2008 Rounds four and five.
2009 *Jan* Saudi and Yemeni branches merge to form Al-Qaeda in the Arabian Peninsula (AQAP).
2009 *Aug–Mar 2010* Round six.
2011 *Mar* Popular protests met by government crackdown.
Nov President Saleh steps down.
2012 *Feb* General Abd Rabbuh Mansur Hadi, vice-president 1994–2012, becomes president after an uncontested election.
2014 *Sept* Houthi rebels seize control of the capital, Sanaa, and overthrow Hadi.
2015 *Mar–Apr* Saudi Arabian bombing campaign – Operation Decisive Storm – not decisive.
Apr Saudi naval blockade.
May Bombing at mosque in Sanaa kills 142 people, injures hundreds more.
June Aid agencies say naval blockade puts 20 million Yemenis in urgent need of water, food and basic medical supplies.

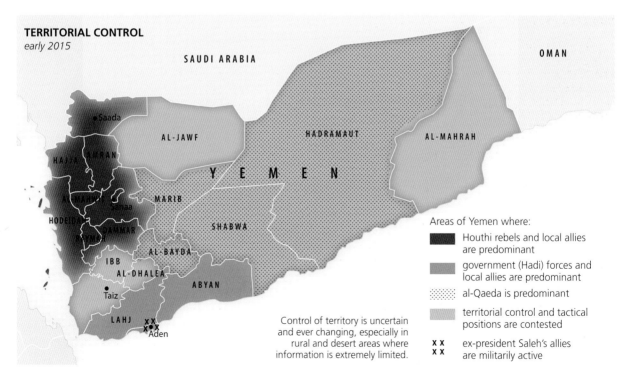

TERRITORIAL CONTROL
early 2015

SAUDI ARABIA

OMAN

Saada

AL-JAWF

HADRAMAUT

AL-MAHRAH

HAJJA AMRAN

Y E M E N

AL-MAHWIT MARIB

HODEIDA SANAA DHAMMAR

SHABWA

AL-BAYDA

IBB

AL-DHALEA

ABYAN

Taiz

LAHJ x x x x Aden

Areas of Yemen where:

Houthi rebels and local allies are predominant

government (Hadi) forces and local allies are predominant

al-Qaeda is predominant

territorial control and tactical positions are contested

x x
x x ex-president Saleh's allies are militarily active

Control of territory is uncertain and ever changing, especially in rural and desert areas where information is extremely limited.

THE GULF KINGDOMS

The six Gulf kingdoms are the richest Arab states per head of population and all are among the richest 10 per cent of countries in the world. Taken together, the six hold over one third (33 per cent) of proven oil reserves worldwide.

Saudi Arabia (see pp 134–139) is the biggest, richest and most powerful of the six and is the strongest voice in the Gulf Cooperation Council (GCC), formed in 1981 for protection against fall-out from the Iran–Iraq war. The five smaller members, however, are also major economic and political players. In recent years, Qatar and the UAE in particular have also taken activist roles in international politics.

Qatar's 2003 constitution says its foreign policy is 'based on the principle of strengthening peace and security by means of encouraging peaceful resolution of international disputes.' Qatar has acted on this by mediating in conflicts in Yemen (2008–10), Lebanon (2008), and Darfur (2008–10), between Sudan and Chad in 2009 and between Djibouti and Eritrea in 2010.

With this experience and resulting credibility, Qatar intervened in the unfolding events of 2011 as an ally of both the West and change. As an ally of the West it supported armed intervention in Libya and later in Syria; as an ally of change it supported Islamists and Salafists – and earned the particular ire of Saudi Arabia and the other GCC states for supporting the Muslim Brotherhood and Mohamed Morsi in Egypt.

In general the GCC states were much more conservative in response to the wave of change in 2011. The pressure for change was greatest in Bahrain and

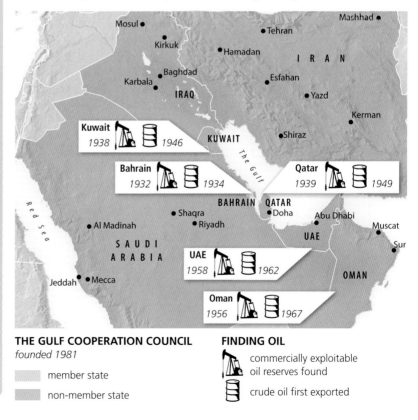

THE GULF COOPERATION COUNCIL
founded 1981

member state

non-member state

FINDING OIL

commercially exploitable oil reserves found

crude oil first exported

Kuwait from, respectively, Shi'a and Sunni Islamist forces.

In Bahrain, where Shi'a are the largest group and have been systematically marginalized, protests in 2011 met a harsh response, with killings, arrests and documented cases of torture. The crackdown was accomplished with the help of security forces from Saudi Arabia, Kuwait and the UAE. Part of the response of Bahrain's authorities was to destroy the pearl sculpture that gave its name to the Pearl Roundabout where the main protest rallies gathered.

Kuwait has long tolerated the relatively open voicing of dissent but the protests of 2011 went further than anything previously experienced. Months of protest induced the resignation of the prime minister and the dissolution of parliament. When elections in early 2012 produced an opposition majority the Emir manoeuvred skilfully to exclude it first from power and then from influence.

Elsewhere events were more muted. In UAE, five activists who attempted to mobilize popular rallies in the manner of the Arab Spring were arrested, tried, convicted, sentenced and then pardoned. Their original rallying cry had not brought large numbers onto the streets and while their supporters welcomed their release, it brought no further reverberations. The overwhelming impression in UAE, as in Qatar, was that the ruling families had provided well enough for most of their citizens and there was unlikely to be any real challenge to their authority. The situation of migrant labourers remained insecure and often worse, highlighted by working conditions in the construction of new stadia for the 2022 football World Cup.

With the Arab Spring held at bay in the Gulf, by 2014 and 2015 the GCC members were turning their attention to playing a regional role in resisting the extreme forces that had been unleashed in Syria, Iraq and Libya.

CHRONOLOGY continued

Oct *Kuwait* Government re-dissolves the previously reinstated 2009 parliament. Tens of thousands of pro-democracy demonstrators in Irada Square, Kuwait City.

Nov *UAE* 'UAE Five' found guilty, given prison sentences of 2 to 3 years, and pardoned the following day.

Dec *Kuwait* New parliamentary elections are boycotted by most Sunni Islamists.

2013 *Qatar* Emir Hamad bin Khalifa al-Thani hands power to his son Tamin.

2014 *Mar* Bahrain, Saudi Arabia and UAE withdraw ambassadors from Qatar to register objection to Qatari support for Muslim Brotherhood in Egypt and other Islamists.

July UAE aircraft bomb militant Islamist forces in Libya.

Sept Qatar pledges to support fight against ISIS. Joins with Bahrain, UAE, Jordanian, Saudi and US aircraft to attack ISIS positions in Syria.

US$
136,727
Qatar

US$
83,840
Kuwait

US$
59,845
UAE

US$
53,644
Saudi Arabia

US$
45,334
Oman

US$
43,851
Bahrain

WEALTH PER PERSON
GDP per capita, PPP
2013 or most recent data

world ranking

SOVEREIGN WEALTH FUNDS *2015*

Middle East rank	World rank	Country	Scale (USD billions)	Source oil & gas / other
–	1	Norway	880	oil
1	2	UAE – Abu Dhabi	775	oil
2	3	Saudi Arabia	750	oil
–	4	China 1	650	other
3	5	Kuwait	550	oil
–	6	China 2	545	other
–	7	China 3	400	other
–	8	Singapore	320	other
4	9	Qatar	255	oil
5	12	UAE – Dubai	175	oil
6	14	UAE – Abu Dhabi	90	oil
7	20	UAE – Abu Dhabi	70	oil
8	21	UAE – Abu Dhabi	65	oil
9	22	Libya	65	oil
10	23	Iran	55	oil

A Sovereign Wealth Fund is a state-owned fund of investment capital, usually accumulated through trade or selling off government assets. At the end of 2014 the combined wealth of a total of over **60 funds** was some **7 trillion US dollars**, of which almost **2 trillion** – some **29 per cent** – is held is by three Gulf kingdoms.

NETWORKS OF GRIEVANCE AND TERROR

The rise of *jihadi* war and terror is reshaping the politics of the Middle East. Where it will end is not yet clear. No single factor explains how and why it has happened.

Key among the threads that created today's networks of activism, zeal and conspiracy is Arab anger at Israel's occupation of Palestine and disillusionment at Arab governments' departure from the standards of a long gone golden age. Indeed, many see these two failures as essentially the same and argue that purer, more Islamic governments would have been able to stop Israel. The failure of Arab governments to deliver development to the majority of people, except when financed by oil income, and the extraordinary extravagance of the Arab oil elites further erode the leaders' legitimacy. Linking these and other factors is the sense of powerlessness they generate, a feeling shared for different reasons by Muslim youth in many other countries in Europe, Africa and Asia, bringing them into the recruiting orbit of the *jihadi* groups.

As well as Palestine, two other Arab countries are central to the rise of modern *jihadism*: Egypt and Saudi Arabia. In the mid-1960s, Saudi Arabia, opposed to Nasser and aligned directly against the Egyptian leader over the war in Yemen, was providing money and arms for a small revolutionary group in Egypt led by the political philosopher Sayyid Qutb. He was in the process of breaking the bounds of Islamism and the political framework of the Muslim Brotherhood and providing philosophical and religious justification for a new level of militancy and violence.

Qutb was too radical for the Nasser government and he was tried, convicted and sentenced to death. At the last moment, Nasser recognized that martyrdom would be a mistake but Qutb welcomed it and refused to make concessions to save his life. The same year, a teenager inspired by Qutb, Ayman al-Zawahiri, started a revolutionary cell in his high school; 45 years later he was leader of al-Qaeda.

The year 1979 was full of epochal events. Khomeini overthrew the Shah; although this was a Shi'a uprising, it was both inspirational and a gauntlet of challenge for Sunni Muslims. Egypt's President Sadat completed a journey of compromise and made peace with Israel; two years later, Sadat was assassinated by members of al-Jihad, which had grown from the cell that teenager had started. The USSR invaded Afghanistan and resistance to it by the mujahideen became an Islamic rallying cry and a training ground for *jihadis*. And militants took over the Grand Mosque in Mecca, demonstrating that for many Arabs the Wahhabist ruling Saud family was not Islamic enough.

By the mid-1980s, Saudi financial support for the mujahideen in Afghanistan, forerunners of today's *jihadis* in Iraq and Syria, was getting up to half a billion US dollars a year. Osama bin Laden, son of a well-connected family, was a prominent early supporter. He first visited Afghanistan in 1984 and on his return proved himself an effective fundraiser, generating $5–10 million in his

New York, USA
Feb 1993 Car bombing of World Trade Center kills 6 and injures 1,040

USA

New York

New York, USA
Sept 2001 9/11: 19 militants, prepared by al-Qaeda, hijack four airliners for suicide attacks on the World Trade Center, the Pentagon, and a further target. Death toll: 2,996

first month at it, apart from what he gave of his own money. But he did more than that; he also organized and mobilized, offering free travel and living expenses for every Arab who went to fight. Late in 1984 he set up a bureau service in Peshawar, on the Pakistan side of the Afghan border – the Arab 'Brigade of Strangers'. And from there he moved on to leading fighters into combat in Afghanistan. During this time he met Zawahiri and as Soviet withdrawal from Afghanistan got underway in 1988, they laid foundations for what became al-Qaeda.

Bin Laden's objectives soon outgrew Afghanistan. He sought a global Islamic revival and a new caliphate – the rule of the Prophet Mohammed's successors. Though he believed in the return to a pure version of Islam, bin Laden avoided taking very dogmatic positions on theology, so as to have as broad an alliance

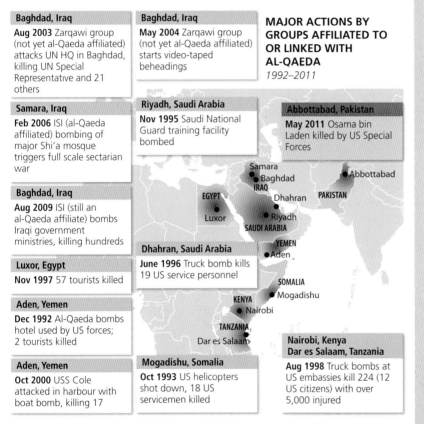

Baghdad, Iraq

Aug 2003 Zarqawi group (not yet al-Qaeda affiliated) attacks UN HQ in Baghdad, killing UN Special Representative and 21 others

Baghdad, Iraq

May 2004 Zarqawi group (not yet al-Qaeda affiliated) starts video-taped beheadings

MAJOR ACTIONS BY GROUPS AFFILIATED TO OR LINKED WITH AL-QAEDA
1992–2011

Samara, Iraq

Feb 2006 ISI (al-Qaeda affiliated) bombing of major Shi'a mosque triggers full scale sectarian war

Riyadh, Saudi Arabia

Nov 1995 Saudi National Guard training facility bombed

Abbottabad, Pakistan

May 2011 Osama bin Laden killed by US Special Forces

Baghdad, Iraq

Aug 2009 ISI (still an al-Qaeda affiliate) bombs Iraqi government ministries, killing hundreds

Dhahran, Saudi Arabia

June 1996 Truck bomb kills 19 US service personnel

Luxor, Egypt

Nov 1997 57 tourists killed

Aden, Yemen

Dec 1992 Al-Qaeda bombs hotel used by US forces; 2 tourists killed

Mogadishu, Somalia

Oct 1993 US helicopters shot down, 18 US servicemen killed

Nairobi, Kenya Dar es Salaam, Tanzania

Aug 1998 Truck bombs at US embassies kill 224 (12 US citizens) with over 5,000 injured

Aden, Yemen

Oct 2000 USS Cole attacked in harbour with boat bomb, killing 17

as possible working together. He identified the USA as the world power that was holding Islam back. To this end, bin Laden's strategy was apparently to provoke the USA into committing itself into war in the region. Based on what happened to the USSR in Afghanistan, the expectation was that, having over-reached itself, the USA would collapse. If the underlying analysis exaggerated Afghanistan's place in the demise of the USSR, the strategy itself was at least partially effective. The USA was provoked into intervention and many observers agreed it over-reached and would pay the price. On the day before US Special Forces killed him, bin Laden had no reason to feel defeated.

CHRONOLOGY *continued*

1989 *Feb* USSR completes withdrawal.

1990 *Sept* Bin Laden proposes and offers to organize a mujahideen army to defend Saudi Arabia from incursion by Iraq after its occupation of Kuwait. Offer is rejected.

1991–92 Bin Laden publicly criticizes Saudi government for hosting US troops and is expelled. Moves to Sudan.

1994 Taliban occupy Kandahar. Saudi Arabia revokes bin Laden's citizenship.

1996 Taliban take Kabul. Bin Laden moves from Sudan to Afghanistan.

1996 *Aug*, **1998** *Feb* Bin Laden issues two *fatwas* against USA and Americans.

2001 *Sept* Al-Qaeda attack on the World Trade Center and Pentagon.

Oct US and allies invade Afghanistan, oust the Taliban and force bin Laden into hiding.

2002 *Oct* Suicide and car bomb attacks on nightclubs in Bali, Indonesia, kill 202 people.

2003 *Mar–Apr* US and allies invade and occupy Iraq, oust Saddam.

May *Jihadi* group led by Musab al-Zarqawi starts operations in Iraq.

Aug Zarqawi group attacks UN HQ in Baghdad, killing UN Special Representative for Iraq and at least 21 others.

2004 *May* Zarqawi group starts videotaping beheadings in Baghdad.

Oct Zarqawi swears loyalty to bin Laden and founds Al-Qaeda in Iraq (AQI).

2006 *June* Zarqawi killed.

Oct AQI reorganized and renamed Islamic State of Iraq.

2007 US 'surge' allied with Sunni Awakening group weakens ISI.

2009 Iraq government targets Sunni Awakening, easing pressure on ISI.

2010 *Apr* ISI's leader is killed by US air strike.

May Abu Bakr al-Baghdadi is named leader of ISI.

2011 *May* Osama bin Laden killed in Pakistan by US Special Forces.

Foreign fighters in Iraq and Syria

By the start of 2015, there were estimated to be over 20,000 foreign fighters in Iraq and Syria coming from a total of 50 countries. It is likely these figures underestimate the number of countries from which fighters have been recruited, and the numbers of fighters are themselves only estimates. According to these generally accepted estimates, about 4,000 fighters came from 14 Western European countries. During 2014 reports indicated that recruitment from Europe and from some Middle Eastern countries including Morocco and Tunisia accelerated. This increased rate of recruitment, if real, was in all probability associated largely with ISIS, its increasing visibility and its victories. However, the total number of foreign fighters includes many who joined other groups.

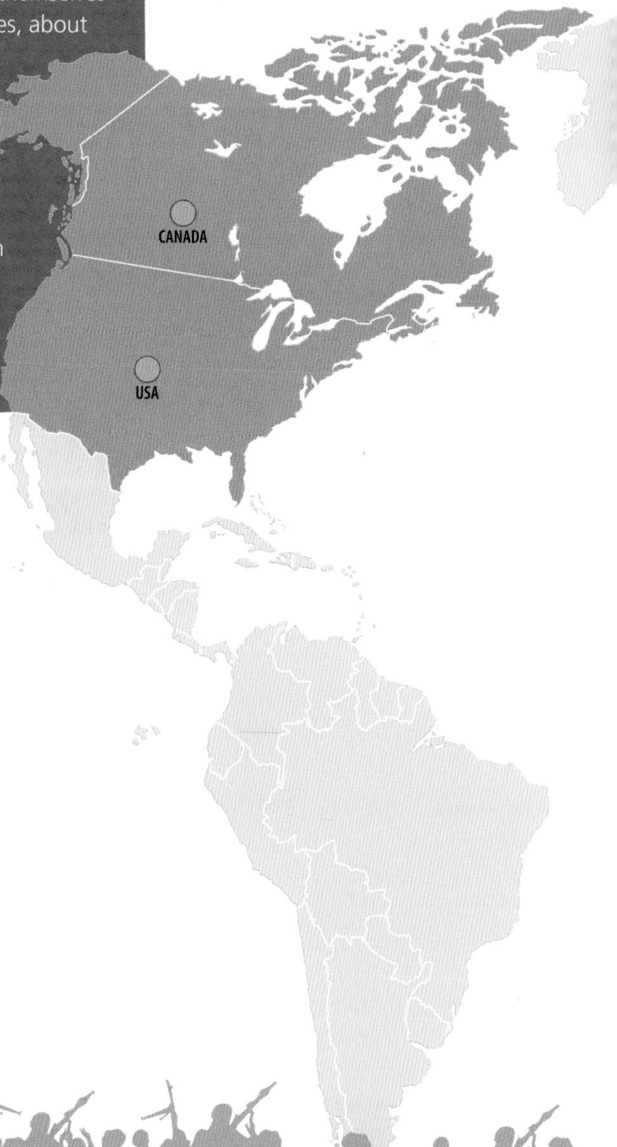

CANADA

USA

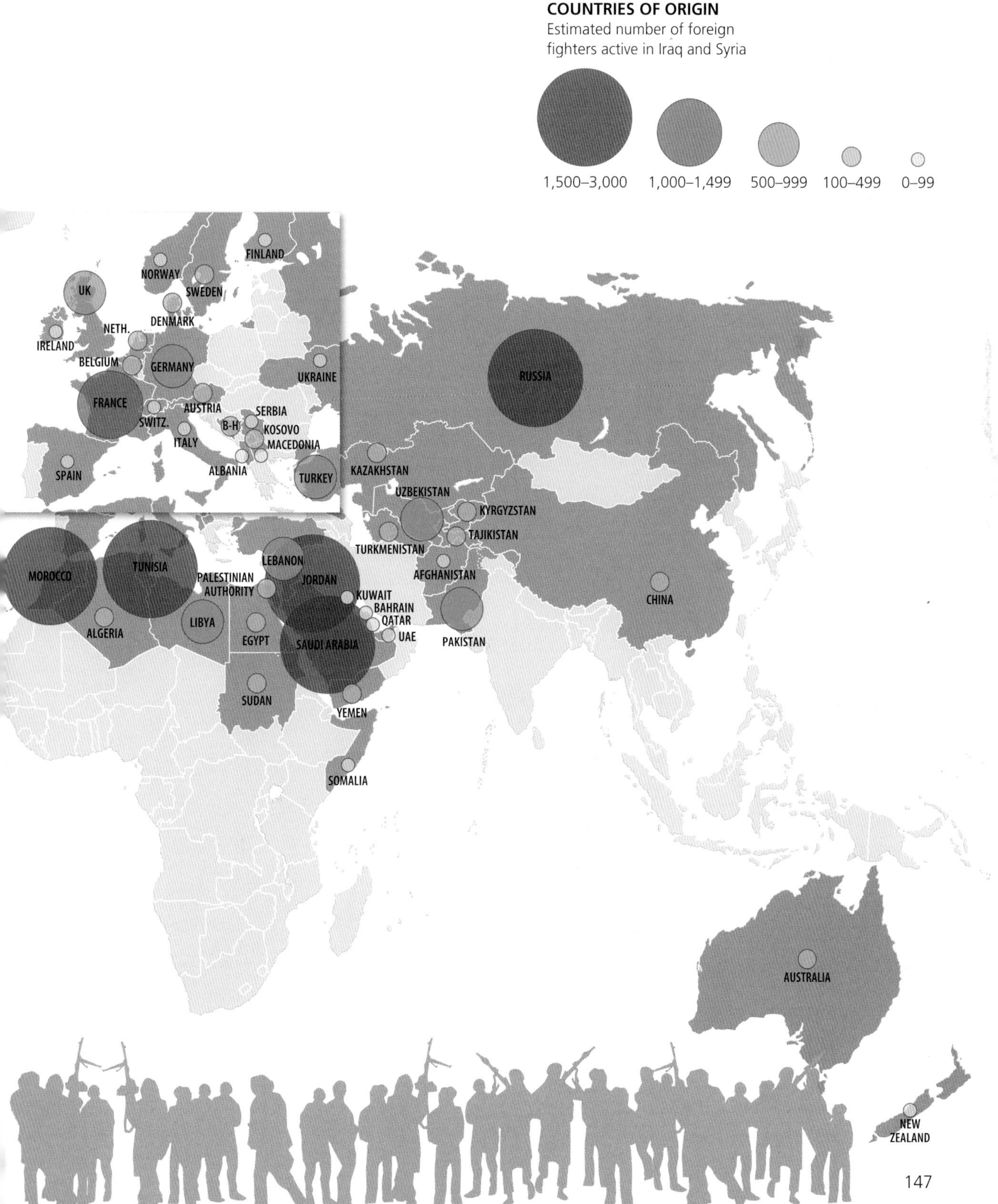

COUNTRIES OF ORIGIN
Estimated number of foreign
fighters active in Iraq and Syria

1,500–3,000 1,000–1,499 500–999 100–499 0–99

FINLAND

NORWAY
UK   SWEDEN

NETH.   DENMARK
IRELAND
BELGIUM

FRANCE   GERMANY   UKRAINE

AUSTRIA   SERBIA
SWITZ.   B-H   KOSOVO
ITALY   MACEDONIA
SPAIN   ALBANIA

TURKEY   KAZAKHSTAN

UZBEKISTAN
LEBANON   KYRGYZSTAN
MOROCCO   TUNISIA   JORDAN   TAJIKISTAN
PALESTINIAN   TURKMENISTAN
AUTHORITY   KUWAIT
BAHRAIN   AFGHANISTAN   RUSSIA
ALGERIA   LIBYA   QATAR   CHINA
EGYPT   SAUDI ARABIA   UAE
PAKISTAN
SUDAN

YEMEN

SOMALIA

AUSTRALIA

NEW
ZEALAND

Divided movement: ISIS splits from al-Qaeda

2011 *Oct* ISI sends group into Syria to join war against Assad regime.

2012 *Jan* The ISI Syria group announces itself as Jabhat al-Nusra – the al-Nusra Front.

July ISI organizes mass prison breaks in Iraq to increase its numbers.

2013 *Apr* ISI announces new name – Islamic State of Iraq and Syria (or Iraq and the Levant) – and states that al-Nusra is part of it. Al-Nusra rejects the claim and asks al-Qaeda for judgement.

May Al-Qaeda orders dissolution of ISIS into two separate organizations.

June ISIS dismisses al-Qaeda's judgement.

Aug ISIS starts systematic attacks on other insurgent groups in Syria.

Sept *Jihadi* groups in Syria form Islamic Front to oppose ISIS and Assad.

Oct ISIS opens an official Twitter account for the first time.

2014 *Jan* ISIS takes full control of Raqqa in Syria and announces it is the capital of the ISIS emirate. In Iraq, ISIS goes into Fallujah and Ramadi, though later pushed out of Ramadi.

Feb Al-Qaeda Central severs all ties with ISIS.

May A returned ISIS fighter kills four people at Jewish museum, Brussels, Belgium.

June ISIS takes Mosul, Iraq's 2nd biggest city, then Tikrit, and then the major oil refinery at Bajji. Al-Baghdadi announces the re-establishment of the Caliphate, renames ISIS the Islamic State and, in *July*, renames himself Caliph Ibrahim.

Aug US starts bombing ISIS positions in Iraq.

Sept US and Arab allies start bombing ISIS positions in Syria.

Some 35 years after the most radical forces in Islam were rallied to support Afghan resistance to Soviet occupation, the *jihadi* movement is rich, powerful, global – and divided against itself.

Al-Qaeda had become the pre-eminent *jihadi* group because of its capacity for the spectacular. Despite all the pressure from the USA and its relentless and ultimately successful hunt for Osama bin Laden, al-Qaeda remained the *jihadi* guiding light for a decade after 9/11. As many commentators noted, its strength was as a network based on a shared, powerful idea – preparing the way for the eventual Caliphate. Other groups were linked and affiliated with al-Qaeda and to lesser or greater degrees accepted the commands of its leader, bin Laden. But many acts by al-Qaeda were neither planned nor even endorsed beforehand by bin Laden.

The cauldron of conflict in Iraq produced something that became in time a stronger force and an even more powerful idea. Not content simply to prepare the way for the Caliphate, in 2014 ISIS declared itself to be the Islamic State and its leader to be the Caliph. It was an al-Qaeda affiliate that outgrew the franchise. Starting in Iraq as al-Qaeda in Iraq and later Islamic State of Iraq, it showed a taste for ostentatious bloodshed that bin Laden and his closest circle were never comfortable with. It successfully escalated sectarian war in Iraq and spread mayhem. But it staggered badly under the pressure of the US surge in 2007 and 2008.

Only when the Shi'a-led Iraqi government put pressure on the USA's main Sunni allies – the Sunni Awakening – precisely because they were Sunni, did ISI recover. Though its leader was killed in an air raid, a new and seemingly more effective leader Abu Bakr al-Baghdadi emerged. Making common cause with officials from Saddam Hussein's apparatus of repression, ISI consolidated in Iraq and then sent forces into Syria that became Jabhat al-Nusra.

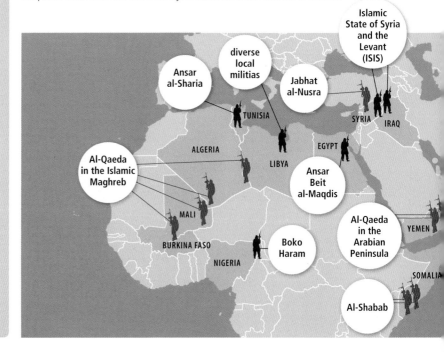

This quickly became the most effective of the anti-Assad groups. But when Baghdadi wanted to confirm his organization's standing in both Iraq and Syria, both the al-Nusra leadership and eventually Ayman al-Zawahiri who had become al-Qaeda's leader after bin Laden's death, demurred. This dispute was quickly turned by ISIS into a civil war within the civil war in Syria – a war of *jihadi* on *jihadi*.

To understand violence between Sunni Muslims who agree on the Caliphate and most matters of religious doctrine, it might be most useful to return to Sayyid Qutb, the Egyptian philosopher hanged in 1966, the inspiration for Zawahiri and many who have trodden the same path. Qutb saw a choice for Muslims, between the purity of Islam in its origins on the one hand and, on the other, Western values and ways of living that had compromised and corrupted ostensibly Muslim societies and rulers for centuries. Seen in this light, much of what seemed or claimed to be Islamic was not. Once somebody or some group has declared the right to affirm what is and what is not genuinely Islamic, and once that right has been contested, the seeds have been sown for continuing conflict.

In June 2014 the forces of ISIS advanced apparently irresistibly in Iraq. When they took Mosul, in June 2014, they took the banks – a haul of about $1.5 billion to add to a trove already standing at about $900 million. With that, ISIS became the richest *jihadi* force. Now it had the wealth to go with its ambitions. Reports suggest there was internal pressure within ISIS that might have led to a challenge to the leader Abu Bakr al-Baghdadi if he had not declared he was the Caliph. And once he was winning, there were many local forces in both Iraq and Syria – as well as other *jihadi* groups around the world – who were ready to support him. How long that would continue if his forces stopped winning was open to question.

CHRONOLOGY *continued*

2015 *Jan* Two gunmen attack office of *Charlie Hebdo* magazine in Paris, killing 12. Both gunmen are killed by French police in the following days.

Mar Three gunmen attack visitors at the Bardo Museum in Tunis, killing 21; ISIS claims responsibility though officials attribute attack to another group. Two of the gunmen are killed by security forces, other alleged conspirators arrested.

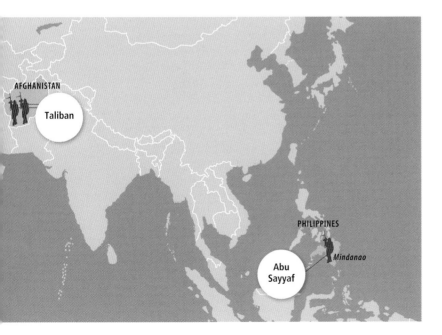

REACH: AL-QAEDA AND ISIS AFFILIATES AND LINKED GROUPS
mid-2015

Key *jihadi* forces' affiliation with:

al-Qaeda   ISIS

CONCLUSION

TRAJECTORIES OF CHANGE

One thing is certain: there will be change. All the rest is unclear. Today the condition of the Middle East is as bad and dangerous as it has ever been – dangerous for the people of the region and for the region's neighbours.

Surveying only the period since World War II on which this atlas focuses, there are more wars simultaneously than ever. The lethality level of today's wars is matched in the last 70 years only by the 1980s when Iran and Iraq were at war and Lebanon was collapsing. Networks capable of causing terror are more developed than they have ever been, and reach further around the world both in recruiting activists and in their capacity to inflict harm.

Today's *jihadis* differ from previous groups who also exported violence, such as Palestinian militants in the 1970s and 1980s, in another crucial respect. Earlier groups had precise if ambitious political demands – Israel out of Palestine, or US out of Saudi Arabia and the Gulf. But the groups born of al-Qaeda, including ISIS, have far-ranging, visionary, totalizing demands that reject without reservation the legitimacy of those of whom the demands are made. For many groups – ruling regimes, Shi'a Muslims, Yazidis, Copts – conceding to the demands of ISIS equates to accepting self-destruction. And as impressive as the fervour with which they pursue their cause is the pragmatic imprecision of what it is that they would put in place of the current set-up. ISIS and al-Qaeda have many differences but both refuse compromise and make it impossible.

Whatever it was that President Bush and his close ally Prime Minister Blair sought to achieve when they invaded Iraq without UN approval in 2003, ostensibly to find and render safe weapons of mass destruction that by then no longer existed, it was not this. What President Bush called a war on terror has succeeded only in producing both. Likewise, whatever President Sarkozy and Prime Minister Cameron, supported somewhat tepidly by President Obama, intended when they intervened in Libya to overthrow Qaddafi, it was not a situation in which 1,800 militia forces rampage across the country. In short, both interventions, both dubbed successes by over-hasty leaders, have failed completely and expensively.

> Whatever the 2003 invasion of Iraq was intended to achieve, it was not this

Of course, whatever the Arab Spring demonstrators in Tunis, Cairo, Benghazi and Damascus had in mind in 2011, it was, with the exception so far of Tunisia, not this either. But there should be more sympathy with people who put their lives and livelihoods on the line to try to achieve change peacefully against a repressive regime, than there is for privileged leaders who sat in safety and gave their orders but had, sadly, got it wholly wrong.

The difficulty at the moment is a deficiency in the options that are available for choice. Between what seemed like the prospect of chaos and the prospect of stability, many Egyptians who had taken the risk of demonstrating and standing up for freedom and democracy chose to support the overthrow of the democratically elected President and his replacement by the head of the military. And if the choice between ISIS and Sisi in Egypt – and comparable choices elsewhere – is unappetising, it is regrettably the case that the outside actors do little to help. They argue among themselves over whom to support, but they mean which group and which leader to support with arms and finance.

That a different approach might be possible has been proven by the patient, quiet and for long periods much-criticized diplomacy in which the USA, EU governments and Russia joined together to find a peaceful resolution with Iran of disputes over that country's nuclear programme. After years of hard work, the outcome is an agreement that, while controversial, has a reasonable chance of working for mutual benefit. Even the benefit of its Arab, American and Israeli critics. And it shows that, when they do not treat force and coercion as the default mode, outsiders can help.

That is important because, in a larger sense, the appearance of no real options is misleading. There are, in fact, clear options for the region – different paths along which it could develop, different trajectories. None is an easy option but then, the region's current condition does not permit easy ways out.

One option is the retention of the *status quo*, which varies across the region in the form it takes. The problem with that is that the forces of change that unleashed the Arab Spring in 2011 are still real, even if currently baulked in most places, so the *status quo* will not be still. And the forces of religiously affiliated militancy, both Sunni *jihadis* and Shi'a militants, are both real and hyper-active. It is in that militancy that the second option takes shape, based on a long, miserable period of strife and warfare. On current evidence, the basis for this in popular consent is weak; Iran is seen by many insightful observers as the most secular of Middle Eastern countries precisely because of the attempted imposition of religious adherence. The problem, therefore, is that it is an option of permanent instability.

The third option is the return in time of the energies and optimism of the Arab Spring and another wave of change. The problem here is that the forces of reaction will also persist and some of that optimism is bound to be disappointed.

The forces of change that unleashed the Arab Spring in 2011 are still real

———

When militant forerunners of today's *jihadis* seized the Great Mosque in Mecca in 1979, the ones who survived the 10 day siege were imprisoned and executed – 63 of them in 8 towns and cities around the kingdom. In Riyadh, the executions were carried out in the market place. The one who went first to face the executioner did so cursing the authorities. As the executioner swung his sword, the *jihadi* flexed his back and his neck rose towards the descending sword.

Twenty-six years later a young Tunisian walked into a hotel on the seafront in Sousse, Tunisia, and started shooting defenceless tourists. Amid the confused accounts that emerged of the massacre, there came out clear narratives of the hotel staff who grouped together and made themselves a human wall between the killer and his intended victims, and of the lone builder who called the killer a dog and flung tiles at him as he tried and failed to make his escape.

They are two moments, each extraordinary, each speaking about valour and commitment – but radically opposite in the intent, in the values expressed through the individuals' action, and in the implications that each one carries if taken as a model for behaviour. Which one wins out in the thoughts and feelings of ordinary Middle Easterners will ultimately define the region's future.

ACKNOWLEDGEMENTS

I have read, listened to and learned from the words of many fine writers and thinkers, researchers and reporters on the Middle East. They are too many and varied to mention here; while many are referenced among the sources I have drawn on for this atlas, there are even more to whom I have also paid attention. Despite the often fundamental and sometimes vitriolic disagreements among them, they form a kind of community of thought and expert knowledge on which a general work of reference such as this must draw. Without them, the dedication they bring to their research, the depth of vision and historical or regional sweep that some of them display, or the focused concern with the detail that others have, the sort of broad overview that I have attempted in this book would not be possible. So it feels appropriate to start my acknowledgements by thanking them.

More directly, this book has both a team behind it and a history, for this is its third edition. Sarah Mullin was a tremendous research assistant for this iteration, hard working and creative, inquisitive and good humoured. While a third edition draws heavily on the preceding editions for some of its material, the pace of change in the Middle East is so fast that Sarah worked on every part of the atlas. At the same time, I have continued to rely on the excellent work that was done for the first edition, published in 2006, by Sarah's predecessor, Trude Strand. Trude's work on the atlas was financially supported by the Peace Research Institute Oslo, and I would like to record my gratitude to the Institute again.

While expressing these thanks, I want also to add that any and all errors of fact and interpretation are mine.

The book and my morale have benefited from the support and interest of publishers on both sides of the Atlantic – Dan Raymond-Barker and Chris Brazier at New Internationalist in Oxford, England, and Emily Murdoch Baker and Matt Giarratano at Penguin Random House in New York.

The editorial and design team at Myriad Editions has worked on this book with the flexibility, professionalism and creativity that I have become accustomed to over the three editions of this book and four editions of the *State of the World Atlas*. Our aim with this book was to tell the story through a variety of means – text, maps, chronologies, infographics – working together. For that to be possible, the editors have to understand the design side of the work and the designer has to have a grasp of the editorial side. I think it is the fact that they achieve that without really noticing it that makes the Myriad team so special. My editors this time were Jannet King and Dawn Sackett. They both brought flair and discipline to the task of editing my raw material. The combination of Isabelle Lewis's cartographic and design work with the artistic coordination provided by Corinne Pearlman is peerless. All of this is led and coordinated by Candida Lacey with style, empathy and integrity. It has been a pleasure working with them all.

REFERENCES

KEY TEXTS
Together, these books and reports provide an excellent overview of the region
and have informed the writing of this atlas:
*Arab Development Challenges Report 2011: Towards the Developmental
State in the Arab Region.* UNDP.
Fromkin D. *A Peace to End all Peace.* London: Phoenix Press, 2000.
Hourani A. *A History of the Arab Peoples.* London: Faber & Faber, 1991.
Human Development Report 2014. UNDP.
Mansfield P. *A History of the Middle East*, 4th edn. Penguin: London, 2013.
Nakash Y. *Reaching for Power: The Shi'a in the Modern Arab World.* Prince-
ton UP, 2006.
Nasr V. *The Shia Revival.* New York: WW Norton. 2007.
Rogerson B. *North Africa.* London: Duckworth Overlook, 2013.
Stern J, Berger JM. *ISIS: The state of terror.* London: William Collins, 2015.
Wright L. *The Looming Tower: Al-Qaeda's road to 9/11.* 2nd edition. London:
Penguin, 2011.

9–14 Introduction
Armstrong K. *A History of Jerusalem.* London: HarperCollins, 1997.
BBC Country profiles. www.bbc.co.uk
CIA World Factbook. Middle East. www.cia.gov
Council on Foreign Relations. Middle East and North Africa. www.cfr.org
Encyclopaedia Britannica. Middle East. www.britannica.com
National Geographic *Atlas of the Middle East* 1st and 2nd editions. National
Geographic, 2003 & 2008.
US State Department. Near Eastern Affairs. www.state.gov
Wikipedia. Middle East. www.wikipedia.org

18–21 THE OTTOMAN EMPIRE & Decline and legacy
Baron JPD Kinross. *The Ottoman Centuries.* New York: Perennial, 2002.
Gilbert M. *In Ishmael's House: A History of Jews in Muslim Lands.* Yale UP, 2011.
Mango A. *Ataturk.* London: John Murray, 1999.
Mango A. *The Turks Today.* London: John Murray, 2004.
Norwich JJ. *A Short History of Byzantium.* New York: Vintage Books, 1999.
Palmer A. *The Decline and Fall of the Ottoman Empire.* London: John Murray,
1992.

22–25 EUROPEAN COLONIALISM & Colonial impact
Palmer A. *The Decline and Fall of the Ottoman Empire.* London: John Murray,
1992.
Yapp ME. *The Making of the Modern Near East 1792–1923.* London: Long-
man, 1987.
Yapp ME. *The Near East Since the First World War.* New York: Longman, 1996.

**26–29 THE NEW MIDDLE EAST AFTER WORLD WAR I & A new regional
order**
Barr J. *A Line in the Sand.* Simon & Schuster, 2011.
Yapp ME. *The Making of the Modern Near East 1792–1923.* London: Long-
man, 1987.
Yapp ME. *The Near East Since the First World War.* New York: Longman, 1996.

**30–35 DECOLONIZATION AND ARAB NATIONALISM, Independence
and unity & The pan-Arab dream**
Dawisha A. Requiem for Arab nationalism. *The Middle East Quarterly*, Winter
2003, 10 (1).
Hourani A. *Arabic Thought in the Liberal Age 1798–1939.* Cambridge: Cambridge University Press, 1962, 1983.
Khashan H. Revitalizing Arab nationalism. *The Middle East Quarterly*, March
2000, 7 (1).
Yapp ME. *The Near East Since the First World War.* New York, Longman, 1996.

**36–41 THE FORMATION OF THE STATE OF ISRAEL, Zionism and anti-
semitism & Flight and exile**
Abu Sitta S. *Atlas of Palestine 1948.* London: Palestine Land Society, 2005.
Gilbert M. *In Ishmael's House: A History of Jews in Muslim Lands.* Yale UP,
2011.
Gilbert M. *Israel: A History.* London: Black Swan, 1999.
HMG, *Palestine: Statement of Policy by His Majesty's Government in the
United Kingdom 1937*, His Majesty's Stationary Office, London. (And State-
ment of same title from 1938 and 1939).
Shepherd N. *Ploughing the Sand: British Rule in Palestine.* London: John
Murray, 1999.
Shimoni G. *The Zionist Ideology.* University Press of New England, 1995.

Shlaim A. *The Iron Wall: Israel and the Arab World.* London: Penguin, 2001.
Uppsala Conflict Data Program / PRIO Armed Conflict Dataset:
www.pcr.uu.se/research/ucdp/datasets/ucdp_prio_armed_conflict_dataset/
REGISTERED PALESTINIAN REFUGEES
UNWRA. www.unrwa.org/

42–45 OIL & The oil market
BP Statistical Review for World Energy June 2015: www.bp.com/content/
dam/bp/pdf/Energy-economics/statistical-review-2015/bp-statistical-review-
of-world-energy-2015-full-report.pdf
CHRONOLOGY
Timelines of History. Oil Timeline.
DATA
BP Statistical Review of World Energy June 2015. www.bp.com/en/global/
corporate/about-bp/energy-economics/statistical-review-of-world-energy/
statistical-review-downloads.html, specific pages are noted below.
PROVED OIL RESERVES WORLDWIDE
Oil – proved reserves.
CRUDE OIL PRODUCTION
Oil production – tonnes.
IMPORTS FROM MIDDLE EAST
Oil – inter-area movement & Oil consumption – tonnes.
OIL CONSUMPTION WORLDWIDE
Oil consumption – tonnes.
WORLD OIL PRICE FLUCTUATIONS
Oil – crude prices since 1861.
THE MIDDLE EAST'S OIL EXPORT MARKETS
Oil – inter-area movement & Oil consumption – tonnes.
OIL ROUTES AND STRATEGIC CHOKE POINTS
World Oil Transit Chokepoints. US Energy Information Administration (EIA).
www.eia.gov/countries/regions-topics.cfm?fips=wotc&trk=p3

46–47 US PRESENCE
Lacey R. *Inside the Kingdom.* Arrow Books, 2010, p291.
Oren MB. *Power, Faith and Fantasy: America in the Middle East 1776 to the
Present.* New York: W. W. Norton & Co, 2007.
Wikipedia: First Barbary War; Iran–Contra affair.
CHRONOLOGY
Main source – BBC news. www.bbc.co.uk
US FORCE IN THE MIDDLE EAST SINCE 1957
Al Arabiya, U.S. bombs ISIS near Baghdad for 'first time', 16 September 2014.
Barrabi T. US Airstrikes in Syria: Timeline of Events that Led Obama to Target
Islamic State. *International Business Times*, 23 September 2014.
BBC. Libya country profile timeline.
BBC. Libya: US, UK and France attack Gaddafi forces. 20 March 2011.
Roggio B. Charting the data for US air strikes in Yemen, 2002–2014. *The
Long War Journal*.

48–49 Angles of influence
BOOTS ON THE GROUND AND BOATS IN THE WATER
June 2014, Sept 2003, Sept 1991. Active Duty Military Personnel by Service by
Region/Country (Updated Quarterly). DoD Personnel, Workforce Reports &
Publications. DMDC. https://www.dmdc.osd.mil/appj/dwp/dwp_reports.jsp
US ECONOMIC AND MILITARY ASSISTANCE
Blanchard CM. Lebanon: Background and U.S. Policy. Congressional Research
Service, 14 February 2014.
Katzman K. Iraq: Politics, Governance, and Human Rights. Congressional
Research Service, 15 September 2014.
Sharp JM. Egypt: Background and US relations. Congressional Research
Service, 5 June 2014.
Sharp JM. U.S. Foreign Aid to Israel. Congressional Research Service, 11 April
2014.
Sharp JM. Jordan: Background and U.S. Relations. Congressional Research
Service, 8 May 2014.
Sharp JM. Yemen: Background and U.S. Relations. Congressional Research
Service, 6 February 2014.
Zanotti J. The Palestinians: Background and U.S. Relations. Congressional
Research Service, 13 January 2014.

52–53 POLITICS AND RIGHTS
POLITICAL SYSTEMS
CIA World Factbook. Algeria.
BBC. Algeria profile – leaders.
Wikipedia. List of countries by system of government.

CAPITAL PUNISHMENT
Amnesty International. Death penalty 2013: Small number of countries
    trigger global spike in executions. March 26 2014. www.amnestyusa.org
INTERNATIONAL AGREEMENTS
United Nations Treaty Collection. www.treaties.un.org:
Convention on the Rights of the Child.
International convention on the prevention of the crime of genocide 1948.
Convention on the elimination of all forms of discrimination against women
    1979.
Convention against torture and other cruel, inhuman or degrading treatment
    or punishment 1984.
HUMAN RIGHTS ABUSES
Amnesty International. Amnesty International Report 2013. The State of the
    World's Human Rights.
Amnesty International. Amnesty International Report 2012. The State of the
    World's Human Rights. Human Rights Watch. World Report 2014.
Human Rights Watch. World Report 2013.

54–55 FAITH
FAITH POPULATIONS
CIA World Factbook.
Supplemented for Bahrain, Kuwait by: How many Shi'a are there in the
    world? www.islamicweb.com/beliefs/cults/shia_population.htm
Supplemented for Egypt, Israel, Oman, UAE, Yemen by:
Sunni and Shia: The Worlds of Islam. www.pbs.org/wnet/wideangle/episodes/
    pilgrimage-to-karbala/sunni-and-shia-the-worlds-of-islam/1737/
International Coalition for Religious Freedom country reports.
    www.religiousfreedom.com/index.php?option=com_content&view=arti-
    cle&id=63&Itemid=29

56–57 ETHNICITY
ETHNICITY AND LANGUAGE
BBC. Country Profiles.
CIA World Factbook.
The Gulf/2000 Project. Middle East Ethnic Groups. gulf2000.columbia.edu.
Vital Statistics: Population Statistics for Israel. www.jewishvirtuallibrary.org/
    jsource/Society_&_Culture/newpop.html
World Population Statistics, Israel Population 2013.
    www.worldpopulationstatistics.com/israel-population-2013/

58–59 POPULATION AND URBANIZATION
TOTAL POPULATION
The World Bank. Indicators. http://data.worldbank.org/indicator/SP.POP.TOT
IMMIGRANTS AS A %..
United Nations Department of Economics and Social Affairs.
http://esa.un.org/unmigration/TIMSA2013/migrantstocks2013.htm?mtotals
POPULATION 1960 AND 2012
The World Bank. Indicators. http://data.worldbank.org/indicator/SP.POP.TOTL
URBAN POPULATION AS % OF TOTAL POPULATION
The World Bank. Indicators. http://data.worldbank.org/indicator/SP.URB.TOTL.
    IN.ZS
URBAN POPULATION GROWTH
The World Bank. Indicators. http://data.worldbank.org/indicator/SP.URB.TOTL

60–61 WEALTH AND INEQUALITY
Mthuli N, John A and Kjell H. Inequality, Economic Growth, and Poverty in the
    Middle East and North Africa (MENA), African Development Bank, Working
    Paper No. 195, December 2013.
Arab Development Challenges Report 2011: Towards the Developmental
    State in the Arab Region. UNDP, 2011.
WEALTH PER PERSON
The World Bank. Indicators. http://data.worldbank.org/indicator/NY.GNP.
    PCAP.PP.CD
WHERE THE WEALTH GOES
United Nations Development Programme. https://data.undp.org/dataset/Ta-
    ble-1-Human-Development-Index-and-its-components/wxub-qc5k
HUMAN DEVELOPMENT
United Nations Development Programme. https://data.undp.org/dataset/Ta-
    ble-3-Inequality-adjusted-Human-Development-Inde/9jnv-7hyp
REMITTANCES
Migration and remittances, World Bank. http://econ.worldbank.org/WBSITE/
    EXTERNAL/EXTDEC/EXTDECPROSPECTS/0,,contentMDK:22759429~pageP-
    K:64165401~piPK:64165026~theSitePK:476883,00.html#Remittances

62–63 GENDER RELATIONS
FEMALE LITERACY RATE AS A PERCENTAGE OF MALE
The Global Gender Gap Report 2013, World Economic Forum, Switzerland,
    2013, Appendix D.

FEMALE EARNED INCOME AS ESTIMATED RATIO TO MALE
The Global Gender Gap Report 2013, World Economic Forum, Switzerland,
    2013, Appendix D.
WOMEN'S RIGHT TO VOTE
A timeline of women's right to vote. The Guardian, 6 July 2011.
WOMEN IN PARLIAMENT
The World Bank. Indicators.
    http://data.worldbank.org/indicator/SG.GEN.PARL.ZS
LIFE EXPECTANCY
The World Bank. Indicators. http://data.worldbank.org/indicator
GENDER INEQUALITY
Human Development Report 2014. UNDP, 2014. Table 3, Gender Inequality
    Index.

64–65 WATER
WATER DEMAND AND SUPPLY
World Bank. Freshwater withdrawals: http://data.worldbank.org/indicator/
    ER.H2O.FWTL.K3
World Bank. Freshwater resources: http://data.worldbank.org/indicator/
    ER.H2O.INTR.K3
WATER USE
World Bank. Agriculture: http://data.worldbank.org/indicator/ER.H2O.FWAG.ZS
World Bank. Domestic : http://data.worldbank.org/indicator/ER.H2O.FWDM.ZS
World Bank. Industry: http://data.worldbank.org/indicator/ER.H2O.FWIN.ZS
Tunisia: CIA World Factbook
DRINKING WATER AND SANITATION
World Bank. http://data.worldbank.org/indicator/SH.STA.ACSN
World Bank. Total population: http://data.worldbank.org/indicator/SH.H2O.
    SAFE.ZS
World Bank. Rural population: http://data.worldbank.org/indicator/SH.H2O.
    SAFE.RU.ZS
World Bank. Urban population: http://data.worldbank.org/indicator/SH.H2O.
    SAFE.UR.ZS
EXAMPLES OF WATER USED AS A WEAPON
Pacific Institute. The World's Water 2014 Vol 8. Water brief 3: Water Conflict:
    Events, Trends and Analysis (2011-2012).
WATER SECURITY: IRAQ AND ISIS EXAMPLE
Maplecroft. Lack of stable supplies may lead to future oil price hikes and
    regional unrest. New Products and Analysis. www.maplecroft.com
Maplecroft 2014; incorporates data from the World Resources Institute ©
    2013 - licensed under the Creative Commons Attribution 3.0 License.
    http://maplecroft.com/about/news/water_stress_index.html
Vidal J. Water supply key to outcome of conflicts in Iraq and Syria, experts
    warn, The Guardian. 2 July 2014.

66–67 REFUGEES
REFUGEES
UNHCR Global Trends 2014. Table 1.
UNHCR Global Trends 2012. Table 1.
UNHCR Global Trends 2011. Table 1.
UNHCR Global Trends 2010. Table 1.
UNRWA. UNRWA in figures 2014, 2013, 2012, 2011, 2010.
    www.unrwa.org/resources
WHERE REFUGEES COME FROM
UNHCR Statistical Online Population Database, United Nations High Commis-
    sioner for Refugees (UNHCR), Data extracted: (03)(07)08/07/2014.
    www.unhcr.org/statistics/populationdatabase
UNRWA. UNRWA in figures. www.unrwa.org/resources
TOP FIVE HOST COUNTRIES IN 2014…
CIA World Factbook. Field listings – internally displaced persons.
UNRWA. UNRWA in figures 2014. www.unrwa.org
UNHCR Statistical Online Population Database, United Nations High Commis-
    sioner for Refugees (UNHCR), Data extracted: (03)(07)08/07/2014.
    www.unhcr.org/statistics/populationdatabase
National populations of Jordan, Lebanon and Syria: UN Department of Eco-
    nomic and Social Affairs, World Population prospects: The 2012 Revision,
    New York, UN, 2013

68–69 WARS
Uppsala Conflict Data Program (Date of retrieval: 22/08/2014) UCDP Conflict
    Encyclopaedia (UCDP database): www.ucdp.uu.se/database, Uppsala
    University. Armed conflict dataset: UCDP/PRIO Armed Conflict Dataset v.4-
    2014, 1946–2013

72–73 ISRAEL AND PALESTINE
CHRONOLOGY
BBC: Palestinian territories profile; Hosni Mubarak profile; Benjamin Netan-
    yahu profile; Q&A: Israeli deadly raid on aid flotilla.
BBC. Israel completes Gaza withdrawal, 12 September 2005.

Beaumont P. Palestinian unity government of Fatah and Hamas sworn in. *The Guardian*, 2 June 2014.
Bronner E. Weighing Netanyahu as Peace Maker. *The New York Time*s, 15 Dec 2009.
Butchner T. Hamas fighters now a well-organised force. *The Telegraph*, 05 January 2009.
Gordon MR, Rudoren J. Kerry Achieves Deal to Revive Mideast Talks. *The New York Times*, 19 July 2013.
Middle East Eye, Timeline: Israel–Gaza conflict.
Schneider H. Israel's Netanyahu Endorses Creation of Palestinian State but Attaches Conditions. *The Washington Post*, 15 June 2009.
Shlaim A. For Israel, the beginning of wisdom is to admit its mistakes. *The Guardian*, 7 Sept 2014.
Report of the United Nations Fact Finding Mission on the Gaza Conflict. 2009. United Nations Human Rights Council.
Wikipedia: Munich Massacre; 1982 Lebanon War.

ISRAEL'S WARS
Gilbert M. *Israel: A History.* London: Black Swan, 1999.
Hirst D. *Beware of small state*s. Faber & Faber, 2010. p116.
Shlaim A. No sentiments in war. *The Guardian*, 31 May 2008.
Wikipedia: List of wars involving Israel; 1982 Lebanon War.

74–75 Land vs Peace
THE SETTLEMENTS
Middle East Peace Institute. www.fmep.org/settlement_info
West Bank 2014: Office for the Coordination of Humanitarian Affairs (OCHA).
Strickland PO. Residents in occupied Golan Heights fear creeping Israeli presence. *Middle East Eye*.
Wikipedia. East Jerusalem and Golan Heights, 2014.
OVERALL POPULATION
Estimated Population in the Palestinian Territory Mid-Year by Governorate, 1997–2016. Palestinian Central Bureau of Statistics.
Israel: Monthly Bulletin of Statistics – September 2014. Central Bureau of Statistics. www.cbs.gov.il/reader/cw_usr_view_Folder?ID=141
OCCUPATION
OCHA. September 2014.
WATER
Average daily water consumption: Palestinian Water Society. Pending Water Issues between Israelis and Palestinians. www.pwa.ps/page.aspx?id=QdC-Coda1607510817aQdCCod
Percentage of West Bank mountain aquifer taken by Israelis: OCHA. Not enough water in the West Bank? Visualising Palestine in partnership with EWASH. March 2013.
Percentage of coastal aquifer taken by Israelis and destruction of Gaza water supply: EWASH. Gaza Strip. www.ewash.org/en/?view=79YOcy0nNs3D-76djuyAnkDDT
Nassar W. In Pictures: Gaza water crisis worsens, *Al Jazeera*. 12 May 2014.

76–77 Uprising
DEATH TOLL
www.btselem.org/statistics

78–79 The Occupied Territories
DAMAGE IN GAZA & INTENSITY OF ISRAELI OPERATIONS AGAINST GAZA
2009–14 Density Comparison of Destroyed and Damaged Structures in Gaza Strip, occupied Palestinian Territory. September 2014, Copyright CNES 2014. http://reliefweb.int/sites/reliefweb.int/files/resources/UNOSAT_A3_DensityAnalysisComparison.pdf
WEST BANK ARCHIPELAGO
West Bank Access Restrictions, September 2014, United Nations Office for the Coordination of Humanitarian Affairs occupied Palestinian Territory. http://reliefweb.int/map/occupied-palestinian-territory/occupied-palestinian-territory-west-bank-access-restrictions

80–81 Force and peace
International Crisis Group, After Gaza, Middle East Report N°68, 2 August 2007.
COMPARATIVE MILITARY POWER
Israel Military Strength: Global Fire Power. www.globalfirepower.com.
The Military Balance 114:1. 2014. Routledge. Accessed at BL 11 Apr 2014.
IRON DOME
Bolton O. Israel's Iron Dome in 60 seconds. *The Telegraph*. 21 July 2014.
Heinrichs RL. How Israel's Iron Dome Anti-Missile System Works. *Business Insider*. 30 July 2014.
Lipin M. Israel's Iron Dome Missile Defence System. 20 November 2012. Voice of America. www.voanews.com
Sharp JM. U.S. Foreign Aid to Israel. Congressional Research Service. 11 April 2014.

The Military Balance 114:1. 2014. Routledge. Accessed at BL 11 Apr 2014 Israel Military.

82–83 LEBANON
Fisk R. *Pity the Nation: Lebanon at War*, 3rd edn. Oxford: Oxford University Press, 2001.
Fisk R. *The Great War for Civilisation*, London: Fourth Estate, 2005.
Harris W. *Lebanon: A History 600–2011*. Oxford UP, 2012.
Hirst D. *Beware of Small States*. Faber & Faber, 2010.
Khatib L, Matar D, Alshaer A. *The Hizbullah Phenomenon*. London: Hurst, 2014.
Norton AR. *Hezbollah: A short history*. Princeton UP, 2011.
Salibi, K. *A House of Many Mansions. The History of Lebanon Reconsidered*. London: I.B. Tauris, 2011.

84–85 Peace and occupation
REFUGEES IN LEBANON
UNRWA, Lebanon, camp profiles and locations. www.unrwa.org
NUMBER AND ORIGINS OF SYRIAN REFUGEES IN LEBANON
www.iiss.org/-/media/Images/Publications/Strategic%20Survey/2014/Syria-Lebanon-refugees-630x506.jpg

86–89 ALGERIA
International Crisis group. The Algerian Crisis: Not Over Yet.

90–93 THE KURDS & The fight for freedom
CIA World Factbook.
Encyclopedia of Diasporas. Springer, 2005.
*The cultural situation of the Kurd*s, European Parliament Report, 2006.
Institut Kurde de Paris. www.institutkurde.org
Jewish center for Jewish-Christian Relations. www.jcjcr.org
McDowall D. *A Modern History of the Kurds*. London: IB Tauris. 2000.
Mango A. *The Turks* Today. London: John Murray, 2004.
van Bruinesen M. Aga, *Shaikh and State*. London: Zed Press, 1992.
KURDISH DIALECTS
McDowall D. A Modern History of the Kurds, Third Edition. London: IB Tauris. 2004.
Kurdish Academy of Language. www.kurdishacademy.org
Zürcher E J. Turkey: A Modern History. London: IB Tauris, London, 1998.
DISCRIMINATION IN SYRIA
Gunter MM. *Out of Nowhere: The Kurds of Syria in Peace and War*. Hurst, 2014.

94–95 IRAN
Akbar MJ. *The Shade of Swords*. London: Routledge, 2002.
ETHNIC DIVERSITY
Iran Primer. United States Institute of Peace. www.usip.org
The Iran–Pakistan Border Barrier. *Geocurrents*, 13 May 2011.

96–97 Revolutionary cycles
CONSTITUTION OF THE ISLAMIC REPUBLIC
N. Rapp. Associated Press.
IRAN'S NUCLEAR SITES
BBC. Iran's key nuclear sites, 15 October 2013.
Beauchamp Z. An expert on nuclear weapons explains the very basics of Iran's nuclear program. *Vox*, 13 November 2014.
IRAN'S NUCLEAR PROGRAMME
BBC. Iran profile.
Timeline on Iran's nuclear program. *The New York Times*, 20 March 2013.
ATTACKS ON IRANIAN NUCLEAR SCIENTISTS
Blair D. Iran nuclear scientist dead: mysterious recent deaths and disappearances. *The Telegraph*, 11 January 2012.
Hasan M. Iran's nuclear scientists are not being assassinated. They are being murdered. *The Guardian*, 16 January 2012.
Kasperkevic J. Someone has been killing off Iranian scientists for five years and it isn't likely to stop. *Business Insider*, 12 January 2012.

98–99 THE IRAN–IRAQ WAR
THE FIVE MOST LETHAL MODERN WARS
Iacina B & Gleditsch NP. Monitoring Trends in Global Combat: A New Dataset of Battle Deaths. *European Journal of Population* (2005) 21. pp 145–166.

100–103 IRAQ & The Ba'ath Party
ETHNIC AND RELIGIOUS DIVERSITY & DIMINISHING DIVERSITY
BBC. Country Profiles.
CIA World Factbook. Iraq.
Encyclopaedia Britannica.
The Gulf/2000 Project. *Middle East Ethnic Groups*. gulf2000.columbia.edu.
Gilbert M. *In Ishmael's House: A History of Jews in Muslim Lands*. Yale UP, 2011.

104–105 THE GULF WARS
UN SECURITY COUNCIL RESOLUTIONS
BBC. Flashback: The 1991 Iraqi uprisings. 21 August 2007.
Draft UN Security Council resolution by Spain, UK and USA, 7 March 2003.
www.casi.org.uk/info/undocs/scres/2003/20030307draft.pdf
Flashback: The 1991 Iraqi uprisings. BBC.
Gulf/2000 Project, gulf2000.columbia.edu/
Jabar FA. Why the uprisings failed, Middle East Report 176, May/June 1992,
Middle East Research and Information Project.
Open Letter to President Clinton, 19 February 1988.
www.centerforsecuritypolicy.org/1998/02/24/open-letter-to-the-president-4/
MAIN COALITION FORCES
Wikipedia. Coalition of the Gulf War.
AFTERMATH
1991 Uprising in Iraq.
http://military.wikia.com/wiki/1991_uprisings_in_Iraq

106–107 Sanctions and the second war
Blix H. *Disarming Iraq.* Bloomsbury: London, 2004.
WAR FROM THE AIR
BBC News.
Wikipedia.
US-LED COALITION FORCES IN THE 2003 GULF WAR
International Institute for Strategic Studies, Strategic Survey, 2005, Routledge/
Taylor & Francis, London.
CASUALTIES
Iraq Body Count. www.iraqbodycount.net/database
Iraq Coalition Casualties. http://icasualties.org

108–109 War after war
IRAQI CIVILIAN DEATHS FROM VIOLENCE
Iraq Body Count. www.iraqbodycount.org/
COMPARATIVE BODY COUNT
Total US-led coalition military fatalities 2003–2015: Iraq Coalition Casualty
Count. http://icasualties.org/
International Crisis Group, Shiite Politics in Iraq: The Role of the Supreme
Council, Middle East Report N°70, 15 November 2007.
International Crisis Group, Iraq's Civil War, the Sadrists and the Surge, Middle
East Report N°72, 7 February 2008

110–111 THE NEW IRAQ
Internal Displacement Monitoring Centre. Iraq.
International Crisis Group, Shiite Politics in Iraq: The Role of the Supreme
Council, Middle East Report N°70, 15 November 2007.
International Crisis Group, Iraq's Civil War, the Sadrists and the Surge, Middle
East Report N°72, 7 February 2008.
CHRONOLOGY
BBC. Iraq profile.
Infoplease. Iraq timeline 2010.
**IRAQI CIVILIAN DEATHS FROM VIOLENCE & IRAQI DEATHS IN OCCUPATION
AND INSURGENCIES**
Iraq Body Count. www.iraqbodycount.or

112–113 Old enemies, new allies
Reuter C. The Terror Strategist: Secret Files Reveal the Structure of Islamic
State, Spiegel Online International, 18 April 2015.
THE STRUGGLE FOR CONTROL OF IRAQ
Map of Control in February 2015. Political Geography Now. February 24,
2015.
Vidal J. Water supply key to outcome of conflicts in Iraq and Syria, experts
warn, *The Guardian*, 02 July 2014.

114–115 TUNISIA
Boukhars A. 2014. In the Crossfire: Islamists' Travails in Tunisia. Carnegie
Endowment for International Peace.
CHRONOLOGY
Ben Bouazza B. Tunisia riots: Islamist Salafist riots lead to 162 arrests. *The
World Post*, 13 June 2012.
Investing in Youth: Tunisia. Paris: OECD, March 2015.
Timelines of history: Tunisia.
NORTH AND SOUTH
Wikipedia: Tunisian presidential election, 2014; Tunisian parliamentary
election, 2014.

116–117 EGYPT
UN Development Programme, Egypt Human Development Report, 2004,
Commercial Press, Kalyoub.
Werrell CE, Femia F. eds. *The Arab Spring and Climate Change.* Washington,

DC: The Stimson Center, February 2013.
**EGYPT – A YOUNG COUNTRY, POPULATION & POPULATION DENSITY BY
GOVERNORATE**
Central Agency for Public Mobilization and Statistics 2013.
www.msrintranet.capmas.gov.eg/?lang=2
Population in Censuses by Sex & Sex Ratio (1882–2006). Egypt State
Information Service.
ECONOMIC GROWTH RATE
The World Bank. Egypt country profile. www.worldbank.org
GDP growth (annual %) World Bank, Data.
http://data.worldbank.org/indicator/NY.GDP.MKTP.KD.ZG/countries/
EG?page=1&display=default

118–119 Pressure for change
Batty D. Egypt bomb kills new year churchgoers. *The Guardian*. 01 January
2011.
BBC. Egypt: Mubarak sacks cabinet and defends security role, 29 January
2011.
BBC. Egypt's revolution: Interactive map, 11 February 2011.
BBC. Egypt unrest: deadly clashes rock Cairo's Tahrir Square, 02 February
2011.
Hauslohner A. After Tunisia: Why Egypt Isn't Ready to Have Its Own Revolu-
tion. *Time Magazine*. 20 January 2011.
L.S. Continuing business by other means: Egypt's military economy. *Mute*. 30
May 2014.
Shenker J. Mohamed El Baradei warns of 'Tunisia-style explosion' in Egypt.
The Guardian. 18 January 2011.
Shenker J, Siddique H. Egyptian government on last legs, says El Baradei. *The
Guardian*. 28 January 2011.
Weaver M, Owen P. Man sets himself on fire near Egyptian parliament. *The
Guardian*. 17 January 2011.

120–121 After the revolution
Al Monitor. Egyptian youth activists need protest plan, 09 December 2013.
BBC. Egypt: Who holds the power? 3 July 2013.
BBC. Cairo clashes leave 24 dead, 10 October 2011.
Dunne M. Egypt's Nationalists Dominate in a Politics-Free Zone, Carnegie
Endowment for International Peace, April 2015.
Sayigh Y. Above the State: The Officers' Republic in Egypt. Carnegie Endow-
ment for International Peace, 01 August 2012.
CHRONOLOGY
Middle East Eye. Egypt: Timeline of key human rights violations since the
2011 revolution, 03 December 2014.
THE COPTS
Brownlee J. Violence against Copts in Egypt, Carnegie Endowment for Inter-
national Peace, 14 November 2013.

122–125 LIBYA & Into chaos
BBC. Libya: The world's 'smuggler state', 29 April 2015.
Black I. The Libyan Islamic Fighting Group – from al-Qaida to the Arab spring,
The Guardian, 5 September 2011.
Gambill G. The Libyan Islamic Fighting Group (LIFG), Terrorism Monitor Vol-
ume 3, Issue 6, May 2005.
Stephen C. Libyan rebels launch dual offensive. *The Guardian*. 6 July 2011.
Tharoor I, Taylor A. Here are the key players fighting the war for Libya, all
over again. *Washington Post*, 27 August 2014.
Wehrey F. Ending Libya's Civil War: Reconciling Politics, Rebuilding Security.
Carnegie Endowment for International Peace. September 2014.
CHRONOLOGY
BBC. Libya profile – timeline.
UNHCR. Libya Factsheet, February 2015.

126–127 SYRIA
Friedman TL. WikiLeaks, Drought, and Syria, *New York Times*, 21 January
2014
Lund A. Islamist Mergers in Syria: Ahrar al-Sham Swallows Suqour al-Sham.
Carnegie Middle East Endowment, 23 March 2015.
Reuters. 'Factbox: Array of combatants deepens complexity of Syria's civil
war'. 29 June 2015.
Syrian Observatory for Human Rights: 310,000 people killed since the begin-
ning of the Syrian
Revolution: www.syriahr.com/en/2015/04/310000-people-killed-since-the-be-
ginning-of-the-syrian-revolution/
UNHCR. Middle East and North Africa.

128–129 The civil war
OPPOSITION AND CIVILIAN DEATHS & CIVIL WAR DEATHS
Violations Documentation Centre in Syria. www.vdc-sy.info/index.php/en/

MOST PROMINENT SYRIAN REBEL GROUPS
Al-Jazeera. www.aljazeera
Al-Monitor. www.al-monitor.com
BBC. Middle East profiles.
Carnegie Endowment for International Peace. www.carnegieendowment.org
Haaretz Israeli News Source. www.haaretz.com
The Guardian. www.theguardian.com
The Independent. www.independent.co.uk
Stanford University. Mapping militant organizations. web.stanford.edu/group/
    mappingmilitants/cgi-bin/
The Telegraph. www.telegraph.co.uk
Reuters. www.reuters.com
Relief Web. http://reliefweb.int

130–131 Chemical weapons
Arms Control Association. Timeline of Syrian Chemical Weapons Activity
    2012–2013.
www.armscontrol.org
BBC. Middle East profile.
BBC. Syria war: 'Chlorine' attack video moves UN to tears, 17 April 2015.
Reuters. www.reuters.com
UN News Centre. www.un.org/apps/news
UN Secretary-General. www.securitycouncilreport.org/un-documents/syria/
Walker PF. Syrian Chemical Weapons Destruction: Taking Stock and Looking
    Ahead. *Arms Control Today*. December 2014.
LOCATION OF CHEMICAL WEAPONS FACILITIES
Syria chemical weapons removal plan. BBC. 16 January 2014.
Graphic: Syria's chemical weapons sites. *The Telegraph*. 10 September 2013.
THE GENEVA TALKS
Explaining the Geneva II peace talks on Syria. *Al Jazeera*. 19 January 2014.
Geneva conference on Syria set for January, UN chief announces. 25 Novem-
    ber 2013.
    www.un.org/apps/news/story.asp?NewsID=46575#.U5bkraNwa1s
Syria – Timeline of Peace Process. Edinburgh Peace and Justice Centre. Issue
    June 2013.
Wikipedia. Syrian conflict peace proposals.

132–133 The state of war
Al Monitor. War-weary Syrians see hope in Homs deal, 13 May 2014.
De Mistura S. UN envoy proposes Syria 'fighting freeze', *Al Jazeera*, 31
    October 2014.
Lund A. Is Assad Losing the War in Syria? Carnegie Endowment for Interna-
    tional Peace, 13 May 2015.
Sciutto J, Crawford J, Carter CJ. ISIS can 'muster' between 20,000 and
    31,500 fighters, CIA says. CNN. 12 September 2014.

134–135 SAUDI ARABIA
Secrets of Al-Yamamah. The BAE Files, *The Guardian*.
Lacey R. *Inside the Kingdom*. London: Arrow. 2009.
Unger C. *House of Bush, House of Saud*, 2004. London: Gibson Square
    Books, 2004.
Wikipedia. Al-Yamamah arms deal.
HAJJ
Al Arabiya. Saudi Arabia has hosted 25 million hajj pilgrims in 10 years, 19
    October 2014.
For Saudi Arabia, The Muslim Pilgrimage Is Big Business. *International
    Business Times*. 07 October 2014.

136–137 Contrary pressures
BBC. Reporting Saudi Arabia's hidden uprising, 30 May 2014.
Cockburn P. Iraq crisis: How Saudi Arabia helped Isis take over the north of
    the country. *The Independent*, 13 July 2014.
WOMEN'S POLITICAL PARTICIPATION
BBC News

138–139 Protecting and projecting power
France inks $3 billion deal with Saudis to arm Lebanon. *Haaretz*. 04
November 2014
SAUDI POWER
Iraq and Syria: Who are the foreign fighters? 03 September 2014.
Cockburn P. Iraq crisis: How Saudi Arabia helped Isis take over the north of
    the country. *The Independent*, 13 July 2014.
Holmes AA. The military intervention that the world forgot. *Al Jazeera*. 29
    March 2014.
NORTHERN BORDER DEFENCES
Spencer R. Revealed: Saudi Arabia's 'great wall' to keep out Isil. *The
    Telegraph*, 14 January 2015.

SAUDI ARMED FORCES
Rosen A, Bender J, Macias A. The most powerful militaries in the Middle East
    [RANKED]. *Business Insider*. 27 October 2014.
Trends in world military expenditure, 2013. SIPRI Fact Sheet April 2014.
The Military Balance. 2014
Saudis lead Middle East military spending. *Al Jazeera*. 15 April 2014

140–141 YEMEN
Abdul-Ahad G. Diary. *London Review of Books*, 21 May 2015.
Borger J. Saudi-led naval blockade leaves 20m Yemenis facing humanitarian
    disaster. *The Guardian*, 5 June 2015.
Clark V. *Yemen: Dancing on the heads of snake*s. New Haven & London: Yale
    UP, 2010.
Hart-Davis D. *The War That Never Was*. London: Century, 2011.
Mutter P. The fight for Yemen, then and now. *The Arabist*, 28 April 2015 &
    30 April 2015.
Woods C. *Sudden Justice*. London: Hurst, 2015.
TERRITORIAL CONTROL
Inton C. *Yemen Control*, Reuters; Izady M. Gulf/2000 Project. 25/03/2015

142–143 THE GULF KINGDOMS
Wehrey FM. *Sectarian Politics in the Gulf*. New York: Columbia UP, 2014.
PER CAPITA WEALTH
The World Bank, GDP per capita, PPP (current international $), April 2015:
    http://data.worldbank.org/indicator/NY.GDP.PCAP.PP.CD?order=wbapi_
    data_value_2013+wbapi_data_value+wbapi_data_value-last&sort=desc
SOVEREIGN WEALTH FUNDS
International Forum of Sovereign Wealth Funds, November 16, 2009, cited
    in The Brave New World of Sovereign Wealth Funds. Wharton Leadership
    Center: University of Pennsylvania, 2010. www.ifswf.org/index.htm
Sovereign Wealth Fund Institute, Sovereign Wealth Fund Rankings, June
    2015: www.swfinstitute.org/fund-rankings/
Qatar
Al-Atiqi S. Brotherly Love in the GCC, Sada. Carnegie Endowment for Inter-
    national Peace. 31 October, 2014.
Ulrichsen KC. Qatar and the Arab Spring: Policy Drivers and Regional Implica-
    tions. Carnegie Endowment for International Peace. September 2014.
Bahrain
Chulov M. Bahrain destroys Pearl Roundabout, *The Guardian*, 18 March
    2011.
United Arab Emirates
Wikipedia. UAE Five.
Kuwait
Oil in Kuwait. Q8.com

144–145 NETWORKS OF GRIEVANCE AND TERROR
Hourani A. *Arabic thought in the liberal age 1798–1939*. Cambridge: Cam-
    bridge University Press, 1983.
MAJOR ACTIONS BY GROUPS AFFILIATED TO OR LINKED WITH AL-QAEDA
Timeline of Terrorism. www.timelineofterrorism.com
9/11 death statistics: Statistic Brain Research Institute.

146–147 Foreign fighters in Iraq and Syria
Neumann PR. Foreign fighter total in Syria/Iraq now exceeds 20,000; sur-
    passes Afghanistan conflict in the 1980s. International Centre for the Study
    of Radicalisation, King's College London, 26 January.

148–149 Divided movement: ISIS splits from al-Qaeda
Chulov M. How an arrest in Iraq revealed Isis's $2bn jihadist network, *The
    Guardian*, 15 June 2014.
Cockburn P. *The Rise of the Islamic State*. NY/London: Verso, 2015.
Malik S, Younes A, Ackerman S and Khalili M. How ISIS crippled al-Qaida, *The
    Guardian*, 10 June 2015.
Zelin AY, Rena ICSR and Fellow SD. ICSR Insight: The State of al-Qaeda.
    International Centre for the Study of Radicalisation, King's College London,
    13 April 2015.

Photo credits

INDEX